Reading Palestine

DATE DUE

DEMCO 38-296

Reading Palestine

Printing and Literacy,

1900–1948

Ami Ayalon

UNIVERSITY

OF TEXAS PRESS

AUSTIN

Requests for permission to reproduce material from this work
should be sent to Permissions, University of Texas Press, P.O. Box 7819,
Austin, TX 78713–7819.
♾ The paper used in this book meets the minimum requirements
of ANSI/NISO Z39.48–1992 (R1997) (Permanence of Paper).

Library of Congress Cataloging-in-Publication Data

Ayalon, Ami.
    Reading Palestine : printing and literacy, 1900–1948 / Ami Ayalon.— 1st ed.
        p.   cm.
    Includes bibliographical references and index.
    ISBN 0-292-70579-4 (cloth : alk. paper) — ISBN 0-292-70593-x (pbk. : alk. paper)
    1. Reading—Palestine—History—20th century.   2. Literacy—Palestine—History—
20th century.   I. Title.
        LB1050.A93   2004
        302.2'244'094694—dc22   2004005733

+━━+

To Bernard Lewis
And to the memory of Charles Issawi
Two masters, two friends

+━━+

Contents

Preface

Did the invention of printing mark the beginning of a "revolution"? If so, has it been properly acknowledged as such? Scholars passionately debate these questions. But even those who feel uncomfortable with the label for one reason or another do not dispute the immense historic importance of the new device. Indeed, it is hard to think of any aspect of human existence that has not been profoundly influenced by it. The mass popular access to texts, which printing made possible, affected political relations by furnishing rulers with better tools of control while availing their subjects of channels for voicing their own views. Printing had an impact on social relations by turning knowledge of new types into a vehicle of social mobility and status. It modified relations between the community's spiritual pastors and their disciples and, more broadly, changed the role of religion in society. It also transformed modes of transmitting knowledge, managing daily affairs, and spending leisure time. Such changes occurred in all societies in which printing was introduced. In the Middle East, the changes were perhaps the more dramatic because of the condensed process in which they took place. Everything happened within a short spell: the adoption of printing, the massive production of written texts, the emergence of a periodical press, the development of distribution channels, the mass imparting of reading skills, and, consequently, the turning of the written word into a central organizer of people's daily routine. All of these changes appeared more or less simultaneously, as one package that was offered to these societies after having evolved more gradually in other places.

Historians of Arab societies have hitherto given limited attention to some vital aspects of these processes. The cultural realm within which written texts and their reading acquired such an essential functional value is yet to be charted: the manifold levels of literacy, the uneven circulation of printed and other texts, the evolution of access mechanisms such as bookstores, literary clubs, public and lending libraries, and the various modes devised by largely uneducated societies for circulating the written knowledge that came flowing in large quantities. The present study seeks to address some of these questions in twentieth-century Palestine, here treated within its mandatory boundaries (i.e., between the Jordan River and the Mediterranean). It highlights the story's main contours and suggests possible directions and sources for further exploration. In its modest scope, however, it is no more than a preliminary incursion into the subject.

Palestine has often been the theater of momentous events, fateful for its own inhabitants, for those of its neighboring lands, and sometimes for humanity. The developments it witnessed during the twentieth century were no doubt among the most dramatic in this history. They were the more striking because they came after an era marked more by continuity than by change. During the first half of that century, the country experienced shifts in every sphere, from demography to politics, from infrastructure to education. Even without the 1948 historic watershed, this would have been a period of profound makeover in Palestine, affecting the life and daily routine of everyone. The 1948 breakdown violently disrupted these trends, turning the change into a cataclysm.

One victim of the 1948 upheaval was historical evidence. Private and public collections of books, newspapers, and documents perished. Personal stories were lost with the people who had carried them in their memories. And just about everything subsequently written on the country, politically or otherwise—by Palestinians, Israelis, and others—came to be slanted and tainted. The student of that society is thus confronted with an unusually intricate challenge, both in obtaining the evidence and in weighing it in a balanced way. A Palestinian effort to recover the past has begun recently, unearthing neglected documents and publishing recently recorded memoirs. Accounts of the latter type, especially, are not free of shortcomings, mostly of the kind that typifies retrospective accounts. Employed with the proper filters, however, they add an indispensable insight into the story. Along with extant contemporary sources—archival materials, Palestinian periodicals, books and leaflets, photographic evidence, and oral testimonies—they allow us to draw a fairly solid sketch of the scene, if not a detailed portrait of it. Its principal outlines are presented and examined in the pages below.

In transliterating Arabic, I have followed the accepted practice in the field of Middle Eastern history, simplified by the omission of superscripted strokes and subscripted dots. Some technical precision has thus been sacrificed for the sake of not scaring away the nonprofessional reader.

As ever, while working on this study I incurred endless debts of gratitude to numerous people, more than I can practically mention here. My thanks to some of them are noted in the proper places throughout the book. A part of the research and a great deal of the writing was undertaken while I was a member of the Institute for Advanced Study in Princeton, from January to August 2001—the ultimate environment for scholarly work in every imaginable sense. I am most grateful to the institute's faculty and staff for having me there and for making my time and work so wonderfully enjoyable and fruitful. Of the many friends and colleagues who provided inspiration and help I wish to single out for special thanks Professors Pierre Cachia, Lawrence Conrad, Michael Cook, Patricia Crone, Rashid Khalidi, Etan Kohlberg, and Salim Tamari, as well as the two anonymous readers of the manuscript for the University of Texas Press. Professors L. Carl Brown, Patricia Crone, Heinrich von Staden, and Michael Winter read parts of the manuscript at different stages, offered indispensable comments, and saved me from many errors. None of these colleagues and friends, however, share with me the responsibility for any faults that might be found in this work, which are all my own. I am also beholden to Rasim Jbarah from Tayyibah, Israel, for allowing me to explore his impressive collection of pre-1948 Palestinian publications; to Dr. Reuven Aharoni for his vital assistance in arranging some of the interviews with Palestinian informants; to Ely Schiller of Ariel Publishing, Jerusalem, for his cordial help in obtaining some of the photographs presented here, including that on the front cover; to Ruthie Beth-Or for her professional advice in selecting and improving the illustrations; to Avigail Jacobson for her efficient and gracious assistance; to Professor Beth Baron, who came up with the title for this book one hazy evening in a Princeton café; and to Amira Margalith, a very dear friend, who passed away prematurely before she could see this book in print. Credible as a rock and ever caring Amira assisted me in numerous ways with this undertaking as well as with all of my previous works. The editorial staff at the University of Texas Press—Sue Carter, Lynne Chapman, and Wendy Moore—handled the task of turning the manuscript into a book with remarkable competence and much grace, thus making my work with them a genuine pleasure. Finally, I wish to record my debt to the many scores of Palestinian Arabs, who told me their captivating stories and willingly responded to my queries even when these questions seemed strange to them. Their names are far too many to register here, but quite a few of them are quoted directly and thus named specifically throughout the text.

The research for this study was supported by a grant from the Israel Science Foundation, founded by the Israeli Academy of Science and Humanities. I acknowledge this help gratefully.

My wife Yael and my sons Yaron and Gil served as an unfailing pillar of support, ceaselessly amazing me with their patience. As ever, again—or perhaps more than ever before—they had to put up with an absentee husband and father who was so often in remote places, geographically and mentally. This book could not possibly have been written without their wonderful love and cooperation.

Reading Palestine

Introduction

The tale of written texts and their use in twentieth-century Palestine is one of spectacular change. Like an engine shifting from first gear straight to fourth, Palestinian society moved within a brief historic moment from near-complete illiteracy to massive reliance on the written word. In Europe, popular consumption of printed products had evolved gradually over several centuries. By the time Arab subjects of the Ottoman Empire began to lend ears to the voices coming from that continent, Europe had already developed a routine of enjoying the fruits of printing in endless ways. In certain parts of the Arab Ottoman region, a similar process started around the middle of the nineteenth century. But Palestine, like most of its neighboring lands, remained on the sidelines of these developments until much later. A handful of early precursors aside, the change it experienced was telescoped into a brief period in the twentieth century.

Only a few decades previously, no portent of this upcoming shift was apparent in Palestine. Under Ottoman-Islamic rule since the early sixteenth century, its society and other Arabic-speaking communities were living through one of the less productive eras in their cultural history. The marvelous Arab legacy of intellectual and scientific creativity had had its zenith in much earlier times. A variety of factors, not least political instability and bloody conflicts on domestic and foreign fronts, had undermined this cultural endeavor and diminished it in scope and quality. Intellectual activity did continue, but it was limited mostly to a small spiritual leadership and marked by a strong religious accent. Writing, reading, the retention and collection of texts—all remained the business of state officials, religious scholars, and an exclusive sociocultural elite. Other parts of the society had little use for such skills and objects. Mechanisms based on oral modes of communication functioned effectively in addressing all their daily needs; writing and reading were redundant. Books, precious and revered items, were irrelevant to the normal routine of most people.

This benign equilibrium was upset, and eventually terminated, by powerful processes that unfolded in two waves. The first was the long-term encroachment of Western imperialism on the societies of the Ottoman Empire. By the nineteenth century, the challenge of Europe, with its lures and threats, had become plain enough in the Arab provinces to stir a response, both from rulers and from their more astute subjects. The reaction came in many forms, among them a vocal demand for cultural revitalization. Europe presented a wide range of attractive ideas and devices—from state-run schools to printing, from newspapers to eyeglasses—which could be borrowed and adapted to local needs. First in the region to experience changes in this field were the provinces of Egypt and Lebanon.[1] The endorsement of printing, emergence of a periodical press, advent of literary societies, enhanced exchanges with foreign colleagues, upgrading of the educational systems—all were signs of the drive for a cultural awakening in them after the middle of the nineteenth century. Palestine was not a locus of such activities at first. But members of its educated elite, a thin social layer, soon became aware of these changes and embarked on a vivid dialogue with their counterparts across provincial lines. It was through this elite that the country first joined the trend that would transform its cultural reality. Involving only a tiny fraction of the people until after the end of the century, modern cultural activities were stepped up following the 1908 Young Turk Revolution, a historic earthquake of major magnitude that shook the region. In the Fertile Crescent lands of Syria, Iraq, and Palestine, hitherto the periphery of cultural awakening, the new sense of opportunity inspired by political changes prompted lively cultural activity. The spread of printing and emergence of a local press in these places were two prominent marks of this new spirit.[2] By the outbreak of the First World War, there were discernible signs of an upcoming cultural transformation in the region, including Palestine.

The second wave was far more intensive than the first. Indeed, more than a wave, it was a massive flood. The traumatic political transition after 1918, from Islamic caliphate to European tutelage, was coupled with the equally disconcerting influx of Zionist Jews, which posed an overt and growing threat to the Arab character of the country. The alarming developments at home were paralleled by fateful changes in the neighborhood, the hitherto familiar environment that was similarly being transformed. These rapid shifts generated a hunger for information that would allow the society to see where it was going. Specifically, the need was of one major kind: news and its analysis. It was this pressing demand for intelligence—now coming not from the elite but from the wide public below—that gave a considerable boost to the circulation of new forms of knowledge.

Information now presented itself in growing quantities, and for the first time in local experience it was offered chiefly in writing and largely in print. It appeared in many formats: books, journals and newspapers, party pamphlets, sidewalk posters, shop signs, commercial ads, rally banners, dissenter handbills. Most of these—indeed all, with the possible exception of books—would fall into the rubric of "mass media," that is, means designed to amplify messages to big crowds through extensive circulation. Accessing the many messages in their novel form required reading proficiency of a scope formerly unknown in Palestine, and the authorities responded with appropriate initiatives. Hesitantly begun during the final Ottoman decades, educational reform was markedly stepped up once a British mandate was established in the country. Governmental efforts combined with the public passion for information to transform the status of writing and reading in Palestinian society. Once an elite domain, written and printed messages came to enlighten and orientate increasing segments of the community. Reading ability became an important asset. A vital tool of navigation in changing waters, it also contained a promise for success in the new reality, a key to lucrative employment and to rapid social mobility.

The extensive introduction of written texts into Palestinian life and the advancement of relevant capabilities thus occurred in tandem. But there was a clear dissonance in pace between the two processes. The spread of written messages in their endless applications was much faster than the expansion of reading ability. This was perhaps inevitable, given the very low point of departure in education and the need to build up a training system almost from scratch. Palestinian society moved ahead tardily in employing the new tools, even though educational development was now considerably more dynamic than in the recent past. Progress was not only tardy; it was also uneven. Large sections of the society, indeed the majority, were left out of the process: members of the older generation who were already beyond school age, much of the rural society, nomads, and women. Moreover, among those who presumably joined the literate circle considerable gaps opened in the level of proficiency, with obvious practical implications. Such an unbalanced development during the early phase of mass exposure to written texts had taken place in other societies as well, of course. And like other societies, Arab communities, including that of Palestine, intuitively

3

fell back on old practices that had hitherto served them for similar if more modest ends: oral communication, by which a single competent reader verbally conveyed written messages to a listening crowd and a single literate family member updated the rest. In Arab societies, relying on such mechanisms had persisted—and had evidently been deemed satisfactory—long after Western societies had adopted more individual modes of accessing written texts. These time-honored methods were now enlisted as temporary complements to the slowly spreading skill of reading, a kind of interim solution until universal literacy had been achieved. In those sections of society that were left out of the process of training at that stage, such traditional collective practices offered the only approach to the coveted information.

The story of print production and consumption in post-1900 Palestine is, thus, one of rapid but lopsided progress. By mid-century, the circle of those capable of independent reading was many-fold broader than at the outset, and continuously growing. Meanwhile, for those still without such training, or with imperfect abilities, the application of old modes to new ends remained an effective way of addressing their needs. Written texts of every kind came to play a central role in communal and individual life, much more so than in the past. It will be clear, however, that the half century explored here represents only one phase of the transformation; the process continued in full swing in subsequent years. But this was the formative and most exciting phase, during which priorities were set and directions took shape. By the end of this period, Palestinian society had come to have high regard for written and printed products as well as a fairly clear idea of how it was going to benefit from them.

Palestine in the First Half of the Twentieth Century

Palestine of the late nineteenth century was a secondary branch of an empire that had known better days. Administratively, its territory consisted of three districts (*sancak* or *mutasarrifiyyah*): those of Nablus and Acre, which formed a part of the province (*vilayet* or *wilayah*) of Beirut, and an autonomous district centered in Jerusalem, whose governing official was answerable to Istanbul. A hierarchical edifice of officials backed by gendarmerie governed the Ottoman control system. Palestine, and especially Jerusalem, had a special status of holiness in this Islamic empire due to its revered place in Islamic tradition, but the practical significance of this status was rather limited. The empire's efforts during the nineteenth century to reinvigorate itself were felt in Palestine in certain spheres of life; but here they were often feeble echoes of louder sounds reverberating elsewhere. It would not be grossly misleading to say that, on the whole, Palestinian realities were marked as much by continuity as by change until close to the end of that century.

The Palestine of 1900 had a total population of c. 600,000. Of these, roughly 75% were Muslim Arabs, roughly 10% Christian Arabs, and the rest were Jews and others.[3] About two-thirds of the population was rural, living in some 800 villages of various sizes scattered throughout the country, mostly in its northern and central sections. Of the cities, most important were Jerusalem (locally referred to as al-Quds), with c. 40,000 people;[4] and Jaffa (Yafa) and Gaza (Ghazza), with somewhat smaller communities. Other towns with more than 10,000 inhabitants were Haifa, Nablus, Hebron (al-Khalil), and Acre ('Akka), and there were half-a-dozen smaller urban centers: Lydda (al-Lidd), Ramlah, Tiberias (Tabariyyah), Safad, Nazareth (al-Nasirah), and Bethlehem (Bayt Lahm).[5] By the turn of the century the country had already begun to experience some change, most noticeably in the economy, which would in due course modify its rudimentary modes of existence. At that point, however, its society still subsisted mainly on domestic agriculture, local handicraft, and limited-scale industry (mostly soap making, in Nablus and Jaffa). Road infrastructure was poor, reflecting but also perpetuating the loose ties between the country's different sections. Urban public services were of a very basic nature,[6] and in the villages they were all but nonexistent. Official and other information was transmitted by the mosque preacher, town crier, and word of mouth; printing was still in the future. Cultural life revolved largely around religious institutions and traditional modes of popular entertainment. Finally, political life represented a variation of the familiar politics-of-notables pattern: prominent urban or rural families vying for local leadership, prestige, and government favor. Descent, wealth, and, to a lesser extent, scholarly eminence—the traditional keys to public status—were very much at play in this scene as the nineteenth century turned into the twentieth.

But if pre-1900 Palestine experienced little of the conspicuous shifts that had taken place elsewhere in the region under ambitious potentates, there were nascent developments that foreshadowed future change. Borne by the Western expansion into the empire, multiple foreign initiatives began to reach Palestine in different ways. The leading states of Europe all opened consulates in Jerusalem as well as in Jaffa, Haifa, and Acre during the nineteenth century. These agencies catered to the growing number of foreign subjects or citizens who engaged mostly in trade and economic projects, and to the pilgrims and tourists, who likewise came in at an accelerated pace. Concurrently, the country was increasingly linked to the world economic system, especially that of Europe, with important implications for its own economy. During the last third of the century, a marked growth was registered in Palestine's foreign trade, which had a manifestly positive effect on its productive sectors (agriculture and industry), services, and infrastructure. Thus, a carriage road was built between Jerusalem and Jaffa in 1868, a few other roads were opened subsequently, and the Jerusalem–Jaffa railway was inaugurated in 1852. Post offices, another channel of international links, were opened in Palestine by several European states, starting with the Austro-Hungarian service in 1869.[7] A development of a different kind, still seemingly insignificant at that stage but containing a grim omen for fateful future changes, was the arrival of Jewish immigrants as part of the Zionist enterprise. Their impact on the country's life would be as profound as that of any other factor.

An important aspect of this widening Western influence was the growing presence of Christian missionaries of many denominations. Setting up cultural and educational institutions in towns and villages, they inspired their pupils with novel ideas and taught them new skills.[8] In part thanks to them, the cultural-literary awakening begun in Lebanon around mid-century and later amplified in Egypt—the *nahdah* (revival)—started percolating into Palestine. Publications produced in the neighborhood reached the country as early as the 1870s, if not before, and members of the small educated elite eagerly opened themselves to the new knowledge and views. Families of this class began to send their children for education in nearby provinces or in places farther away, where they were exposed to similar cultural effects. None of these changes before 1900 was of major scope in itself; some were all but invisible. But after the turn of the century they would combine to generate a budding transformation.

The years between the onset of the century and the First World War were a period of more lively developments. The political ground was shaking, exploding in the summer of 1908 with a promise for reform and freedom in the empire and its provinces, but sustaining some aftershocks that served to cool down expectations. Still, constitutional life in the Ottoman capital was resumed, Palestine was represented, and government-sponsored projects moved ahead more energetically. State and foreign initiatives further boosted the country's economy. Exports and imports continued to grow, agricultural and industrial ventures expanded, and there was evident progress in communications, including the building of paved roads and railways and improvement of the Jaffa and Haifa seaports. These changes spurred a slow but palpable rise in the standard of living, especially in the cities. Evolving unevenly, as ever, these last shifts opened and increased socioeconomic gaps among different sectors of the society—another familiar mark of modernization.[9] A person born in Palestine on the eve of the war was thus met with an environment markedly more dynamic than his predecessor a generation earlier, especially, again, in the urban areas. More dramatic changes lay ahead, after the war.

The disintegration of the Ottoman Empire and the British conquest that came in its wake meant more than the substitution of one yoke by another. It also marked the replacement of an Islamic order by a non-Islamic—and profoundly alien—one, making the changeover highly problematic. The mandate on behalf of the League of Nations was meant to prepare Palestinian society for self-rule in the modern world. But the British also had other motives in assuming the task, which sometimes took precedence over those pronounced by the international community, an approach for which Palestinian Arabs and others would censure them, often bitterly. At the same time, the three decades of their rule were also a period of undeniable progress and much gain in many areas, which Palestinians would explicitly acknowledge. To an extent, this may also be said of the expanding presence of Zionism in the country: it was a source of endless troubles for Palestine's Arab inhabitants, but indirectly also an impetus for material development and growing communal awareness. Palestine now departed from its secondary-province status and relatively calm routine of public life and became the focus of foreign concern and domestic agitation.

As so often happens, these changes were felt most prominently in the political arena. In the face of a mighty foreign government and the small but highly motivated Zionist rival, Arab Palestinian politics were transformed. In deviation from patterns known since time immemorial, a national leadership now emerged in the figure of Hajj Amin al-Husayni, the mufti of Jerusalem, who embarked on unifying the community in a passionate struggle against the invaders. Given traditional political norms and the intricacy of the challenges, such a new leadership could hardly have expected to remain without domestic opposition. Thus, alongside coordinated strife against external foes, Arab political action under the mandate was also marked by deep friction, pitting two large camps and many subcamps against each other. Political groupings organized themselves as political parties, a novel phenomenon in the country. On the whole, political life in mandatory Palestine was incomparably more intensive and passionate than during the late Ottoman era. A series of bloody encounters with the Jews—in 1921,

1928–1929, and, more dramatically, 1936–1939—served as major milestones of the period. Other historic benchmarks were born from the conflict with the British: the appointment of a Zionist Jew as first High Commissionaire in 1920 and periodic changes of his successors; a set of government "White Papers" designed to determine the country's fate, in 1922, 1930, and 1939; several inquiry commissions; and a British plan to partition the country, in 1937. With political realities changing so quickly and with the expansion of new media such as newspapers, posters, and written proclamations, increasing circles of the public came to be involved in these struggles, both actively and passively.

The Arab population of Palestine, Muslim as well as Christian, more than doubled during the first half of the twentieth century, reaching c. 1.3 million by the end of the mandate. This was an unusually rapid growth rate, occurring largely thanks to improved sanitary conditions and a concomitant decline in deaths, and marginally also due to immigration. There was a clear trend toward urbanization: the relative share of urban population in the Arab community (Muslims and Christians) grew from 27.5% in 1922 to c. 36% in 1946. The expansion was particularly felt in the biggest cities: Jerusalem's Arab population grew from 28,000 in 1922 to 65,000 in 1946; in Jaffa it grew from 27,000 to 61,000; and in Haifa from 18,000 to 71,000. In that, there was no symmetry between Muslims and Christians: while only 28–30% of all Muslims lived in towns and the great bulk of them in villages, the great majority of Christians, about 75–80%, were urbanites.[10] The rising importance of the urban centers was not merely a function of their growing size but also of the ever closer ties between cities and their respective rural hinterlands. Whereas in the past such relations were loose, more and more villagers were now coming to the towns for employment, study, even entertainment. Simultaneously, urban commercial endeavors and cultural products found their way into the countryside. Meanwhile, the country's Jewish population increased dramatically, from c. 80,000 on the eve of the First World War to c. 610,000 at the end of the mandate, mostly due to Zionist immigration[11]—nearly an eight-fold increase that perforce had a mighty impact on every aspect of the country's daily realities.

Rapid demographic development went hand in hand with accelerated economic progress. Between 1922 and 1947 the economy of Arab Palestine grew at the impressive rate of 6.5% annually on average. According to one study, in terms of average per capita growth it ranked second among the world's economies during the period (the first being the economy of Palestine's Jewish sector).[12] With urbanization, industrialization, and upgrading of the services sector, the share of agriculture in the economy was gradually reduced, from c. 65% in 1922 to c. 54% in 1945.[13] Though Arab Palestine continued to rely on agriculture as its largest economic sector until the end of the mandate, this was clearly a period in which the economy dynamically moved toward structural change—a trend whose particulars are beyond our concern here.[14]

The British brought with them new standards of physical infrastructure and public services. They built paved roads all across the country, increasing their total length more than four-fold during the mandate.[15] They replaced the anarchic array of parallel postal services by one central system in 1920–1921 and connected Palestine by telegraph to London, Cairo, and Beirut in 1921. Telephones came to be used in the country in the middle of 1920, and by 1921 a few newspapers and other businesses were proudly publicizing their two- or three-digit telephone numbers in their announcements.[16] Electricity was first introduced in private homes in the large cities in the mid-1920s, but the process was slow and the most common residential lighting devices throughout the decade remained oil or gas lamps, or, for those who could afford them, residential generators.[17] In smaller towns and in the villages, these would remain the only means of lighting until mid-century and often beyond. Cinema entered the country in the early 1920s, and by the second half of that decade newspapers were regularly publicizing theater schedules. Stationers, opening after the First World War, began marketing typewriters from the early 1920s and, as one ad suggested, these machines quickly came to be used "in all banks, offices and government departments."[18] Early in the following decade, when radio broadcasting began in neighboring countries, businesses in Palestine started marketing battery- and electricity-operated receivers. The inauguration of broadcasting from Cairo, on 31 May 1934, provided an opportunity for promotion,[19] and Palestinian newspapers regularly carried the Egyptian radio broadcast schedule. This was followed, in early 1936, by the launching of Radio Palestine.[20]

Residential electricity, telephones, radio receivers, gramophones, typewriters—these were affordable only to the small sector of the well-to-do, mostly, again, in the better-off urban neighborhoods. Endorsing such technology was slow not merely because of the expenses involved. It also required departing from past habits of benign convenience and accommodating to a new, more dynamic routine—a shift that occurred slowly. "As for telephones," a foreign visitor to Jerusalem noted early in the period, highlighting a cultural constraint, "who that can shout from roof to roof and down the echoing streets should trouble himself to whisper into a funnel?"[21] Still, the impact of these changes gradually reached beyond the wealthy urban residences. The appearance of novelties such as electrically lighted spaces and radio in public places made them accessible to many that did not have them at home. This included villagers in growing numbers, whose visits to towns brought them in touch with the changing conditions. Even in faraway corners there was a nascent sense of transition.

There were two other important spheres in which considerable shifts occurred, beginning in the late years of Ottoman rule and accelerating under the mandate. One was the proliferation of printed texts, once the exclusive province of the learned few but gradually becoming public property. The other, involving the government as a central agent, was the laying of solid foundations for a modern schooling system, which placed Palestinian society on the road to comprehensive literacy. These changes and their repercussions will be at the center of discussion in the chapters below.

Recapturing Past Reading

Intellectual history was once dominated by the study of abstract ideas—the literary output of eminent thinkers and writers and their public impact. More recently, scholars have moved to probing a hitherto neglected aspect of the cultural endeavor: modes of reading and the transmission and assimilation of written products. For several decades now, students of cultural history in different eras, mostly exploring Europe and its offshoots, have been seeking to reconstruct patterns of text assimilation in the past. Studying writings while ignoring the readers, they have come to reckon, would be as smart as analyzing an economic system by focusing on producers while ignoring the buyers. It has become clear that the interrelationship between a written text and its consumer is a vital part of the text—its contents, style, and impact. First addressing their probe to questions of circulation, scholars focused on readership size, social composition, and geographical distribution, hoping in this way to gauge the popular influence of certain writings. This entailed scrutinizing book title lists, lending-library records, and files of book dealerships (when found), as well as assessing literacy levels. More imaginative search then called attention to historic changes in the very mode of reading itself, which carried substantial implications. In different times and places, it was shown, people had read under different physical and mental circumstances, and with different intents. The techniques employed in the practice had also varied, and the results had, quite likely, varied accordingly. Studying these circumstances and techniques came to be deemed essential for a closer assessment of the public impact of written products. In recent years, therefore, students of the history of reading, by now a well-recognized subdiscipline of cultural history, have centered largely on the issue of "how"—the manner in which people read. This kind of search has been expected to carry us to the very essence, the protons and electrons, of the experience of writing and reading. Raising these questions has often invited micro case studies that have dealt with small communities during short periods of time, or even with individuals. Studies of this nature have lately permeated the small but animated field.

Questions of this last kind in particular, but also other issues in this subdiscipline, confront the historian with an intricate challenge. Evidence is ever a problem; more often than not it is partial, fragmentary, and murky. As repeatedly noted in introductions to such studies, students of literary history have texts lying ready for their analysis, while the practice of reading is rarely documented. Extracting its tale from the sources thus requires, beyond erudition, some detective instincts and imagination. Still, testimonies do exist, sometimes even in substantial quantities and surprising quality. In many cases they are of an inadvertent nature, hidden in clues, popping up as unintended details in a narrative whose concern is elsewhere, or veiled in suggestive anecdotes that need to be decoded inventively. When uncovered and put together, the findings sometimes make it possible to reconstruct the main contours of the story of texts and reading in a given society—and occasionally even more than that. In a great many cases, however, the picture would suffer from gaps, leaving room for inference and speculation.

Considerable progress has been made in this subdiscipline, mostly, again, in the study of Western societies. To a large extent, the achievements resulted from the availability of sources that students of non-Western societies can only envy. Scholars have embarked on the task by putting forward a set of intriguing questions: not only how many people read, what they read, and who read what, but also where they read; when; how; in what circumstances and physical setting; to what end; and with what effect. Some of these questions have been easier to answer than others. But they have all been examined, spurring creative investigation. Students have screened lists of estate inventories, library sales catalogues, reader records of public and personal book collections, private individual reading diaries, autobiographies, readers' letters to authors and editors, even police (and the Inquisition) interrogation files. Relevant economic aspects have also been examined: prices of written texts and their affordability to various social groups; availability of suitable physical conditions such as comfortable quarters, sufficient lighting, and adequate furniture; and the architecture of spaces intended for reading, potentially hinting to modes of the practice for which they were designed. Other types of evidence have been exploited: artwork and belles lettres depicting situations of reading, useful sources when treated with due caution; and the physical shape of written texts, including handwriting or typeface quality, page layout, use of illustrations, which can be searched for clues about the intended audience. Dealing with such queries has brought historians closer to sociologists, anthropologists, and ethnographers, on whose arsenals of methods and jargon they have come to draw for weaving their stories together. These efforts have helped in producing quantities of evidence whose very bulk has often compensated for limitations in quality. In such cases the results have been quite impressive.[22]

A good illustration of the potential inherent in this variety of sources is James Smith Allen's study of reading in France between 1800 and 1940. Allen starts by posing some standard questions, such as the size of the public that had access to education and acquired literacy; the number of titles that were printed, including their print run and circulation; and the activities of lending libraries. He was able to procure data on the numbers of students attending school in each stage of education throughout the period; the number of books printed every year, with a breakdown by genre; circulation data for specific journals at different points in time; the numbers of school libraries and details on the volumes they lent each year; estimates on the number of active readers in France during the period; and profiles of reading audiences of specific authors. To reconstruct these last profiles, he had at his disposal more than 10,000 letters written to leading French authors of the period, filling many boxes in the archives, out of which he only used a modest sample of some 1,500. Allen then moved on to probing additional sources that shed more light on his statistical findings. He examined works of art—paintings, lithographs, sketches—depicting reading in every conceivable condition by people from all walks of society: aristocrats and peasants, priests and shopkeepers, men and women, adults and children. A corpus of no fewer than 500 of these was available to him for the period. His study of these artworks revealed a gradual shift over time in certain typical features of the practice, primarily from collective to individual mode, as well as many other details on the physical conditions in which reading was conducted. Literary novels were another rewarding source of describing reading experience at different stages in life, from childhood to old age. Private diaries and memoirs, often recording daily routine, exposed other facets of the reading habits of authors and their family members. Having gathered all this wealth of testimonies and employed it in charting the story of text production and consumption in France, Allen could offer an interpretive discussion of his rich findings, in the second, more analytical, part of his book.[23]

Studies like Allen's have shown not only what the sources can teach us if capably exploited, but also what they usually cannot. As has repeatedly been demonstrated, it is easier to conduct such a probe into the better-educated segments of society—the urban, upper-class, more conscientious consumers, who are more likely to leave a record of their experience. It is harder, sometimes impossible, to study the less sophisticated (and often much bigger) parts, about which we inevitably know less. Another limitation that has been exposed lies in the fact that any evidence one can procure on the subject, even when rich and elaborate, as in Allen's study, would perforce be indirect and "extraneous." At its fullest, it usually comes short of conveying the infinitely varied human experience at the moment of reading, with its emotional and intellectual effects. Such lacunae would be particularly significant for studying reading in group, as in the traditional mode: the makeup of the forum, the physical setting of the place, the quality of the reader's voice, the reader-audience encounter in the course of the session—all are factors that produce a quality which accounts rarely reveal. To a somewhat lesser extent, this is also true of instances of individual reading. Both limitations no doubt restrict our ability to fathom the experience of reading and hence to assess its full impact. They should be kept in mind as borderlines circumscribing the potential scope of the field. Within these confines, however, it is still possible to tell a meaningful story.

In nineteenth-century France, the interior ministry demanded periodic reports on the use of local libraries, arranged by categories of readers.[24] Painters, primarily but not exclusively of the Impressionist school, took special interest in human conditions and recorded them artistically.[25] Writers conducted correspondence with thousands of readers and preserved their letters, which were subsequently deposited in archives in Paris and elsewhere.[26] A student of the cultural history of the Middle East, by contrast, can only dream about such a corpus of evidence. In the Ottoman Empire, of which the Arabic-speaking countries had been a part from 1516 –1517 onward, printing was introduced only in the eighteenth century (certain non-Islamic minorities had started earlier). It became an important way of producing texts only in the second half of the following century, and that only in a few locations: Istanbul, Egypt, and Lebanon. Other places had to wait until the twentieth century for that development. A local periodical press, the most important medium of exposing the wider public to the written word, was consequently a late product in the region. Similarly, organized systematic education, initiated by the state or by missionaries, began for the most part around the middle of the nineteenth century, a fact with obvious implications on the local level of intellectual skills. Consequently, public and lending libraries, as well as bookstores and stationers, appeared in these places only in the late nineteenth or early twentieth centuries.

Studying the history of texts and reading in Arab societies from the mid-nineteenth century onward is, thus, akin in some ways to exploring that field in Europe during the decades following the invention of printing. Indeed, many of the Western cases that inspired the discussion in this book deal with that period in Europe. But even for the era of printing, exploring text production and consumption in Arab societies is ever problematic. The age-old tradition of careful manuscript collecting did not apply to the preservation of such publications as newspapers and printed pamphlets—ephemeral yet centrally important items in the local history of printed texts—and a great many of them disappeared without a trace. Nor was there a demand for, or a routine of keeping, user registers in the few libraries that existed. Records of text circulation, book catalogues, and library reader lists are therefore extremely rare. Nor yet was there a habit of artistic documentation of human situations; and private memoirs, even novels, describing such situations are similarly scanty. On top of it all, in most places the political and socioeconomic circumstances during the nineteenth and twentieth centuries were inhospitable to the preservation of evidence on individual and collective daily life. Such was the case in twentieth-century Palestine, where stormy events had a devastating effect on the retention of the country's written legacy.

Still, if a far cry from the situation in Europe, the state of sources for the modern history of Arab writing and reading is not hopeless. For some sections of the scene it is even quite promising. State, colonial, missionary, and local archives contain information on education in these societies—on schools, teachers and students, curricula and textbooks. Books in private collections, few as they are, and those in the libraries of religious institutions (which in some cases have been surveyed and catalogued), reflect fields of interest, acquisition policies, and sometimes even preservation standards and norms of usage. So do inventory lists of estates endowed as Waqf (religious endowment), which often contained books. The periodical press, of which a partial corpus does exist, represents an arena of vivid dialogue, open or implicit, between writers and audience. Designed for mass circulation, it comprises ample clues about readers' fields of concern and often also about ways in which they transmitted the knowledge they acquired. Ads in the papers—for printing presses, imported and locally produced publications, and bookstores and libraries, as well as reading-related devices such as lamps and typewriters—are another useful source, as are notices on the literary activities of clubs and associations. Even the language of these publications, their vocabulary and style in addressing the potential customers, often contains clues about readers' education level and the manner in which they expected to receive information. Autobiographies and memoirs, though few, likewise include relevant descriptions—on educational experience, modes of access to texts, family and public routines of conveying news and knowledge, and the practice of reading, collective or private. Accounts by foreign observers, recording what they considered curious Middle Eastern habits, frequently bear useful allusions. All of these may be complemented, for recent decades, by a focused gathering of oral testimonies. Finally, photographs, present in the Middle East since the mid-nineteenth century, contain pleasant surprises for the probing scholar—from evidence on the existence of texts in public places, such as shop signs and bulletin boards, to scenes of newspaper reading in cafés. None of these sources is sufficient in itself for this kind of inquiry, and all too often they are too patchy or shaky to teach us much. Carefully gathered and cross-checked, however, they may add up as a basis for a useful picture.

The present study relies on an exploration of many of these types of sources. Being a preliminary foray of its kind into this territory, it does not pretend to be comprehensive either in its findings or in the range of questions it poses. As already noted, pre-1948 Arab Palestine is a particularly difficult trail to blaze because of the 1948 destruction and its horrendous impact on the evidence. Questions that would have been tricky to address anyway have become so much more intricate that they are often impossible to tackle. This study aspires to identify and chart the main constituents of the evolution of printed texts and their reading during the era of rapid change in Arab Palestine. It certainly leaves much room for further exploration and elucidation.

CHAPTER I

Literacy and Education

"Culture in this country is dead!" the owner of the Jerusalem weekly *al-Munadi* proclaimed in 1912. In an intensely pessimistic editorial, he depicted a dismal state of affairs in Palestine. Having abandoned science and learning, people had sunk in ignorance bordering on unbelief, indeed in unbelief itself. Nothing concerns them but vain talk and senseless squabbling, he noted in dismay. This editor was not alone in his gloom. Many others voiced frustration with the country's cultural realities at the outset of the twentieth century. "The readers shall know," stated Raghib al-Khalidi, a prominent Jerusalem notable, "that two forces have a grip over the Islamic community in Palestine, the force of despair and the force of poverty." Khalidi might well have added a third force, that of illiteracy, reflected in widespread apathy and ignorance of which he and his colleagues complained. Such phenomena were inevitable, 'Isa Da'ud al-'Isa of the Jaffa-based *Filastin* soberly noted, "in a society of which merely two percent are literate."[1]

This last assessment by 'Isa, obviously no more than a raw speculation, is nonetheless of some interest to us. In a study dealing with a community adopting reading habits, literacy rate is of the essence. The editor of *Filastin*, of course, sought to convey a sense of anguish rather than to offer a solid estimate; Palestine would have to wait another two decades before its first orderly survey would address the issue systematically. The tiny rate 'Isa quoted may thus have been deliberately minimized, but perhaps not grossly so.[2] The first authoritative evaluation of literacy at our disposal comes from the general census of 1931, conducted by officials of the British mandatory government, who applied modern methods. The survey put the overall literacy rate among sedentary Arabs, 7 years old and up, at c. 20%. Among Muslims it was c. 14% (men c. 25%, women c. 3%), and among Christians

c. 58% (men c. 72%, women c. 44%).[3] This reflected the situation after a decade of enhanced educational endeavor. A reasonable assessment by a seasoned observer in 1947 put the overall literacy rate in Palestine's Arab community at 27%: 21% for Muslims (men 35%, women 7%), 75% for Christians (men 85%, women 65%).[4]

Such figures—we are unlikely to get any better—may or may not have been close to the mark. But what was the mark? More practically, what was the concrete meaning of "literacy" and "literate," and what did the figures signify with regard to the bulk of society, which was left out of this rubric? We may assume that in defining 2% of society as "literate," 'Isa Da'ud al-'Isa intended fully educated people who could read texts of any kind, as well as write; or, more to the point, those who would have made up the potential reservoir of readers for his pioneering newspaper. But what about the 98% he excluded? Were they utterly incapable of deciphering any written text, not even of the simplest type? Not even the headline of a public notice, or a street sign? Were they unable to decode an inscription in a mosque, or a passage in a prayer book? Were they able neither to read nor to write, or even sign their names? Maybe some of them did have some such skills, but perhaps not enough to place them among the "literate" whom the editor of *Filastin* would have as his readers?

'Isa, again, was merely airing his despondency, and we should not read into his statement more than that. The authors of the 1931 census, by contrast, aspired for a more reliable picture. They presented a host of tables on the state of literacy in Palestine, with a breakdown by religion, age, sex, district, urban/rural origin, and so forth, as elaborate as one could possibly hope to get. Yet the surveyors did not pretend to resolve questions like those posed above, nor did they directly address them. Rather, they acknowledged that "literacy is a condition with a wide range, so that its definition for the purpose of an inquiry is a matter of considerable difficulty."[5] When conducting the census, they chose to determine "literacy" on the basis of answers to two questions which they posed to those surveyed: (1) "Do you read and write?"—whereby the person concerned was left to determine his/her own classification; (2) "Have you attended a school? If so, for how many years?"—an equally problematic yardstick, as we shall see. A brief reading/writing test to ascertain the findings, a procedure sometimes employed in such surveys, was not applied. The difficulties in a classification based on these methods are all too obvious, and one could not agree more with the authors of the survey, who, having discussed these dilemmas at some length, eventually submitted that their findings were "crude."[6]

The problem, however, is more complex than that which results from inadequate surveying tools. Even if the British had applied the measures necessary to verify the answers they were given, they would still have a quandary on their hands. As has been demonstrated in numerous studies—and as the present study will show for pre-1948 Palestine—both "literate" and "illiterate" are loose concepts that, between them, represent a gamut too wide for any census to handle satisfactorily. Basically, "literacy" is intended to denote the possession of skills allowing independent access to written texts and extracting meaningful messages from them. Accordingly, the differentiation between a literate person and an illiterate one is determinable by the possession or absence of such skills. But this simplistic dichotomy, though still popping up here and there, has long since been discarded by social scientists and historians. Once believed to be quantifiable—a luring advantage to historians—the notion of literacy has repeatedly been proven to obscure more than reveal. Along with the equally sticky division between "literacy" and "orality," this blank distinction has thus given way to a more nuanced approach. It has been shown that, far from being a skill people either possess or lack, literacy is context dependent: its meaning varies from one society to another, from one period to the next, and, perhaps most important, according to the specific function it is expected to fulfill in any given context.[7] A complete reading ability and a total absence of it are merely two situations at the opposite ends of a rainbow. In between there are many intermediate levels of reading competence. They include situations of literacy acquired and then partly or wholly forgotten, an ability to read only certain kinds of text to the exclusion of others, an ability to read but not write (or vice versa), a capacity to make out words from written letters without comprehending their meaning (literacy and comprehension, though interrelated, are distinct attributes, and it is possible to obtain either one without the other), and more. This intricate scene becomes the more complex in times of accelerated change, when standards of reading are transformed, as was the case in twentieth-century Palestine; or when the language itself undergoes a crisis and rapid shifts, as happened to Arabic from the mid-nineteenth century onward.

Literacy is a matter of central importance to the present study. The considerable pliancy of this concept is mirrored in the multichannel course along which the cultural history of Palestine unfolded until 1948. Faced with an inflow of written texts unprecedented in scope and nature, this society was armed with a mixed array of abilities whose serviceability fluctuated perpetually. People who had been literate by traditional standards became handicapped readers; and those who had relied on the community's sages for guidance now found themselves listening to children, whose newly acquired tools seemed to be more relevant. It was a time of kaleidoscopic fluidity. The standard vehicle for attaining independent access to written texts was education, but here, too, there was considerable variance, not only in methods but also in goals. Once geared to obtaining a fairly clear set of objectives, the tasks of education were redefined and its structure accordingly reformed, in order to address the formidable challenge of the time as quickly as possible.

The discussion below focuses on the development of education as a vehicle for literacy in its narrow sense of being a practical ability to access written messages. Needless to say, schooling is often geared to attaining higher goals, such as teaching critical thinking, expanding intellectual horizons, and imparting social skills. The focal concern of the present study, however, requires that such other objectives remain outside the boundaries of the discussion.

Education: Phases of Development

"In Palestine, we were fortunate in beginning with a *tabula rasa*," recalled Humphrey Bowman, the first director of education for the British mandatory government; "so little existed that was worth preserving that we were able to start afresh."[8] Bowman may have earnestly believed his own words, though he seems to have somewhat overstated the case. Students of Palestinian history generally agree that in the later part of the Ottoman era the state of education there was deplorable, reflecting a marked decline from the better days of a remote past. An essay in the *Palestinian Encyclopedia* (*al-Mawsu'ah al-Filastiniyyah*), to name one source of many, uses expressions such as "retrogression" (*taraju'*) and "degeneration" (*taqahqur*) when discussing education during that period.[9] At the point where our story begins, however, the nadir of this trend was already in the past. There was a palpable awakening, in which the authorities and others began to address the issue of education so as to reverse the state of decline. Some progress had been achieved before the downfall of the Ottomans. The ensuing era of British rule was one of a far more energetic advancement in this arena, something over which scholars generally agree, regardless of much anti-British criticism on the part of many of them. By the middle of the twentieth century, Palestine had come to display an educational reality substantially more developed than in 1900, even while leaving so much to be desired.

The story of education in pre-1948 Palestine has been the subject of numerous studies, some of them more credible than others. Many of these contain extensive data, of which there is no dearth, especially for the British period. There is thus no need to retell the story in detail; we may make do with laying out its main contours before focusing on aspects that are most relevant to our discussion.[10]

At the base of the Muslim educational system in the Palestine of 1900 — and for centuries before—was the network of traditional Qur'anic schools known as *kuttab* (pl. *katatib*). With deep roots in Islamic history (and, in terms of organization, probably going back to pre-Islamic times), the *kuttab* was an integral part of the community's religious life. It was a voluntary, unorganized, and unsupervised institution that taught its pupils to be good Muslims by training them to recite sections of the Holy Book. *Kuttab*s existed all over the country, in both towns and villages, accommodating mostly boys and occasionally a few girls in separate classes, for several years of edification. Apparently a few hundred of them existed in Palestine at the beginning of the period under discussion. An assessment from 1914, to be taken with some caution, mentions 379 "private schools" in Palestine with c. 8,700 pupils (including 131 girls), whose overwhelming majority was no doubt *kuttab*s.[11] The itinerary and functioning of the *kuttab* is of particular import to this discussion. They merit a separate examination, to which we shall come later on.

A traditional complement to the *kuttab* was the *madrasah* (pl. *madaris*), an institution normally adjacent to a mosque and designed to engage its students—all *kuttab* graduate males—in learning of a higher order. Only very few of those who had attended a *kuttab* went on to continue their training in the *madrasah*. Here, too, the focus was religious, with particular emphasis on Islamic law (jurisprudence—*fiqh*), along with subjects such as Qur'an, Hadith, and exegesis, as well as the Arabic language and its grammar. *Madrasah*s had prospered in Palestine in earlier times, and, although the evidence we have on their state in the final Ottoman century is scanty, it is quite clear that they were in a state of decline in both scope and quality. Learning of this kind, however, continued to be carried out in and around mosques—above all in al-Aqsa in Jerusalem, as well as in the central mosques of Nablus, Acre, Safad, Jaffa, Hebron, and Gaza.[12]

Both *kuttab* and *madrasah* were non-state institutions. Until the last third of the nineteenth century, the government adhered to the old tradition of leaving its subjects to care for their own education. Then, as a part of extensive reforms in the empire, the state launched a new initiative. The

1869 Ottoman education law required the opening of elementary schools in every community and secondary schools in every large town in the empire. The government meant business, and schools began to spring up in Palestinian towns and villages. According to an oft-quoted statistic—again, perhaps no more than an indication of scale—by 1914 the authorities had opened 95 new schools in Palestine. Most of them were on the primary (*ibtidāʾi*) level, designed for a three-year course of study. In addition to reading and writing in Ottoman Turkish, their pupils were also trained in some arithmetic, Ottoman history, and geography. This number also included upper-level primary schools (*iʿdadi*), 8 in all, that were opened in certain district towns, which students attended for another three years. Here they were trained in additional fields, such as geometry, chemistry, and drawing. Finally, in each of the three district cities of Jerusalem, Nablus, and Acre, higher-level schools (*rushdi*) were established (all three were in place by 1900), offering another four years of further extended education; the one in Jerusalem would later become the country's first full-fledged high school.[13] In 1914 these institutions accommodated a total of c. 8,250 pupils, including 1,400 girls, who represented c. 10% of the country's Arab school-age population at the time (narrowly defined by the authorities as children aged 7–11).[14] The state's educational endeavor at that early stage thus left nearly 90% of all Arab children out of the circle of school-goers.

Not all of those left outside the system necessarily remained without learning. Among Muslims, in addition to *kuttabs*, local enterprising men took their cue from the government and began setting up private schools based on modern methods and curricula, most prominently *rawdat al-maʿarif* (1906) and *al-madrasah al-dusturiyyah* (1909), both in Jerusalem. Initiatives of this kind would play a bigger role after the First World War. The country's many Christian factions had their own autonomous educational institutions. These included schools operated by foreign missions—French, Italian, Russian, British, German, Austrian, and American—and an array of local communal schools that were sometimes aided by foreign religious organizations. Begun before the middle of the nineteenth century, this activity was markedly accelerated during the second half of the century. Quite like their Muslim counterparts, Christian schools lay much emphasis on religious edification. Most of them were primary schools, but there were also more advanced institutions. The latter included Russian teacher-training seminars for men (in Nazareth) and women (in Bayt Jala), and a German seminar for men (in Jerusalem). The information on the number of these schools and their enrollment is often confused and contradictory.

An official Ottoman source from 1914 put the total number of Arab Palestinian pupils in local private and communal schools at c. 12,000, to which one should add several thousands who attended missionary institutions of learning.[15]

These figures, shaky as they are, give us a sense of the proportion of Palestinians who received any kind of education at the beginning of the twentieth century. Apart from several thousand pupils in the basic *kuttabs*, the total number of Arab students in state and private schools, including the foreign ones, may have reached between 15,000 and 20,000 in 1914.[16] A group of that size would represent some 2.5–3.3% of the country's Arab population of c. 600,000 or, more significant, some 20–28% of the Arab school-age population. Again, we can safely assume that at the starting point of our story, back in 1900, the number was smaller.

No institutions of higher education existed in Palestine (with the partial exception of the teachers' seminars). But there were such institutions in the neighboring countries, and those who could afford it and were properly qualified sometimes took advantage of them. At least some members of the country's socioeconomic elite were already attending higher institutions abroad before the end of the nineteenth century. They went to al-Azhar in Cairo, the Syrian Protestant College and St. Joseph's College in Beirut, the Ottoman university (Dar ül-fünun) in Istanbul, and the University of St. Petersburg. A small trickle even reached France and the United States. Some of them settled permanently abroad; others returned and took part in the efforts to modernize their society, among them some of the prominent figures in the country's modern cultural and educational history.[17] This was a tiny group at the top of the community's social structure, an aristocracy of infinitesimal size whose cultural cosmos was quite apart from that of the rest of society.

The period of British rule, unlike the Ottoman era, is rich with extant documents and data. There is a wealth of readily accessible figures and descriptions, both contemporary and of later publication. At the same time, the status of education during this period is the subject of bitter controversy, and thus information is often presented selectively and with differences in accent, dictated by various agendas. Assessing British performance in this arena, however, is of little concern to us here. Instead, we will focus on the results of developments during this phase.

Having assumed the formal responsibility of advancing the country toward self-rule along League of Nations guidelines, and "determined as far as possible to avoid the mistakes made elsewhere" under their rule,[18] the

British gave education a higher priority than their predecessors had. They set up a system modeled on the one at home, appointed British and local administrators to run it, allocated funds, built schools, devised curricula, and imported textbooks. Eliminating functional illiteracy was the primary objective—it was the declared official aim of "a sufficient minimum of education"[19]—and to that end they sought to expand lower-level schools as widely as possible. But they also invested resources in advancing secondary education, developed programs for teacher training, and opened institutions for agricultural, trade, and vocational instruction. A welcome change over the Ottoman period was the introduction of Arabic as the language of teaching, in lieu of the Turkish, which had been previously used in all state schools, to the chagrin of their Arab students. In the new order, many of the town *kuttabs*—though only a few of those in the villages—were absorbed into the official system and for the first time came under state control.

Statistical data on schools, teachers, and students during the mandate period indicate constant growth (see Table 1.1). The number of Arab schools in the public (state) system rose from 244 in 1920–1921 to 308 in 1930–1931 and to 514 in 1945–1946 (the last year for which we have comprehensive statistics). The number of teachers in these years climbed from 525 to 744, then jumped to 2,156 for the same years; and the number of students rose from c. 16,000 in 1920–1921 to c. 24,000 in 1930–1931, then reached c. 81,000 in 1945–1946 (including c. 16,000 girls, some 20% of the total). The student body continued to expand and reached c. 103,000 in 1947–1948, by an official estimate. This last figure represented more than a six-fold growth in state education in the Arab sector during the mandate, while the total Arab population during these years only doubled. Since the British emphasized lower-level education, some 90% of all students in the state system attended elementary schools, usually for five years in towns and for four in villages. Private Arab schools likewise expanded, not due to direct government initiative but certainly encouraged by its activities. There were some 180 of those after the First World War and about 310 after 1945, with a dominant Christian constituent—c. 75% of all private schools at the beginning of the period, c. 60% toward its end.[20] The number of students in private schools had reached a total of c. 44,000 by 1945–1946, about two-thirds of them Christian and the rest mostly Muslim. At that stage, in the mid-1940s, Arab students in state and private educational institutions together made up about 40–45% of the country's school-age population.[21]

These achievements did not result from British initiative alone. The post-Ottoman Palestinian community demanded education and was prepared

Table 1.1. Development of Arab Education in Palestine, 1914–1948

Year	Arab Population	State Schools			Private Schools			Total		
		Schools	Teachers	Pupils	Schools	Teachers	Pupils	Schools	Teachers	Pupils
1914	600,000	95	236	8,250	500[a]	719	12,150[b]	595[a]	955[c]	20,400[b]
1920–1921[d]	660,000	244	525	16,442	181	802	14,239	425	950	30,674
1930–1931	850,000	308	744	24,288	318	1,680	21,603	626	2,424	45,891
1940–1941	1,100,000	403	1,364	54,645	377	1,680	35,165	780	3,924	89,810
1945–1946	1,250,000	514	2,156	81,042	313	1,900[e]	43,883	827	4,056	124,925
1947–1948	1,300,000	555	2,700	103,000	—	—	—	—	—	—

Sources: Tibawi, *Education*, pp. 270–271; Husri, pp. 6–9.

[a] mostly *kuttabs*
[b] not including pupils in missionary schools
[c] not including teachers in missionary schools
[d] data for private schools are for the year 1921–1922
[e] data for teachers are for the year 1944–1945

to shoulder some of the cost. Facing the mighty challenges of massive foreign presence and expanding Jewish settlement, as well as attractive opportunities in the new state apparatus, many Palestinians, hitherto largely apathetic, came to view education as a key to success. This was especially noticeable in the villages, where two-thirds of all Arab (and 70% of all Muslim) Palestinians lived throughout the period. Required by the authorities to pay half the cost of building a school structure, villagers in many places raised the necessary funds and repeatedly called upon the government to increase and improve the system. "We have put together 150 pounds out of our meager resources," wrote a man from the Muslim village of Madamah, near Nablus, so "our children do not have to remain in dark ignorance in the epoch of light, when the entire world from end to end is striving to eliminate illiteracy."[22] Such aspirations and demands, however, were often beyond the mandatory government's plan, according to which only villages with 600 souls or more justified the opening of a school. Hundreds of other places—more than half of all rural communities—were left without education or with only the local *kuttab*. Nor were the schools in the towns able to accept all applicants, and a great many of the latter were rejected or "deferred" (by one estimate in 1945, 47% of all Arab children who had applied to urban schools until then had been turned down).[23] Despite the impressive growth of the education system, then, there were still limits on its absorption capacity. As a result, most Arab children of school age were left out of the state and private school systems under the mandate. Only a third, or slightly more, received the minimal education of four to five years. The rest were left, in the words of a British official, "without a ghost of a chance of learning the alphabet."[24]

The results of the mandatory government educational policy were thus considerable but clearly unsatisfactory to many. Developments during this phase showed the familiar symptoms of the sociocultural infancy diseases that often accompany the introduction of organized education into a traditional community for the first time. In Palestine the government in charge was alien and there was a stormy national conflict that affected this arena in more ways than one. A great deal of criticism was leveled at the British authorities: for allocating insufficient funds to education, for pursuing an unbalanced educational strategy motivated by political considerations, and, in the final account, for failing to meet their mandatory responsibilities on this front. Arab educators who were part of the endeavor were particularly harsh in their censure, accusing the British of both bad faith and impotence. Again, we do not need to engage in this controversy, whose focus is beyond our concern here. But the changes that actually took place are of direct interest to us, and we may now turn to examine them more closely.

Kuttab

Most of those who have told the story of their *kuttab* days have expressed mixed feelings about the experience. Often they have acknowledged that it was a useful chapter in their edification. Equally often, however, it has remained as an unpleasant memory, an inevitable ordeal.

Kuttab was the main framework of education throughout the Muslim parts of the Ottoman Empire and it remained so long after the introduction of organizational changes toward the end of the nineteenth century. It was designed to equip its students with what society regarded as the basic package of skills required by every believer. This was sometimes supplemented by training in the rudiments of the three Rs. For the majority of Muslims who attended *kuttab,* this was the first and last station in the schooling course. Few went on to expand their training in other institutions. Muslim *kuttab*s had their Christian (and Jewish) parallels: rudimentary classes with religious emphasis, which differed from the *kuttab* in the contents of the texts taught in them but not in their basic goals. In Palestine, this remained the prevalent form of learning until the end of the Ottoman era, notwithstanding promising beginnings of a more modern system. When a new educational program was launched under the British, the *kuttab*s in the towns and large villages, most of which were integrated into the state system, were thereby gradually modernized. Many others, however, mostly in the smaller rural places, remained unchanged or changed marginally.[25] Educational frameworks in Palestine were thus transformed piecemeal, and at no stage during the period did they feature clear-cut categories, which could have made our exploration simpler. As we are mainly interested in the kinds of skills graduates of the schooling system took with them, our distinction will be between institutions that offered the limited *kuttab* training and those that sought to equip their students, more ambitiously, with additional tools needed in a modern society. In this context, "*kuttab* training" refers at once to Muslim institutions and to their Christian equivalents. It refers to the basic schools in the old Ottoman order as well as to those schools in the small villages and remote town quarters that continued to function along the same lines even when other parts of the system were being reformed. Existing statistics do not address themselves to such parameters, so that for the quantitative aspect of these developments we will have to make do with an informed estimate.

*Kuttab*s were conducted in private homes, in mosques, or in other public buildings usually associated with religion, such as a *turbah* (a house built over the burial place of a shaykh). There was no standard age for admission: children normally began to attend sometime between the ages of 5 and 8, when their parents decided the time was ripe. "Children" here meant boys with few exceptions, although here and there girls in small numbers were also edified in this way. The length of attendance was likewise loose: *kuttab* pupils would stay for a number of years, then depart, having attained their objectives in full or in part. The age group of *kuttab* students was thus in the range of 5 to 14 years, and occasionally even beyond that. Many graduates of the system have depicted the experience of this learning in lively colors. One of them is Muhammad 'Izzat Darwazah, later a leading Palestinian educator and politician, who attended a *kuttab* in Nablus during the last decade of the nineteenth century. Most such places, he recalled, were "dark and damp":

> The *kuttab* of Shaykh Mas'ud was in the center of town, on the southern street stretching from East to West, in a big *zawiyyah*[26] adjacent to the tomb of Shaykh Badran. You would descend two or three stairs to the *zawiyyah,* which had a big window on the street level. Through it you could see the tomb, with a green turban and a green veil on it, adorned with some Qur'anic verses and text of the *shahadah* . . . The kids would sit on shabby mats on the ground in rows and clusters, their ages varying from six to fifteen. They would hold tin boards in wooden frames on which they would write their lessons, the alphabet, Qur'anic verses, and readings which the shaykh and his more advanced students would write for them. Often pupils would teach each other. They would all recite what the shaykh said, rocking right and left. On [the shaykh's] side were sticks of varying sizes for goading and jolting pupils in the rows and clusters, the long for the remote ones, the short for the near. He would heap abuse on them, employing obscene language; those moving too much would be yelled at or beaten hard.[27]

The ingredients making up this picture—the *kuttab*'s proximity to a holy site, its rugged physical conditions, the classroom jammed with kids of various age groups, peer teaching, the use of tin writing tables, collective recitation, the teacher's rudeness, corporal punishment—were all standard features of this institution. References to them occur repeatedly in personal accounts of the *kuttab* experience. They are thus depicted at the outset of our period and, with little variance, toward its end.[28] The region's general poverty entailed poor material conditions. The fact that many places had only one classroom and one teacher often meant crowdedness and a gamut of age groups under one roof. This, in turn, called for young pupils being trained by their older peers and for the use of an assistant to the teacher, or monitor, known as *'arif* (pl. *'urafa'*, literally, "one who [already] knows"). Such circumstances and solutions, of course, were not unique to Palestine; they obtained everywhere in the region.[29]

Another characteristic indirectly implied in Darwazah's account and explicitly stated in many other reports was the usually poor quality of teachers. Public respect for this calling had long been very limited, as reflected in popular proverbial expressions, such as "stupider than a *kuttab* teacher" (*ahmaq min mu'allim kuttab*) and "stupidity is with weavers, teachers, and yarn spinners" (*al-humq fi'l-haka wa'l-mu'allimin wa'l-ghazzalin*).[30] As so often happens, popular depreciation of the profession and the poor quality of those engaged in it reinforced each other in a vicious circle. "The negligence and incompetence we have witnessed have become common among teachers," noted the authors of a report on northern Palestine during the First World War; "asking [teachers] to show some fervor and zeal in executing their duties would be a fatal blow to their dull brains and idiotic minds. This truth is well known."[31] The rough style and use of corporal punishment as a matter of course did not necessarily result from the teachers' "dullness" and "idiocy." Rather, they were common educational conventions at the time. Palestine was no exception. It was widely believed that "the stick is the remedy for every disease, that it will cure idleness and laziness, the shabbiness of books, stupidity, stubbornness and deceit, and every kind of mental and cultural illness."[32] Some of the less competent teachers were depicted as excessively cruel; creativity in inflicting bodily punishment seemed to be their main claim to professional fame. "The teacher Salim Zaghlul, who came to us from Ramallah, was a drunkard," recalled one graduate of his days in Bir Zayt in the 1890s. "He beat me with a cane on my face and nearly knocked out my eye. My father got angry and took me out of that school."[33] In the overcrowded classrooms the shaykh's task was often limited to implementing the disciplinary regime through beating, typically with the famous *falaqah*, or bastinado. For those who had tasted it, memories of the *kuttab* came to evoke a strong association with pain. Bahjat 'Ata Sukayik (Skeyk), who attended a *kuttab* in Gaza in 1920, spoke about that experience as "terrifying and dreadful." The shaykh, he recalled, hit children on the soles of their feet so hard that the stick would fly from his hand to the ceiling after each blow. Having witnessed this harsh ordeal of edification on his first day there, he returned home with his "head bent down, full of horror and fright," and fell ill with high fever for the next three days.[34] There were, of course, also more compassionate teachers, with a gentler pedagogic approach, just as there were students who, being diligent and well behaved, suffered little of their shaykh's roughness.[35] But for many *kuttab*-goers the experience was harsh.

The sorry reality described by Darwazah and other contemporaries was confronted by the mandatory educational authorities, which placed many of the *kuttab*s under their supervision. The physical conditions were improved, with desks replacing mats and notebooks replacing slate tablets. Books were introduced, and an inspection system went into operation. Yet, in many places such changes were only partial or minimal. The problem of incompetent teachers could not be resolved overnight, and quite a few of the shaykhs with poor ability remained in the system. They often had difficulties adjusting to the new tasks, especially to modern books, and many of them reportedly continued to employ outdated practices. In the small and remote locations, which the Department of Education failed to reach for financial and other reasons, the old modes remained largely unchanged. There, more than in the towns, traditional social conventions hindered the shift.

The primary objective of the *kuttab* was to train the children in memorizing the Qur'an (*hifz*, literally "retaining" in the mind), in its entirety or in part. A secondary priority was teaching them how to read, write, and, if possible, also teaching them some arithmetic. The primacy of learning the Qur'an, which lent the *kuttab* much of its standing in the community, was based on the belief that to practice one's faith properly, one needed to be able to spell at least some parts of the Holy Book out of one's memory. The Qur'an—literally "vocal reading," "calling," or "proclaiming"—had an existence above all as a recited message. It was as a vocalized text that it made sense as the verbatim speech of God, and reciting passages from it was a major expression of fulfilling one's faith. This required learning the holy text "by heart," or, as one graduate of that system has put it, "commit[ting] the spoken word to memory in an abiding way."[36] Training the children in memorization was thus the thrust of *kuttab* teaching. This can be seen in the fact that once memorization was attained, the course of study was normally terminated. A festive ceremony would mark the *khatm* or *khatmah*, literally the "sealing" of this noble training, with more modest ceremonies celebrating interim achievements.[37] A child who had completed memorizing the Qur'an "was regarded as qualified in knowledge (*mu'ahhal 'ilmiyy^{an}*), as if he had obtained a secondary school diploma," related a graduate of the system. What was left for him at that point was learning some vocation, so his father would take him to any of the men-of-trade, who would teach him a craft of one type or another. Sometimes, he recalled, "a child who had completed his course of memorizing would remain in the *kuttab*, being too young to learn a trade. The shaykh would start reading the Qur'an with him all over again. Once he finished, it would be as if he attained [the title of] Magister."[38]

Beyond coaching in recitation, *kuttab*s sometimes taught other skills. Children were taught the alphabet, practiced reading and at times writing, and in a few more fortunate places even a little more. Traditionally such learning was likewise conducted without any written text. In the twentieth century, as books became available, some *kuttab*s were able to introduce primers or readers. The methods were the same as those by which recitation was taught, based on repetition and memorization and normally handled in a rigorous atmosphere. Students were using whatever writing tools they had at hand—tin or slate tablets and slate pencils at first, notebooks and lead pencils later on.

For the mostly oral learning, the physical presence of a written text could be useful, but it was not absolutely essential. For a variety of economic and technical reasons, books were rare and sometimes nonexistent in schools—more so in the villages than in towns, more so at the outset than at the end of the period in question. But this did not necessarily impair training in recitation, which largely relied on the text being retained in the shaykh's memory. When a written text was available—a copy or copies of the Qur'an in this case—it would be more convenient and would also lend some authority to the process of learning, but this was not crucial. Nor was the shaykh's personal involvement necessary at all times: once he had taught a passage or section, he could lie back (often literally) and entrust the *'arif* with conducting the recitation drills. Moreover, it was not absolutely essential that the shaykh himself knew how to read or write. In principle it was sufficient that he knew the Qur'an by heart, or even—if a man with such proficiency was unavailable—that he knew only parts of it, which he would impart to his pupils.[39] It was possible for students to go through the entire course of training in reciting the Qur'an without using a written text and without learning how to read it, let alone how to write. We will never know what part of all *kuttab* graduates received this kind of limited training and ended their studies without being able to decipher a written text. But many references would seem to suggest that the phenomenon was not rare. It may well have been widespread.

The difference between acquiring the ability to recite the Holy Book, or even read parts of it, and acquiring the skill of independent reading and writing is of far-reaching significance. The distinction is sometimes blurred by the fact that the Qur'an—the text that usually served for training in both spheres—is written and vocalized in the language of the Arabs. In Islamic countries where other tongues are spoken and a non-Arabic script is employed, the division between memorization of the Qur'an and training in reading and writing in the vernacular is all too obvious.[40] But even for Arabic-speaking communities, the language of the Qur'an represents a different quality, indeed largely a different language, from the spoken idiom. It is possible for one to know sections of the Holy Book by heart without understanding the full meaning of the text, even if one's own language is an Arabic dialect. It is also possible for one to recite large parts of the Holy Book without being able to identify written passages of it when these are present—since one's training has been in memorization, not reading. Finally, it is possible for a person who has studied the Qur'an using a written text to identify any given passage in it when it is presented to him and start reciting correctly from that point, while still being incapable of actually reading anything else. In this last case, the person would be identifying the passage by the shape of the written or printed letters, or the page layout, then reciting from memory.

Jabra Ibrahim Jabra, an acclaimed Palestinian writer, described such limited-purpose technical practice in his Catholic school in Bethlehem in the 1920s. The children's chorus, he related, was positioned in two separate wings, with the text of the hymns they were singing placed in the middle. This required half of the chorus to read the text upside-down, a practice in which they were expected to train themselves. "I thus learned to read any text, in Syriac or Arabic, straight or upside-down equally well. . . . We all learned how to do it, but only a few of us comprehended these texts, or even a part of them. We were in fact praying in a largely incomprehensible language although capable of reading it straight, upside-down or sidewise, in light or dark."[41] This kind of acquired proficiency in identifying and spelling out a "largely incomprehensible language" did not automatically translate into a capacity to read anything else. Rather, it was an ability of a very limited kind.[42] For Jabra, it was not this specific skill but other parts of his training at the school that instilled solid literacy in him. But for many others, there were no such other parts.[43]

What were the results of this training? The Palestinian educator and scholar 'Abd al-Latif Tibawi noted that "despite its primitiveness and all its limitations, the *kuttab* succeeded on the whole in achieving literacy. . . . The explanation of this success is to be sought in the fact that the process of instruction had a definite religious setting and purpose actively aided by society."[44] This seems to be an upbeat appraisal, which apparently applied to only some of the cases. The more gifted among the students, or those who happily learned with more gifted teachers, were able to gain a practical reading capability. Sayf al-Din al-Zuʿbi, who attended a *kuttab* in the village of Nayn near Nazareth around 1920 and who was evidently a talented person (he would later become mayor of Nazareth), related how being trained in the *kuttab* prepared him for reading stories to his uncle. He was taught the alphabet through traditional texts and became able to apply this knowledge to other kinds of writings. "Having learned the Qur'an has benefited me much [later on], in fine articulation (*nutq*) and excellent reading (*qira'a*)," he noted.[45] Another graduate of the system in the early 1920s likewise acknowledged that "we made considerable strides in writing and reading" and suggested that "the method of teaching in the *kuttab*s in their improved format . . . was more effective and useful than the modern methods" employed later on.[46] Statements of this last kind would substantiate Tibawi's depiction of *kuttab* education as achieving success in cultivating literacy.

Other testimonies, however, indicate that the success was less than universal. Low standards of the educational system and poor material conditions combined to yield limited results in many places. "It was clear to me that my schooling throughout the year would be useless," reported Niqula al-Khuri, who had attended such a place in Bir Zayt around the turn of the century. His education continued "without any benefit worthy of mention. I practiced reading with the help of my father."[47] Khuri's case of learning to read outside the *kuttab* was hardly unique, nor was it limited to the earlier part of the period. Many years later, Hanna Abu Hanna—who was sent to a *kuttab* in Isdud (near Gaza) in the 1930s—still had to learn to read from his father since, in his words, "the *kuttab* did not teach me anything."[48] A major point to remember here is that the value of this training eventually depended on whether or not the *kuttab* graduate subsequently moved on to a higher stage of study in another institution that would help him retain and refine his skills. For the many that did not, Tibawi's assessment may well have been too optimistic.

Modern Education

The schools considered in this section were distinct from the *kuttab*s mainly in the higher priority they accorded to imparting knowledge unrelated to religion. Such knowledge was regarded in the new system as essential equipment for modern life. The training pupils received in these areas—primarily, reading and writing, arithmetic, and certain other basic fields such as grammar and history—was overall better than in the old places of learning. Schools of this newer kind began to appear during the last Ottoman decades, the venture of a state seeking to invigorate itself, as well as of private interests. At first launched mainly in the larger towns, their development was considerably enhanced under British rule, when they broadly expanded to other parts of the country.

The new program of study was geared to attaining proficiency in these elementary fields. Such was already the case in the schools built as a part of the Ottoman educational reform. For instance, an elementary school in Nablus during the last decade of the nineteenth century featured a four-year program that included the study of writing, reading, and arithmetic, in addition to history, geography, chemistry, and physics. In some of the courses, printed books were in use and pupils practiced writing not just on slate tablets but also on paper notebooks, with pencils and pens.[49] A private school, *rawdat al-maʿarif*, set up in Jerusalem in 1906 by Shaykh Muhammad al-Salih, boasted a program based on "modern fields of learning and . . . the study of Arabic language, its intimate elements and literature." In addition, the school bulletin announced, "several foreign languages are taught through excellent techniques and the modern methods that have been tried in the best of schools."[50] Another famous private school in Jerusalem, Khalil al-Sakakini's *al-madrasah al-dusturiyyah*, developed a similar curriculum and even published its own newspaper in 1910–1911, entitled *al-Dustur*, a mark of its modern educational approach. These were modest but promising beginnings meant to produce the kernel of a modern educated class, better equipped than the graduates of the older rudimentary institutions.

The more organized system introduced by the mandatory government was pronouncedly aimed at eliminating or minimizing illiteracy as its primary goal. Based on experience gained elsewhere,[51] the British assessed that four to five years of learning would suffice to instill permanent literacy, namely, of the kind that is not lost even in a person who does not practice it subsequently. Accordingly, they set up a standard system of elementary schools with a five-year program in towns and a four-year program in the villages. Some 90% of those educated by the state in mandatory Palestine attended these schools and nothing beyond them.[52] The old Turkish programs and textbooks were discarded forthwith as unfit, due to "their incompatibility with the spirit of the time," and the government borrowed teaching schemes from Egypt, where an organized system had long been in place. The official curriculum, laid out in 1921, included many hours of Arabic language teaching, namely, reading, writing, pronunciation, composition, and syntax—about half of all the hours taught during the first two years and about a third in the next two. In addition, about a quarter of all class hours for the third and fourth years were to be devoted to learning English, especially reading. More hours were earmarked for arithmetic, history, and geography. Notably, only a sixth of class time was allocated to the study of religion.[53] From the start, the Department of Education brought school texts from Egypt and Lebanon in sufficient quantities to meet the country's needs—a novelty whose importance in imparting literacy hardly needs elaboration. Used exclusively in the early years, they were later supplemented and eventually supplanted by books which local educators authored (most famously Khalil al-Sakakini, 'Umar al-Salih al-Barghuthi, Khalil Tawtah, and 'Izzat Darwazah), primarily in history and Arabic language. More books became available in libraries that were set up in schools and, in some parts of the countryside, by state-operated circulating libraries.[54]

In considering the role played by these more modern schools, we should keep in mind the inevitably slow pace of the shift from old to new modes, despite the considerable resources invested. Many of the previous problems continued to impede progress in the modernized system as well. Contemporary accounts of the newer schools often depict poor physical conditions, incompetent teachers, deficient or irrelevant curricula, and the continued application of outmoded pedagogic methods. The official introduction of a modern course of study did not necessarily mean its full (let alone successful) implementation everywhere, nor did the introduction of periodic inspection guarantee high-quality instruction. Control of students' attendance was lax, and parents' cooperation with the system was often problematic. Accounts of such problems, frequent in the late Ottoman and early mandate years,[55] also appeared for the later part of the period.[56] Yet, despite such understandable difficulties, the new system clearly reflected efforts on the part of the state to pull the society ahead and make it more enlightened. Graduates of the system took with them skills and knowledge of a kind that had been unavailable to previous generations, with few exceptions.

For the most part, urban centers were well covered by the new educational net. But the majority of all Palestinians lived in villages, and the scene there was more problematic. By the late Ottoman years, state schools had already been founded in some of the larger villages. But they had been plagued by the many ills besetting the *kuttabs*, and in practice had barely differed from them. Under the mandate, the number of rural schools increased substantially, and a dual objective was defined for them: educating the peasant to be more productive, thereby raising his standard of living; and "eliminating the darkness of illiteracy," so he can "comprehend what he reads and write what he wants."[57] A special program of study was prepared, similar but not identical to that of town schools,[58] and libraries, permanent or mobile, were brought to some of them. It should be remembered that rapid developments in the country triggered demand for more education by villagers, who were ready to share the cost involved to the best of their abilities. In some places they even took independent initiative in opening classes and hiring teachers where the government failed to do so.[59] Villages close to towns—to wit, a walking distance of up to a couple of hours—often sent their children to study there, if the village itself had no school or if the one in the town was better.[60] On the whole, the demand for education in these places was higher than the government's ability to provide it, and by the end of the period schooling was still beyond the reach of a great many rural communities.

There were more problems in village education, beyond the massive exclusion. As already noted, the rural curriculum was designed for a four-year course of study, unlike the town schools' five. The reasons for this were probably practical, but it was rationalized as a matter of social principle: the peasant was "that innocent man, marked by simplicity, remote from the intricacies of civic culture . . . [who merely] needs to be guided in his work."[61] Out of this reduced program, a part of the time was devoted to agricultural training and manual work, mostly to practical labor in the school's garden, at the expense of classroom instruction.[62] In many of the places, schools offered only a partial program of less than the four years, for lack of teachers or due to various material constraints. Most villages with education had one school building of one or two classrooms and one teacher, whose own skills usually left something to be desired. "We beg you to examine the village teachers," ran an open letter to the Department of Education, in 1925:

We know of a teacher who seems to have no knowledge of teaching principles. He is probably incapable of writing a letter for himself. Look into the matter and you will find that his being a teacher is harmful. Out of reverence for knowledge and education, we urge you to test him. If he fails, send him away and appoint instead someone fitter for the post.[63]

There was also the perennial problem of student absence, mostly during agricultural seasons but also at other times. Sending a child to school was usually a sacrifice for the family, which would be doing without his (or her) valuable help in the field and at home. When the high season came, families often could not afford the sacrifice. (Such circumstances, of course, were hardly unique to Palestine—or to the Middle East for that matter: they bore a striking similarity to the social and cultural problems that obtained in rural communities of eastern and western Europe until very recently.)[64] "Enthusiasm for education in our village was limited," a man from Qaqun (near Tulkarm) related, "since the people, being farmers, wanted their sons to help them in fruit-picking and irrigation."[65] Sometimes the phenomenon was so disruptive of the course of studies as to force the authorities to close schools "on account of unsatisfactory attendance."[66] High expenses were frequently involved, which peasants found it difficult to pay: writing tools, school uniforms, even shoes—a compulsory item they would not necessarily buy otherwise. In addition, "there were also the fines imposed on the families when their children damaged school equipment or furniture," recalled Faysal Hurani, a graduate of the system in one small rural community, "and there were the various forms of gifts to the teachers, required by tradition." No wonder, he suggested, "that only the well-to-do could send their children to school. The poor could not, or would only send some of the kids while keeping others at home, to shoulder the burden."[67] Such constraints were also responsible for a high dropout rate.[68] Mahmud al-Qadi, another product of the rural schooling system during the mandate, offered this description of his experience in Surif (near Hebron), in the 1930s:

> In those days, the teacher would not devote his time to educating his students. Rather, he would leave them to teach each other, while spending most of his time wandering among the many guesthouses in the village. We [the author and his brother, who attended the same school] therefore did not persevere in learning our lessons regularly. Instead, we often worked in [our father's] shop during [our] father's absence, when he went to the town or to the neighboring village for his business. Sometimes we accompanied the shepherd to help him guard the sheep from the wolves. I therefore completed my course of studies in 1936, that is, completing the fourth grade, which was also the last grade, at the age of thirteen.[69]

Obviously, such difficulties undermined the goal of achieving literacy, let alone attaining a permanent reading ability. The implications of this are clear: such circumstances rendered the value of rural education in Palestine quite dubious in terms of the particular proficiency we are considering here. The length of a training period required for obtaining permanent literacy was a matter of controversy: when arguing that four years of study were sufficient for the purpose, the mandatory authorities came under heavy fire. But even the authorities concurred that the goal could be achieved within such a period only under optimal conditions. Conditions in the great majority of villages were less than optimal, with the result that many of those who learned how to read and write in village schools left with a rather shaky competence. The subsequent utility of these skills and the chances of retaining them depended on the scope of exposure to the written word and on opportunities to practice reading. But the rural environment, seldom providing such opportunities, was not conducive to the retention, let alone consolidation, of these usually partial skills. By certain pessimistic assessments, the loss of reading competence in rural Palestine was so massive that the level of illiteracy there hardly decreased during the mandate.[70]

Another generally weak link in the system was girls' education, primarily in the Muslim community. Here, too, the change was particularly slow. Traditional reasons accounted for the scant presence of girls in the schooling system throughout the period discussed here, and for the fact that even toward its end only 28% of the country's school pupils were girls.[71] "I like my child to learn to read and write," said parents who agreed to send their daughters to school at the beginning of the twentieth century; "but—they admitted—I like it better that she is taught to kiss my hand when she comes home."[72] Such an outlook, entertained even by the more liberal families, left the great bulk of the country's girls out of the system. Those who did attend schools with their parents' consent were mostly sent to missionary institutions.[73] This approach began to give way to a more positive attitude following the shift from Ottoman to British government, yet the departure from age-old norms was anything but quick. "She is not going!" exclaimed the father of a Jerusalem girl in the 1920s, when her mother pleaded with him to let the daughter get some education. "What does she need school for? It will only make her strong-willed," he charged, voicing a popular conviction.[74] Another girl from Jerusalem in the same period, whose brothers were sent to study in the best of institutions, attended a girls' school near al-Aqsa for one year, but then her education was cut short. "My father took me out of school after the first grade. He bought me a sewing machine. . . . My father said it was better for me to learn to sew."[75] The persistence of such principles was chiefly responsible for the wide gap between boys and girls in the educational system, a gap that narrowed only belatedly. In the rural community, in particular, traditional conventions of this kind remained all but unchanged throughout the entire period, and often beyond. When a British official came to the village of Qaqun in the 1940s and proposed opening a school for girls, the idea was abhorred: "We fear," said one of the elders, "that should they become educated they might tomorrow start writing letters to the boys."[76]

Nevertheless, more schools for girls were opened under the mandate. In state schools, the boy:girl ratio decreased from 5:1 in the late Ottoman years to 4:1 by mid-century.[77] This meant that, as against several thousand girls in schools around the turn of the century, tens of thousands were getting education toward the end of the mandate—an impressive development, no doubt. Two other related facts should be noted in this context. First, educational progress among girls was much less balanced than among boys. Here disparities between towns and villages and between Muslims and Christians were far sharper. By mid-century, the number of town girls in schools was greater by four-fold than that of rural girls. Similarly, while in Christian schools the number of boys and girls was roughly equal, in the Muslim sector the ratio was 1 girl for every 4 boys.[78] Second, in many educational institutions for girls, especially in Muslim and village schools, the focus of study was different from that of boys: less on enlightenment, more on practical skills, such as housekeeping, hygiene, and sewing—a training that would "make them successful and diligent housewives and mothers," in the words of education planners.[79] Still, basic reading and writing skills were imparted, and girls with education could potentially join the country's reading audience, if their subsequent careers allowed them the appropriate conditions for it. For some of them the experience was even gratifying: Fadwa Tuqan, who attended the Nablus girls' school in the 1930s, recalled her days there as distinctly pleasant—"I cannot remember a single teacher who left a painful memory in me"—and closely associated with her love for language and literature.[80] But Tuqan, later a celebrated poet and writer, was not necessarily typical.

Finally, we should briefly consider the private schools, clearly a category apart, and on the whole above, the other systems in the country. Muslim private schools were maintained by the Supreme Muslim Council or other private and public organizations, and were somewhat better than the state schools in their infrastructure, equipment, and educational regime (though not in their teacher:student ratio). The much bigger Christian private school system, however, was clearly of a higher quality. Christian institutions were wealthier and better equipped, their teachers more numerous and better trained, and they often enjoyed the powerful backing of a mother organization abroad.[81] A recent study of one such school, the French Catholic St. Joseph College for boys in Jaffa, depicts an impressive scene of first-rate education already in the Ottoman period and, of course, subsequently. It included the study of reading and writing in both Arabic and French, along with a variety of other subjects offered from the very beginning. The school had elementary and secondary classes, which during the mandate prepared students for Palestinian matriculation and for study abroad. At first it attracted mostly Christian students—c. 80% of the total during the Ottoman period—but the number of Muslims grew, reaching close to a third of the student body during the mandate. It was clearly an elitist institution: over half of its population came from upper- or middle-class families (among Muslims, close to 90% came from these classes).[82] In that it was typical of the many foreign schools in the country, which had conspicuously foreign, almost extraterritorial characteristics.[83] Students of these schools acquired solid linguistic and literary tools and the habit of working with texts, which would make them a central segment of the reservoir of upper-echelon educated Palestinians and of the country's reading audience.

The Impact of Education: Profile of the "Literate" Community

With the enhanced pace of educational development, the number of Palestinian Arabs able to read and write, negligible at the outset, grew manyfold during the first half of the twentieth century. But the precise scope of this growth and the quality of skills acquired by this educated segment are difficult if not impossible to assess. Data on school attendance and gross estimates of literacy level, the best we have in this respect, do not address the variations that concern us here. The most reliable available figures are quoted in the opening pages of this chapter; but they all fall short of illuminating for us the multilayered setting of abilities created by the different schooling systems, and by different schools within each system, since they were in flux throughout the period. Considerable disparities in the method, nature, and duration of learning—the outcome of a hastened transition—inevitably produced highly disparate results. Gaps were often evident even between schools in two neighboring villages or within the same city. The scene at the end of the period, besides being more promising than at the beginning, was also immensely more varied.

The figures we have, however, do seem to tell us one important thing: most Arab Palestinians were excluded from the "literate community," no matter how we define it. More than half of the country's Arab school-age population was left out of the enterprise we have examined. And since public education on a massive scale was a novelty, the bulk of Palestinians who were already beyond school age when the system evolved were likewise left out. As for those included in the multicolored scene, the data permit only the use of very broad categories in profiling it.

At the top of the ladder stood the educated elite, whose members received the most advanced schooling the country could offer. A small core of this elite had existed in Palestine in the late Ottoman decades, the metaphoric "two percent" referred to by 'Isa Da'ud al-'Isa. This group expanded during the ensuing phase, but even toward the end of the period it still represented a tiny minority of society. It consisted of notable and well-to-do families, who would buy for their children the best education as a key to integration in the state bureaucracy or commerce and to success in a changing world. They sent them to state or, better, private schools in the towns—or, better still, to any of the foreign institutions—took private tutors for them and sometimes arranged for them to complement their training abroad. Also included in this category were most of the other graduates of private, primarily Christian schools, who similarly benefited from high-quality training. Those who belonged to these groups would be considered fully literate anywhere and by any standard, with unqualified ability to use texts of any kind independently, in their own language and more.

At a level below was the much bigger group of state school graduates, comprising mostly middle- and lower-class children, whose parents had come to value education and had managed to place them in the system. For obvious reasons, this category consisted mostly of the society's younger generation. It was predominantly urban, but it also included a rural segment consisting of those that happily had a good school in their village or were sufficiently close to a city to get their education there. Aside from being wider, this was also a more diverse group, featuring a broad range of proficiencies. In principle all of them were trained in reading, writing, and more. The better students, or those who were fortunate to have better teachers, acquired a solid command of reading and writing, and if they remained in an environment where texts were present they could improve their abilities still further. But there were also those who had attended weaker schools—in small towns or villages, or in the few places where Bedouin education was available—and those who had not completed the full course of elementary training. Such graduates sometimes took with them imperfect abilities, including a limited knowledge of reading, of the kind that would allow them to decipher short and simple texts but perhaps not high-level, complex ones. For them—and for those considered in the next category—literacy did not necessarily mean comprehension (let alone critical thinking). Even that restricted knowledge was at risk of being lost if not practiced for some time. It was a kind of temporary and conditional literacy, so to speak, always in danger of regression to functional illiteracy. This category was the archetypal product of the educational efforts during this period, and its immense diversity clearly mirrored the fluidity of the entire enterprise.

At a yet lower level were *kuttab* graduates who did not pursue their education further. This was a very large mass that, unlike the previous group, included not only young people but members of the older generation as well. It was similarly a varied category. The more intelligent among them would sometimes be able to make practical use of the training they had obtained, including the ability to read writings of a simple nature. The rest, apparently the great majority, would normally be capable of reciting the texts they had learned and little else, and in practical terms there was small difference between them and those who had never had an opportunity to study.

Other social parameters, already alluded to in different contexts, may be mentioned in further characterizing this colorful "literate community." The most significant division line seems to have been between town and country. On the whole, urban residents had access to better schools, while those in villages received education of a lesser quality, due to both administrative and sociocultural factors. Among urbanites, those living in bigger towns—Jerusalem, Jaffa, Haifa, Nablus, Acre, Gaza—also had postelementary schooling locally available to them. Villages adjacent to towns and benefiting from this proximity had an advantage over the more remote places, where education was on the whole deficient. The objective of "encouraging village pupils' desire for reading, so they can advance themselves by consulting newspapers, books and journals,"[84] which a leading educator in 1935 defined for the village school, was for the most part more wishful than realistic. And villagers were, furthermore, at a greater risk than urbanites of losing whatever knowledge they had acquired.

Two other important and interrelated distinctions were those between men and women and those between the Arab-Muslim and Arab-Christian communities. As a rule, men received more education than did women. As a rule, again, Christians invested more efforts in education, both because they could rely on foreign resources and because as a minority they sought a qualitative edge. Education in the Christian sector advanced rapidly, and by the end of our period it had become nearly universal, comprising 90% or more of the relevant age groups, as against less than half of the Muslims. The number of Christian girls who received education grew concomitantly, and by the end of the period their presence in schools was more or less equal to that of Christian boys. Among Muslims, by contrast, girls attending schools remained few until the end of the period: in the mid-1940s they included 60% of all town girls, but only 10% of those in the villages.[85]

Urbanites, men, Christians—these were the categories that received better training and were prominently represented in the country's literate segment, however defined. It goes without saying that such divisions often cut across each other: a town Muslim boy was likely to get better education than his village counterpart, let alone more than a Muslim girl anywhere— but perhaps not quite as good as a Christian girl in the city, or even in a village missionary school. To these typical traits of the literate community we should finally add another obvious characteristic. At any given point in time, the younger the person, the better was his/her chance to be educated, due to the constant expansion of the system at the lower ages. The literate community was young; and in a society where education was gaining esteem as a measure of status, this last fact was bound to have profound repercussions for social and, eventually, political relations.

The expansion of literacy, itself a change of primary significance for Palestine, was merely one facet of the cultural transformation. The skills imparted by education permitted increasing segments of the society to quench their growing thirst for information, obtainable from written sources of many kinds. This craving for knowledge and the expanding ability to access it evolved in tandem with an unprecedented proliferation of written texts in the country—a development that at once enhanced and was boosted by the growing thirst and spreading skills. Eventually, the confluence of these processes would lead to actual dependence on written products by a public that only a few decades previously had little use for them. The multiplying presence of such products is the subject of the next chapter.

CHAPTER 2

Texts: Imported, Produced, Viewed

Texts of every kind were in lively circulation in the Palestine of 1948. They changed hands in libraries and bookstores, enriched private collections, enlightened pupils in urban and rural classrooms, and pervaded the public domain in large towns and small, in endless shapes. Half a century earlier, hardly any of that could be seen in the country. There had been no printing press in Palestine until the last decade of the nineteenth century (with the exception of some small missionary shops), and hence no local production of books, journals, or public announcements. Manuscript texts had been kept in closed private and mosque libraries accessible to few, and only a tiny elite had been importing and reading publications produced abroad. Nor had writing been normally used in open places—in street signs, shop names, or advertisement—except sparingly and then in foreign tongues. In all of these, dramatic changes occurred during the first half of the twentieth century. They evolved slowly at first, a trickle blocked by illiteracy, poverty, and old habits. But with foreign inspiration and local enterprise, they gradually turned into a considerable stream that modified the landscape.

Traditional Stocks: The Augury of Change

We begin with a view of the elite, looking at the very slim sector in which intellectual and literary activity was routine even before 1900.

Collecting books has been a time-honored tradition since very early on in Islamic history. Books were a mark of faith, learning, and wisdom that lent prestige to their possessors. Rulers from Umayyad times onward are known to have founded libraries, often seeking to outshine their predecessors in collection size and the uniqueness of their treasures. Some of these libraries are said to have comprised tens of thousands of volumes or, according to certain accounts, hundreds of thousands. Mosques and *madrasah*s enhanced their reputation as centers of learning by expanding their book stocks; individual scholars attained fame with impressive private libraries. Until the introduction of printing, and for a while thereafter, the common means for increasing one's collection was buying more items—a practice that sustained a vivid book trade—or having duplicates made by a copyist (*nassakh*), a respectable calling. Considered valuable assets, books were often bequeathed as Waqf, earmarked for the use of other scholars in the mosque or *madrasah* of the collector's hometown. It is to a large extent thanks to elaborate book lists in Waqf documents that we have a notion of the scholarly activity in different times and places.[1]

Libraries whose contents have come down to us from early Islamic periods give us an idea about the subjects that had concerned public and private book collectors. Mosques and *madrasah*s normally kept texts in the various branches of religious studies: Qur'an, Hadith, exegesis, and law, as well as *adab*, the Arabic language, and history. In private libraries the variety was usually bigger, including entries in every field of knowledge: philosophy, logic, geometry, astronomy, medicine, and so forth. For example, the library of Ibn Ta'us, a thirteenth-century Shi'ite scholar from Iraq, consisted of 669 manuscripts, which, while particularly rich in religious subjects, also comprised a broad array of other topics, from medicine to meteorology, from alchemy to archery.[2] When eventually bequeathed to mosques, such individual collections would enrich these public libraries in size and variety.

The fate of libraries in the region following the 'Abbasid demise is yet to be systematically explored. Meanwhile, available studies suggest that this was on the whole an era of decline for libraries. This was partly due to political instability, military turmoil, and natural disasters. Decline was also due to poor maintenance, massive robbing (or acquisition) of written treasures by foreigners, and, no less damaging, the abandonment by the spiritual leadership of its scholarly openness in favor of adherence to an ever-smaller range of texts. Assets accumulated earlier apparently fell to pieces, and later Arab scholars would lament this loss of resources that had been "carried away from their place by unfit people, who sold them for a pittance due to their own ignorance and lack of appreciation for texts and their meaning."[3] Such was apparently the fate of public and private stocks alike, which, under the hands of less conscientious inheritors, disintegrated and dwindled to insignificance. By and large, this was the state of affairs throughout the

Ottoman era in the region. For example, in eighteenth-century Aleppo, formerly a thriving center of learning, members of the educated elite reportedly possessed "what is reckoned in that country a considerable collection of books: but it should be remarked, that the number of volumes in an Aleppo library, might easily be contained in a small book case."[4] By the nineteenth century, libraries in much of the Islamic world had become a pale shadow of their past glory.

Palestinian collections could hardly fair any better. Testimonies on institutional libraries there in the late nineteenth century depict a disheartening scene. Important public libraries had previously existed in the main mosques, but many of their assets had apparently diminished. The country's most prominent book stock around 1900 was that of al-Aqsa in Jerusalem, comprising several thousand volumes, and there were other mosque collections in Acre, Jaffa, Gaza, and Hebron, with several hundred manuscripts each. There were also private and family libraries, belonging to members of the social elite, who had sometimes studied in al-Azhar and who, pursuing an old tradition, managed to assemble tens or hundreds of books. A few important collections were started during this otherwise unfruitful period: the libraries of Shaykh al-Khalili and the Khalidi family, both dating from the eighteenth century, and that of Shaykh al-Budayri, from the early nineteenth century—all in Jerusalem; the Qamhawi family library in Nablus, apparently from the nineteenth century; and a few other, more modest, stocks in both of these towns and in Safad.[5]

Palestinian scholars in recent years have undertaken to explore the scene of private book collections in towns and villages of the country, sometimes purporting to present a complete picture of it.[6] Others have suggested that such collections may have been too dispersed to record. Dr. Mahmud ʿAli ʿAtallah from al-Najah college in Nablus, an authority on Palestinian manuscripts and editor of several catalogues of private and mosque collections, has noted that there are "tens of libraries considered to be private collections of Palestinian families," most of which are still awaiting exploration.[7] For example, Dr. Muhammad ʿAql, from ʿArʿarah (in the Wadi ʿArah region), discovered several such collections in his home village in the mid-1990s. ʿAql, a historian concerned with the cultural legacy of his village, unearthed stocks of books in three local homes dating from the beginning of the twentieth century. One of these, belonging to the al-Khatib family of 'ulama', comprised some 60 items; another, likewise owned by an eminent shaykh, had 49; the third, once containing "many" books, had disintegrated and its contents were scattered all over the village.[8] Loose as this picture is, it may well be indicative of the state of affairs in many other places both in towns and in the countryside. Such private collections were normally kept behind closed doors, inaccessible to the public. Anyone seeking to read more than the spiritual pieces available in mosques would have thus faced serious difficulties finding such texts.

In 1900, or shortly before, the first public library in Palestine—the Khalidiyyah—was opened in Jerusalem.[9] It featured literary treasures collected by several generations of one of the city's most respected families, the Khalidis. Backed by a Waqf endowment, these works were now put at the public's disposal. The Khalidiyyah offers a splendid view of the scholarly interests and literary tastes of the country's educated class on the eve of the twentieth century. It attests to its owners having been men of intellectual passion in the best classical tradition of Islamic learning. It also indicates that they concerned themselves, in addition, with modern, nontraditional, matters, thereby marking a nascent cultural trend in Palestine.

We have a fairly accurate notion of the contents of this collection at the departure point. The Khalidiyyah published a catalogue of its most important holdings upon its inauguration, and scholars have documented other parts of the collection and its subsequent development.[10] The original stock belonged to Raghib al-Khalidi, founder of the library, who had inherited most of the books from his ancestors. Other family members—Yusuf Diya', Ruhi, and Nazif al-Khalidi—also bequeathed their substantial collections to it. The original library comprised 2,168 items, of which 1,156 appeared in the published catalogue and another 1,012 in an unpublished list. Works of a traditional nature constituted the bulk of it. Nearly half of the total dealt with religious subjects. Other texts were of a more secular nature, a component equally consonant with the tradition of private book assembling—on medicine, mathematics, astronomy, history, geography, philosophy, grammar, literature, and poetry. The library boasted many old and precious manuscripts, some going back to Mamluk times and a source of much pride to their owners. Remarkably, however, an even greater segment of the collection was printed works, obviously imported from abroad—a portent of the technological changes that would soon transform the scene. Thus, out of 213 books of history, 206 were printed volumes, as were 104 out of 127 in *adab,* 84 out of 119 in exegesis, and 48 out of 83 in Sufism. A survey indicates that as many as 4,500 printed books, among them some 1,000 in European languages, were already part of the stock before the First World War.[11] At least 1,138 of these had been in place by 1900; the rest were in the possession of family members, who donated them to the Khalidiyyah between that year and the war.

The presence of a new type of writings received from neighboring provinces and from Europe is of particular interest. The 1900 catalogue recorded, among these imported works, modern history books authored in Egypt, including studies on European history such as *Ta'rikh bunabart al-awwal* (History of Napoleon I) and a translation of François Guizot's *Histoire de la civilisation en Europe,* entitled *Tamaddun al-mamalik al-urubawiyyah.*[12] Later contributions included works on European history and politics; dictionaries and grammar books of all the important European languages; Arabic, English, French, and German translations of the Bible; the complete works of Plato and Voltaire, and texts by Josephus, Dante, Montesquieu, Darwin, Gibbon, Milton, Hugo, and Shakespeare. There were also studies by Western Orientalists, as well as a variety of periodicals in scores of volumes, both bound and unbound, that had been published in neighboring countries.[13]

For Arab men of letters, to amass valuable manuscripts was consistent with tradition. For them to display interest in the histories, idioms, and ideas of Europe was not. This was a concern of a novel kind, which, judged by the dates of the items acquired, had begun several decades before the onset of the twentieth century. The Khalidi collection deviated from the old model in other ways as well. Not only did it contain books on hitherto "alien" matters, in hitherto ignored languages, produced by a hitherto overlooked technology; it also comprised a host of foreign periodicals that had been received regularly. The presence of this last kind of items reflects a different concept of collecting: the successive arrival of journals and newspapers changed not just the contents of the stock but also the pace of its development, rendering it considerably more dynamic than before. Encompassing old manuscripts that represented conventional intellectual endeavor at its best alongside such modern works, the Khalidi library augured an upcoming transition in the country's cultural landscape. While no doubt exceptional in its richness and variety, this library was probably not unique in assuming such a role. Sometime during the second half of the nineteenth century, Palestinian intellectuals—then still a precious few—began to echo the sounds originating across the provincial boundaries. Quite a while before the country joined the new trend in a massive way, members of its elite were becoming enthusiastic consumers of the literary products arriving from the vicinity.

Impact of the Neighborhood

Exciting cultural changes occurred in three centers of the region during the second half of the nineteenth century: Istanbul, Lebanon, and Egypt. Those in the latter two, in particular, are directly relevant to our story. Known as the *nahdah*—"awakening," or "revival"—this set of changes was reflected in an impressive blossoming of literary, journalistic, scholarly, and educational activities. It started in Lebanon around mid-century, the initiative of a group of local Christians, mostly educated by European and American missionaries. Inspired by foreign ideas and eager to ameliorate their uneasy minority standing, they set out to redraw the parameters of cultural activity, reviving old treasures of language and literature and borrowing whatever seemed useful in Western culture. Christian Lebanese formed societies of learning; opened printing presses; wrote and translated works of science, history, and literature; and started the region's earliest private journals. This last enterprise was perhaps the most vibrant mark of the awakening: 21 private journals appeared in Beirut during the third quarter of the century,[14] becoming a lively channel of public edification and discourse far beyond the confines of Lebanon.

In the last quarter of the nineteenth century, another center of cultural ferment emerged on the banks of the Nile, quickly overshadowing the one in Lebanon. In Egypt, potentates who were bent on consolidating their autonomous power base by borrowing implements of power from Europe expanded education, built a printing industry, developed communications, and even permitted private publication. By the last quarter of the century, their efforts were further invigorated by an inflow of gifted Lebanese fleeing political instability in their own country. The literary output resulting from this confluence of Egyptian venture and Lebanese skill was remarkable. In a recent study, the Egyptian scholar 'Aydah Nusayr has shown that during the second half of the nineteenth century, Egypt produced a striking 9,538 book titles, with a total print run of no fewer than 7 million copies (as against 1,849 titles in 725,000 copies during the century's first half). About 300 titles annually, sometimes more, were published there in the last two decades of that century.[15] Journalistic endeavor in Egypt was equally dynamic, with a total of 627 different newspapers appearing in Cairo and Alexandria from 1880 to 1908 (and many more in other towns of Egypt), reaching a circulation of perhaps 100,000 copies by the end of that period.[16] The enterprises underpinning such activities—printing shops, publishing companies, bookstores, literary societies, reading rooms—made concomitant strides forward.

Palestine experienced none of this sort of revival until much later. But it was in the neighborhood and, like other parts of the region, it enjoyed the cultural light radiating from Lebanon and Egypt. In the last quarter of the nineteenth century, books and journals from Lebanon and Egypt (and to a lesser extent Istanbul) reached Palestine and circulated among members of its small, educated elite. Accounts on the presence of such publications in the country, seldom more than the mention of names, are insufficient for a quantitative assessment of their inflow, still less of their readership. But that local intellectuals became attentive to the new voices around them, had access to the literary output of their neighbors, and even engaged in a dialogue with them is solidly confirmed by ample evidence. We have already seen that the Khalidis avidly acquired works printed abroad, on both traditional and modern matters. A recent exploration has also revealed numerous volumes of each of the leading Arab journals of the time in the Khalidiyyah: 7 volumes of Ahmad Faris al-Shidyaq's semiweekly news journal *al-Jawa'ib* (Istanbul, published 1861–1883); 8 of Butrus al-Bustani's literary biweekly *al-Jinan* (Beirut, 1870–1886); 26 of *al-Muqtataf*, the scientific monthly of Ya'qub Sarruf and Faris Nimr (launched in Beirut in 1876 and continued in Cairo from 1884 to 1951); 8 of Jurji Zaydan's historical-literary biweekly/monthly *al-Hilal* (Cairo, begun in 1892 and still going on today); and more. In addition, there was a large number of incomplete volumes and single issues of these and other journals.[17] The same study has shown that the al-Aqsa library—which, likewise, comprised several private stocks bequeathed to it by individuals and families—had in its holdings even bigger runs of the same imported periodicals.[18]

More clues are provided by the imported journals themselves.[19] When Butrus al-Bustani invited readers of his biweekly *al-Jinan* to subscribe to a new universal encyclopedia, *Da'irat al-ma'arif,* which he was about to launch in 1876, no fewer than 115 people from Palestine applied, in spite of the high cost involved. The journal made it a point to mention each of them by name (as it did with the many hundreds of applicants from other parts of the region). About 70% of these prospective buyers came from the three towns of Jerusalem, Jaffa, and Acre, but there were also interested people in Nazareth, Haifa, Ramlah, Nablus, Gaza, Bethlehem, Lydda, Bayt Sahur, and Shafa 'Amr. We may assume that most, if not all, of those who applied did indeed read and perhaps subscribe to *al-Jinan,* the journal promoting the project. Letters to the editors of periodicals abroad provide additional evidence. Some of the journals in the region had regular sections devoted to patrons' queries, in which the inquirers' place of residence and often their personal names were mentioned. Needless to say, the authenticity and representative nature of letters to the editor are ever in doubt; but coming in bulk, they would suffice to confirm the phenomenon of reader-editor dialogue, if not its scope. Two of the leading Arabic periodicals examined for the present study, *al-Muqtataf* and *al-Hilal*, received questions from all over the region, from Aden to Adana, as well as lands farther away, during the period between their inception and 1900. Palestinians, too, engaged in such a dialogue: during the 24 years of its publications until 1900, *al-Muqtataf* handled 81 queries from Palestine, while *al-Hilal*, launched only in 1892, responded to queries of 20 different Palestinian readers. Other foreign periodicals of the time that carried similar sections likewise received queries by Palestinian readers, among others. The extent of Palestinian presence in the questions-and-answers sections was, unsurprisingly, markedly smaller than that of Lebanese and Egyptian readers. It was also smaller than the presence of queries sent from Damascus, Aleppo, or even Baghdad.[20] Still, though limited in scope, such involvement did reflect active Palestinian interest in the fruits of the *nahdah*.

The arrival of other periodicals into Palestine in the late Ottoman years has also been mentioned by their readers: the Egyptian *al-Bayan, al-Diya', al-Muqattam, al-Ahram, al-Mu'ayyad,* and *al-Falah;* the Lebanese *al-Jannah, al-Mashriq, Lisan al-Hal, Thamarat al-Funun, al-Safa',* and *Bayrut;* and the Syrian *al-Muqtabas.*[21] The names of over 30 different agents acting in Palestinian towns for these and other foreign journals prior to the First World War—found in a cursory, far-from-exhaustive search—further attest to this flow.[22] Again, most subscribers were urbanites; but evidence also suggests that journals from neighboring provinces were ordered by literate people in the countryside. Thus, receipts from the western Galilee village of Yarka indicate that the notable Shaykh Marzuq Ma'addi paid the subscription fee for both *al-Janna* and *Lisan al-Hal* as early as 1882; for *Bayrut* in 1888; and for *al-Safa'* in 1898–1899. Similarly, a receipt from the village of 'Ar'arah, dated 1893, attests to the payment by Muhammad al-Qasim, a local resident, of his dues for subscribing to "the official paper of the province" (*jaridat al-wilayah al-rasmiyyah,* apparently the state bulletin *Bayrut*).[23] It is clear, then, that while the country on the whole had to wait until after the Young Turk Revolution to feel the full impact of cultural change already affecting some of its neighbors, a few of its intellectuals experienced this change much earlier. They availed themselves of texts purchased abroad, ordering books and subscribing to journals. Such imported publications sometimes had to bypass state censorship by being dispatched via the foreign mail services that operated uncontrolled in the empire. They were read, bound, and integrated into private collections. Similarly, the handful of Palestinian writers who sought to publish works they had composed did so in the printing shops of Beirut, Cairo, and other places.[24]

The emergence of a printing industry in Palestine itself after 1908 would alter this scene, a change that will be examined below. Yet, even when this last shift was under way, the arrival of written works from abroad did not subside. If anything, it expanded. Egypt—politically freer than other countries, with a richer press tradition, more advanced infrastructure, and the region's largest pool of talent—remained the main source. After the First World War, Egypt witnessed a tremendous literary prosperity in scope, quality, and variety, fed by unprecedented political and intellectual ferment. A struggle for national independence, issues of state building, questions of communal identity and cultural orientation, traditional political rivalries—all spurred lively public exchanges in print. The periodical press was, again, the most colorful channel for this activity. By the mid-1930s, according to one survey, over 250 papers in Arabic and 65 in other languages were in circulation throughout that country.[25] At that stage, some 10,000 copies of Egyptian daily newspapers and 15,000 copies of other periodicals were being sent regularly to the countries of the Fertile Crescent, Palestine among them, according to a contemporary assessment.[26] Egyptian—and, to a lesser extent, Lebanese—journals served as an arena for cross-regional discourse on many levels, from politics to the arts. In book making, too, Egypt remained a leader. ʿAydah Nusayr's above-mentioned study on Egyptian production in the nineteenth century is yet to be paralleled by one on the twentieth century. But there is little doubt that the energetic literary activity there persisted and even intensified. In the literary scene of the post–Ottoman Middle East, Egypt was the chief pivot of activity, Lebanon a secondary axis. All other countries were peripheral, their cultural-intellectual life depending to a large extent on the output of these two centers.

Available evidence on Palestinian consumption of imported writings confirms its role as a literary satellite in the Egyptian and Lebanese cultural orbits. Such, for example, are promotional ads by booksellers and journal vendors in Palestine, who served as agents for foreign publications. They tell us, for example, that the Jerusalem bookstore of Bulus and Wadiʿ Saʿid carried "all scientific and cultural books, Arab and foreign"; that Tawfiq Jirjis

Nasir's shop in the same city sold "Palestinian, Egyptian, Syrian and foreign newspapers and periodicals," and that Fu'ad Nassar's store in Nazareth featured even Iraqi periodicals "and all other Iraqi publications."[27] Palestinians who read foreign Arab journals in that time often mention the experience in biographies and memoirs. Thus, Ibrahim Snubar, an educator in Gaza in the early 1920s, tells us that he had used to read "al-Muqtataf, al-Hilal and a third literary journal whose name escaped" him. Niqula Ziyadah, a student in Jenin and Jerusalem and then a teacher in Acre in the 1920s and 1930s, used to "read al-Muqtataf and al-Hilal regularly; in the years in which al-Siyasah al-Usbu'iyyah appeared in Egypt, it became a second school for me after al-Muqtataf and al-Hilal." Fawzi Yusuf, a student in Jerusalem in the early 1930s, usually spent his school breaks selling "Egyptian newspapers, such as al-Muqattam and al-Ahram." And Ihsan 'Abbas, a high school student in Haifa in the mid-1930s, relates how every student in his class subscribed to al-Risalah, upon their teacher's advice.[28] In 1936, Zionist leaders, seeking to set up an Arabic newspaper that would counter Arab anti-Zionist propaganda, acknowledged that it would be difficult to compete with the quality of imported Egyptian publications like al-Ahram and al-Jihad, to which "the Arab educated class is accustomed."[29] In the late 1930s, as the political atmosphere in and around Palestine became tenser and the country's ties with its neighbors closer, demand for imported publications increased commensurately. The situation sometimes led the mandatory government to ban the entry of Arab newspapers into Palestine to protect British interests. Obviously, a decree prohibiting entry does not necessarily indicate that the paper actually reached Palestine. But it does imply that the banned item might have had some influence in Palestine, through direct circulation or in some indirect way. During the period from 1934 to 1939, such measures were taken against 36 papers: 11 from Egypt, 12 from Lebanon, 9 from Syria, 3 from Iraq, and 1 from Tunisia.[30] Such scattered clues, again, do not indicate scale. But added up they do allow us to form some general sense of the scope of the phenomenon.

The leading periodicals to circulate in Palestine (and in most other Arab countries) were the Cairo-based al-Hilal and al-Muqtataf (beginning in the late nineteenth century); al-Siyasah al-Usbu'iyyah, al-Musawwar, and Ruz al-Yusuf (from the 1920s); al-Risalah and al-Thaqafah (from the 1930s); and the Beiruti al-Adib (1940s). The Egyptian al-Ahram, al-Muqattam, al-Balagh, al-Jihad, and later al-Misri were the main dailies.[31] Imports expanded constantly, aided by improved means of transportation. By the 1940s, leading Egyptian newspapers were flown into Palestine on the day of publication, reaching the cities and sometimes finding their way into the villages as well.

Palestinian ties with the press of the neighborhood grew into a recip-rocal exchange. This was typical of the culturally peripheral Arab coun-tries, whose literary activity was closely linked with and inspired by cultural developments in Egypt and Lebanon. Themes discussed in publications across the borders were reviewed at length in Palestinian newspapers, some-times by means of special supplements.[32] One observer of Palestinian cul-tural history has noted that the educated public "would impatiently await the arrival of [Egyptian journals]. They would read them thoroughly and critically then split into thinking groups and parties, supporting one author or another and engaging in passionate debates of the ideas brought up in the journal."[33] Other forms of dialogue with the foreign press were also used. Letters by readers and articles by local writers published in the papers of Jerusalem, Jaffa, and Haifa often addressed matters discussed in Arabic journals abroad, usually starting with a reference to the journal in ques-tion: "We have read in [such and such] Egyptian [or Lebanese, Syrian, etc.] paper that . . ."; they would then offer their commentary. As before the First World War, Palestinians continued to send queries to the editors of journals in other countries. To pick a random example, the readers' ques-tions section in the 1928 volume of *al-Hilal* contained 6 queries by Pal-estinians, sent from Jerusalem, Jaffa, Haifa, Bethlehem, Ramallah, and Tulkarm.[34] Other interwar volumes of that journal carried letters from read-ers in Nablus, Acre, Nazareth, Gaza, Samakh, Baysan, Bayt Jala, and Majdal-'Asqalan—an impressive distribution.[35] Palestinian writers also contributed articles, essays, and poems to journals abroad. Kamil al-Sawafiri, one such author who used to write for the Egyptian literary monthly *al-Risalah,* has counted no fewer than 14 compatriots—authors and poets—whose writ-ings had appeared in that journal alone during the 1930s and 1940s.[36]

Foreign books, like foreign journals, had already reached Palestine be-fore 1908. Books printed in the region itself were often promoted in the Egyptian and Lebanese press, and those who could afford it ordered them straight from the publishers. When journals began to appear in Palestine, they immediately became conduits for such promotional ads. Khalil Baydas's literary monthly *al-Nafa'is al-'Asriyyah,* launched in 1908, advertised books printed in Lebanon and Egypt and advised his readers to purchase them from their authors or printers. The regularity with which he offered this advice, and the fact that it commenced from the journals' inception, would indicate that direct ordering from abroad was already common among the elite.[37] Many of the imported books in the Khalidi family collection and in those of others from the same class came in through such a procedure.

Postwar issues of *al-Nafa'is* continued to announce the sale of foreign printed books, and Egyptian publications, especially historical works and novels by Jurji Zaydan, Niqula Haddad, Farah Antun, Ibrahim al-Yaziji, and others, were now marketed directly from the journal's office.[38] The postwar literary monthly *Zahrat al-Jamil,* published in Haifa, did the same.[39] Bookstores—new businesses that expanded rapidly after the war—carried the imported publications of neighboring countries and advertised the fact in the local press. In the immediate postwar years, there was little local output to counter or supplement the sale of these foreign items. But even later on, when a text industry had emerged in Palestine, it could hardly have undermined the inflow of the far-superior products from across the borders. Fawzi Yusuf, who in 1935 opened a bookstore in Jerusalem named *maktabat al-andalus,* relates in his memoirs how he used to go to Cairo regularly to replenish his stock. Like other businesses in the trade, his was largely based on selling Egyptian imports, though he also carried whatever was available of local making. There was enough demand for Egyptian books to justify the opening of an office in Cairo, he noted, a move that allowed him to offer his Palestinian customers the attractive service of handling orders for Egyptian books within 24 hours. This, in turn, generated more demand for them. At the height of this endeavor, on the eve of the Second World War, his Cairo branch would dispatch books, packed in predesigned boxes, by train to Jerusalem every day, leaving Cairo at 5 P.M. and reaching Jerusalem the next morning at 8—an impressive enterprise, if true.[40]

Palestinian papers occasionally devoted columns to reviewing and thus promoting books published in other Arab countries. To pick, again, a random example, the 5 February 1929 issue of *Filastin* featured a literary section in which three new books were discussed: an Arabic translation of Gustave Le Bon's *The World Unbalanced;* a work by Hanna Khabbaz, a Syrian author, on the Syrian anti-French revolt; and a study of holy Islamic sites by 'Abdallah Mukhlis. The first two were printed in Cairo, the third in Damascus; readers were urged to order them directly from the publishers abroad or from a Jerusalem bookstore.[41] Egyptian, Lebanese, and Syrian booksellers took their own measures to promote their merchandise in Palestine. In the early 1920s one could find their catalogues in the country's bookstores[42] and their ads in its press, often with post-box addresses and telephone numbers. A typical ad in 1924 announced the sale of As'ad Khalil Daghir's study on language errors and their rectification, entitled *Tadhkirat al-katib;* published in Cairo, it was obtainable from Bustani's famous *maktabat al-ʿarab* on Faggalah street in that city. Another, from 1934, advertised three books on sale at ʿIsa al-Babi al-Halabi's Cairo bookstore, a work translated into Arabic and two originally written in that language.[43] The high frequency with which such notices appeared in the Palestinian press—one could find a few of them running at any given moment from the late 1920s onward—indicates that this was indeed a thriving business. In addition, as we have already seen, school textbooks were also brought in. At first relying almost exclusively on imports from Egypt and Lebanon for lack of a local alternative, the mandatory Department of Education used to buy the texts and distribute them among pupils in its schools. They were also sold in stores, alongside other works of foreign origin.[44]

Literary works by the Arab luminaries of the time and by lesser writers circulated in mandatory Palestine. Their authors had keen admirers there who fervently read their books, journal articles, and press interviews and bought their publications whenever they could. They were also prominently represented on the shelves of public and lending libraries. Egyptian writers such as Qasim Amin, Tawfiq al-Hakim, Taha Husayn, ʿAbbas Mahmud al-ʿAqqad, Ahmad Amin, Ibrahim al-Mazini, ʿAli Adham, Mustafa Sadiq al-Rafiʿi, Zaki Mubarak, Ahmad Shawqi, and Hafiz Ibrahim; the Lebanese Jubran Khalil Jubran; the Iraqi Maʿruf al-Rusafi; and others.[45] "In the years between 1931 and 1940," recalls Fadwa Tuqan, who was a teenager at the time, "I read . . . al-ʿAqqad's *al-Fusul, Saʿat bayn al-kutub* and *Mutalaʿat fiʾl kutub waʾl-hayat.* I also read [works by] Taha Husayn and Ahmad Amin's *Fajr al-Islam* and subsequent volumes. Then, for a while I concerned myself with reading Mustafa Sadiq al-Rafiʿi on the one hand and May Ziyadah on the other."[46] A recently discovered stock of books, gathered from several club libraries in pre-1948 Jaffa, has been found to contain works by all of these authors and more, in both hardcover and paperback editions from the interwar period.[47] Another aspect of the elite Palestinian experience involved occasional visits to Palestine by authors and poets from Egypt, Syria, Lebanon, and Iraq. They delivered lectures, offered public readings of their works, and met with groups of intellectuals.[48] In more ways than one, then, the Palestinian educated elite engaged in the regional cultural discourse, whose center of gravity was elsewhere.

A word on the scope of these developments is in order. Personal recollections, traces of commercial campaigns, bookshop advertisements, and similar haphazard fragments rarely indicate quantity. They teach us little beyond the names of imported papers, the places where they were sold in Palestine, and the identity of casual individuals who bought and read them. Nor do British or Zionist accounts contain systematic data on such imported products, and it is unlikely that a record of this kind was ever kept anywhere. Published mandatory government statistical accounts, which contain minute details on a very broad range of matters, happen to be of little value for the present purpose. For example, from a British statistical survey of imports to Palestine we learn that the country bought "printed books" from Egypt to the tune of 3,490 Palestinian pounds in 1928, 4,353 pounds in 1929, 5,692 pounds in 1935, and 2,634 pounds in 1936. There are also figures for such imports from Syria, including Lebanon (roughly a third of the Egyptian level), and far smaller figures for Iraq and Tunisia. The rubric designed to indicate numbers of items, in which figures are quoted for most other types of imported goods, is void in the case of books, and it is thus all but impossible to draw responsible inferences from the given data. Nor do these data distinguish between school texts—which apparently made up a sizeable segment if not the majority of all imports—and other works. The tables quote accurate figures for "advertising and printed matter" imported from abroad, but this definition of the category is in itself too ambiguous to be of much use.[49]

We thus have to make do with a general view of the scene and with speculating about its boundaries. The evidence at hand seems to suggest that the exposure of the Palestinian elite to the literary influence of its neighbors was, on the whole, quite substantial. Avid acquisition of foreign texts, dialogue with educated counterparts abroad, festive hosting of visiting authors, all made for an exciting scene. Of course, this was a small group, remaining so even when it was growing. This point is not always clear in studies on the period, which, focusing on the ever-brighter spot of light under the lamp, overlook the darkness around it. Here and there, patchy data at our disposal hint to the limited dimensions of the vibrant literary scene during this period. A Jewish observer in 1936, for example, noted that *al-Ahram* was circulating in Palestine in 1,000 copies and *al-Jihad* in 800[50]—figures comparable to those for the weaker Palestinian newspapers of that year, as we shall see. Another observer referred to the Egyptian series of inexpensive booklets called *Iqra'* (Read), which is said to have been the most popular type of text imported into Palestine in the 1940s: a total of c. 3,000 copies of items from that series were brought into the country in 1943 and c. 4,500 in 1944.[51] The number of titles included in these totals is not mentioned, but we may assume that the few thousand copies represented a few hundreds for each of several titles sold in Palestine in these years. If such was the case with relatively affordable books toward the end of our period, then the image of a small—if increasingly glowing—light surrounded by extensive dimness may well be apt.

Local Production

Printing reached the Arab lands late, several centuries after its explosive spread throughout Europe. Cultural, political, and other considerations informed the Ottoman policy against adopting the invention, a line that was abandoned only in the eighteenth century.[52] Even when permitted, printing progressed only sluggishly in the empire for another century or so. But during the second half of the nineteenth century, with the cultural awakening in Lebanon and Egypt, it began to make big strides and became a thriving industry. In Palestine, however, such prosperity had to wait until the twentieth century.

Christian societies, having blazed the trail in introducing printing elsewhere in the region, brought it to Palestine as well. The Franciscans, Anglicans, and Greek-Orthodox set up printing shops in their Jerusalem missions (the Franciscans, starting as early as 1846, ran the most active operation in this field).[53] Several other presses were founded before the end of the century. These were small plants with simple steam-driven machines, or, in some cases, leg- or hand-operated devices and a few boxes with movable letters. Some of them had Arabic characters, but they limited themselves to producing mostly educational/evangelical material. A handful of privately owned Arab presses are reported to have emerged in the early 1890s.[54] One of them, about which we know a bit more than the rest, was that founded by the Greek-Orthodox Jerusalemite Jurji Habib Hananiyya, in 1894. "Our town Jerusalem, like other [towns], was thirsty for knowledge and science . . . [which] are spread and circulated only by the printing press," he later rationalized his enterprise.[55] More to the point, Hananiyya may have sensed a potential for making a living in this business, an option that had not existed until then. At first possessing only Latin characters, he kept busy for three months a year during the tourist season. Some two years later, having acquired Arabic letters, he made forays into Arabic and Turkish printing, which brought upon his head the wrath of the authorities. But he persevered, performing printing jobs for some influential officials who protected him, working days in his printing shop near the Old City's Jaffa Gate and nights clandestinely at home. In February 1898 he eventually managed to secure a license to print in Arabic, reportedly in return for a heavy bribe. Hananiyya, who in 1908 began publishing his paper *al-Quds,* reported that

The Franciscan printing shop in Jerusalem, 1893.
From Ely Schiller and Menahem Levin, *Tsilumei eretz Israel ha-rishonim*
(Tel Aviv: misrad ha-bitahon, 1991). © Ariel Publishing. Courtesy of Ely Schiller,
Ariel publishing Ltd.

between the foundation of his press and that year he had printed a total of 281 books, including 83 in Arabic.[56] This is an impressive but somewhat dubious figure, for which we have no supporting evidence anywhere.[57] If true, the majority of these publications must have been ephemeral leaflets rather than real "books." Whatever the true scope of this activity, it took place, significantly, prior to the 1908 dramatic collapse of the state censorship dam, a historic event that triggered an outbreak of feverish activity in this area.[58]

The downfall of the wall blocking free expression after the demise of Sultan ʿAbd al-Hamid resulted in an immediate upsurge in publication in Palestine. This increase indicated a latent demand for printed items that had apparently evolved during the later years of severe censorship. It was seen in the feverish birth of newspapers and journals, which in turn prompted the hasty foundation of printing shops in Jerusalem, Jaffa, and Haifa. Printing machinery, often old and secondhand, was usually imported for the specific purpose of producing newspapers. Periodicals were the mainstay of most presses in Palestine before the First World War and for a while thereafter: Hananiyya printed *al-Quds;* Iliya Zakka printed *al-Nafir* (Jerusalem, 1908, and later Haifa); Najib Nassar printed *al-Karmil* (Haifa, 1908); Bandali Gharabi printed *al-Akhbar* (Jaffa, 1909); and the ʿIsa cousins, Yusuf and ʿIsa Daʾud, printed *Filastin* (Jaffa, 1911). These enterprises were often a one-man project or family business. Once the machines were set rolling, their owners would look for more printing jobs, which the market then was slow to provide. The printing shop at the German (Schneller) missionary orphanage (*dar al-aytam*) in Jerusalem seems to have been better equipped than its competitors (the orphanage also ran a printing training program for its students).[59] While the early history of printing in Palestine is yet to be fully explored, it would seem—given the paucity of commercial and political activity—that the local printing of texts other than newspapers was infinitesimal in pre-1914 Palestine.

As in every other respect, here too the pace of development was accelerated after the war. The intensification of public life, the expansion of economic activity, and progress in education all called for more printed products. New presses emerged and engaged in more massive production in response to demand. Besides journals and books, to which we shall turn next, they also provided other products, previously familiar in Egypt and Lebanon but little known in Palestine. An ad in a Jaffa-based newspaper, promoting its own press just after the war, offered services in printing "personal [visit] cards (*kart fizit*) and envelopes (*zuruf*) as well as paper bags and all [printed] needs for pharmacies."[60] A Haifa newspaper offered printing services for "all commercial documents and personal cards" and "letting and renting deeds (*sanadat ijar wa-istiʾjar*)."[61] Another printing shop in the same city invited the public, around Easter time, to order its holiday greeting cards (*bitaqat al-ʿid*), produced in Arabic and foreign letters on high-quality paper.[62] And a Jerusalem paper, which in 1920 had likewise offered all of these services, added a new option in a 1921 commercial: printing wedding invitations (*daʿwat ʿusr*).[63] Presses periodically announced the upgrading of their equipment, featuring printing in Arabic, Latin, and Hebrew characters, and boasted of improvements in professional execution, something that was reflected in the ever-better graphic appearance of the ads themselves.[64] Within several years after the war, a broad range of printed products came to be used in Palestine, primarily by the urban population, but—if the growing intensity of such promotional ads is any indication—also by expanding circles of other consumers. Most important of these products were the ones designed for mass consumption, which served as the backbone of the entire industry: newspapers.

The Periodical Press

One predictable result of the vigorous presence of Egyptian and Lebanese publications throughout the region was the weakness of local text industries in other provinces. It was hard, and in some fields quite impossible, to compete with the quality of the products flowing in from Cairo or Beirut. To a large extent, this was the reason why journals in Damascus and Baghdad, as well as in Jerusalem and Jaffa, failed to take off and prosper. Complaints by their owners affirmed the impact of this foreign inflow. "We are the first to rejoice about the press renaissance of our Egyptian neighbor," the editor of *Filastin* stated in 1929. "But does our delight with foreign journals—Egyptian or otherwise—warrant the poor state of our own press, to the extent that it is denied its due share in this blessed journalistic awakening?"[65]

The emergence of the Palestinian press was a development of major importance to our story. Fairly well documented in existing scholarship,[66] its many details need not detain us too much and we may limit our attention to its main stages. As we have seen, a segment of the country's elite had previously been exposed to journals imported from abroad. But the appearance of indigenous publications and their availability in mass numbers surely marked a new phase. A few feeble attempts at starting newspapers were made in Palestine toward the end of Sultan 'Abd al-Hamid's tenure. But it was the change of political regime in August 1908 that prompted the first substantial wave of publication. As many as 15 periodicals appeared in a vigorous surge of journalistic activity before that year was over. Another 20 were published before the outbreak of the First World War, and c. 180 more before the end of the mandate.

That so many papers appeared within such a short period, growing out of a tabula rasa, reflected their owners' urge for self-expression and their assessment that the market was waiting for such products. It also reflected the fact that starting a newspaper was a simple and inexpensive matter. In Palestine, as elsewhere in the region, a private person with limited resources could put out a periodical by executing all of the necessary duties—editorial, technical, and administrative—single-handedly (such, we may note in passing, had likewise been the case in seventeenth- and eighteenth-century Europe). That person could gather the information by himself, appropriating materials from other publications and writing his own editorials and essays. It was not absolutely necessary to purchase printing equipment, which could be costly; instead, one could collaborate with a local press. Even the distribution of the final product could be performed personally, or by hiring urchins for a pittance. Anybody adequately ambitious and resourceful could thus join the new trade. Launching a newspaper, however, was far easier than sustaining its publication for long, and the great majority of papers started in Palestine, as well as elsewhere in the region, turned out to be ephemeral. Only a few, especially those set up by members of the better-off socioeconomic class, remained in the market long enough to have an impact.[67]

To the unaccustomed public, newspapers represented a new idea, distinct from the traditional types of writings. There was, first, the novelty of format: large, unbound sheets, portable, foldable, and, more curiously, disposable, produced in mass numbers and designed for popular—not elite—consumption. Like no Arabic text hitherto, they dealt with daily matters of a transient nature, each issue rendered largely obsolete by the next. They also confronted their readers with a new kind of authority, that of the anonymous writer (who, in Palestine, was most often a Greek-Orthodox Christian). Newspapers seemed to speak for a cause unlike that normally promoted by men of the pen. Conceivably, the very novelty of the medium and the anonymity of its authors could have alienated a traditionally disposed audience. Such shortcomings, along with material and educational constraints, were obvious obstacles to the development of the press. But in the long run they were offset by their undeniable—indeed indispensable—advantages. The mighty encroachment of foreign forces, the increasingly intrusive state, the manifestly expanding market economy, the imposing presence of novel ideas and their infringement on old values—all called for a new compass. Local papers provided fresh news and commentary on daily developments, economic data, enlightenment on modern subjects, and a host of other useful services. The opening of newspaper columns to readers' comments lent them the additional attraction of an interactive dialogue, thereby somewhat reducing the effect of anonymity. Soon overcoming its initial misgivings, the local society made the press a popular conduit of communication.

The appearance of newspapers in Palestine was a mark of the excited response to the shifting landscape in and around it. Most papers were primarily devoted to news reporting and to airing political views, with a boldness of contents and style previously unthinkable.[68] Of these, the Jerusalem-based *al-Quds* and *al-Munadi,* Haifa-based *al-Karmil,* and Jaffa-based *Filastin* were at first the most vocal. There were also some modest attempts to publish literary journals, such as *al-Asma'i* in Jaffa and, more successfully, *al-Nafa'is al-'Asriyyah* in Haifa, geared by definition to a more sophisticated audience. The nascent press suffered from a variety of problems—economic, technical, and professional—which rendered the majority of papers ill-executed and short-lived. Illiteracy, indigence, and undeveloped infrastructure all checked their public acceptance. But the press was meant to be a mass commodity, and its owners made it their business to awaken the market and habituate it to the new merchandise. Palestinian papers, shabby products of low material quality—a humble replica of their proud Lebanese and Egyptian counterparts—competed with each other over a small reservoir of potential customers. Up until the First World War, most of them were published with a modest print run of 200–300 copies per issue (one or two papers printed more—perhaps up to 1,500 copies—but many of these were sold outside the country).[69] By one reasonable assessment, the total number of newspaper issues circulating in Palestine in 1914 was a meager 4,500–5,500.[70] Still, even the lower bracket of this estimate, if true, marked significant progress: from an apparent use of several hundred imported copies by an exclusive group prior to 1908 to an expanding public consuming thousands of them within some five or six years.

Journalistic endeavor and the market for its fruits broadened rapidly after the war, enhanced by the historic changes at home and in the region. The 1920s was a formative decade for the Palestinian press. It consolidated its presence in the public domain and became by far the most important type of text in use. Some 40 papers appeared during that decade, usually at a weekly pace; daily newspapers would emerge only later. Expanding beyond the three main cities of Jerusalem, Jaffa, and Haifa, newspapers now came to be published also in Acre, Gaza, Bethlehem, and Tulkarm for varying periods of time. They served the public with news and analysis, offering themselves as an arena for debating and intramural squabbling. Political factionalism, a perennial ailment, was ever-manifest, and papers took on the color of one camp or another; occasionally, they changed colors. They also rendered their consumers other useful services: publicizing official notices, circulating commercial ads, alerting readers to upcoming social and cultural events, and entertaining them in their literary columns. Demand for newspapers increased gradually. Rather than the few hundred copies of the prewar era, individual papers in Palestine of the 1920s circulated typically at 1,000–1,500 copies. *Filastin,* the most popular publication, reportedly sold ca. 3,000 copies per issue toward the end of the decade. By 1929, the leading papers had reached a combined circulation of 12,700, according to a British assessment. Again, this last figure may not seem large given the overall size of the community, by now c. 850,000 people. But the rate of readership was increasing more rapidly than the population itself. During the 15 years between 1914 and 1929, the country's Arab community grew by some 40%, while the number of Arabic newspaper copies in the market more than doubled.[71] That the press had become a standard channel of communication in Palestine of the 1920s was further confirmed by the fact that court announcements as well as individual notices had come to assume binding legal status by being posted in them. To illustrate, a man from Abu Tur placed a "notice to the merchants" in a 1924 paper, warning them not to employ his son Ibrahim or sell him anything on credit—"and I am absolved of responsibility by having published this notice [in the paper]."[72]

Local newspapers continued to head the list of texts produced and consumed in Palestine until the end of the mandate. With experience and technological improvement, the best of them became solid products, gradually approaching the level of their better counterparts in the neighborhood. Most of them were political publications; there were more attempts to produce literary and cultural journals (e.g., the Jaffa-based *al-Fajr*, in 1935, and *al-Diya'* in 1946), which failed after a short while. As a Jewish observer at the time noted, "[Palestinian] Arabs do not read weekly [journals]; at most they read an illustrated magazine. By contrast they read—and especially listen to—daily newspapers, due to their being highly politicized."[73] This was basically so, although one ought to bear in mind the high-quality literary publications of neighboring countries consumed by the Palestinian educated class. But papers of news and views, with their obvious advantages over imported items, made impressive progress. With political tension sharply escalating, the local press was propelled to a new phase. Following the Muslim-Jewish encounter over the status of holy places in Jerusalem in the fall of 1928, and the bloody clashes of fall 1929, papers began to be published daily and in ever-bigger numbers.

Strikes, street demonstrations, violent confrontations—against the British, the Zionists, or domestic rivals—were not merely reflected in the press but also inspired by journalist preaching. Newspapers served as manifestoes for the many groups and individuals engaged in the ideological, political, and personal contentions that made up the public agenda. Eager for up-to-date intelligence and commentary, the public increasingly relied on the press as a lighthouse in a stormy sea. This was especially evident in the cities, where most of the action took place: people witnessing or participating in protests read about them in the press both before and after these events occurred, taking their cue from the headlines and drawing courage from passionate editorials. Much of the tension and the concomitant need for news reached the rural areas as well, where a handful of copies would suffice to keep a whole community abreast of developments. The Palestinian press came to play the familiar role identified for it by Benedict Anderson in his *Imagined Communities,* that of cementing a dispersed public into a self-conscious community. In Arab Palestine, one may assume, the mighty challenges posed by alien forces would have acted as generators of communal identity even without newspapers, given the country's physical compactness. But the press was there and naturally assumed the obvious and by far most important function of articulating the essence of these struggles and their lessons for the local society.[74] It instilled in its readers a Palestinian-Arab awareness in the face of foreign intruders. At the same time, serving partisan causes of one kind or another, it also contributed to factional consciousness and sharpened intramural rivalries.

No longer an upper-class phenomenon in the 1920s, the Palestinian press became a still more popular commodity during the second half of the mandate. Circulation figures mirrored this trend: the two leading dailies, *Filastin* and *al-Difaʿ* (the latter, launched in Jaffa in 1934, quickly matched the former in popularity) each sold 4,000–6,000 copies daily in the mid-1930s, a figure comparable to the country's total press output of two decades earlier. By the mid-1940s, the same two dailies sold as many as 7,000–10,000 copies each. In addition, many other papers circulated in more modest quantities, with some of them—e.g., *al-Jamiʿah al-ʿArabiyyah* and *al-Jamiʿah al-Islamiyyah*—selling more than 1,000 copies daily.[75] Moreover, as we shall see later on, efficient transmission mechanisms allowed the copies in circulation to have an impact far beyond their actual numbers. Progress was also reflected in the quality of these products. Back in its early years prior to the First World War, the Jaffa-based *Filastin* offered its readers low-quality sheets that were comparable to the lesser products of neighboring countries. The small-format, four-page issue of 3 January 1914—to pick a random instance—contained a couple of political commentaries, a few domestic and foreign news-bits (the latter drawn primarily from the foreign press), a single letter to the editor by a Jew, a notice by the deputy-mayor of Jerusalem, and about a dozen ads, mostly by foreign companies. It was cursorily edited and crudely executed, the different items spread out over five sparse columns on each page, separated from each other by monotonously uniform headings. Two decades later, *Filastin* was a far better product. The 8 April 1933 issue—a random example once again—had eight pages of six columns each, with a wealth of essays, up-to-date domestic and international news (the latter drawn from news agencies and local and foreign correspondents), a section reviewing the country's Jewish press, and an array of official and personal notices. By now it was a daily paper, its editorial standards high and its setting attractive, with daily topical photographs and an aesthetic graphic layout—a truly appealing product. It also featured an illustrated weekly supplement. So did *al-Difaʿ*, a latecomer to the field but a first-rate publication from the start. Other papers had likewise raised their professional level considerably. To be sure, shoddy products remained a part of the scene; but they were now secondary. The constantly increasing reading public of the later mandate years had at its disposal quality newspapers which drew on the better part of the country's talent and energy.

Books

A discussion of the book industry in pre-1948 Palestine is bound to be leaner than that of the parallel journalistic activity. Unlike the periodical press, book production remained meager. The small size of the community's educated class combined with the ease with which foreign texts were brought into Palestine were both responsible for this. With less experience, fewer cultural resources, and an inferior infrastructure, the Palestinian literary endeavor could scarcely compete with the vigorous output pouring into it mostly from Cairo. To a public immediately concerned with the burning issues of the day, books were obviously less rewarding than the press, even when they tackled the same issues in a broader manner. On the whole, the less urgent needs that books normally addressed were largely satisfied by imported products. The number of Arabic books published in mandatory Palestine was consequently scanty, a fact all the more conspicuous in light of the energetic Hebrew book industry of the country's much smaller Jewish community. Still, this humble story will be considered here at some length, since it has scarcely been treated in previous studies.

Full-fledged publishing houses—of the kind that handle everything from editing to marketing—did not appear in Palestine until after the end of the mandate. The publishing endeavor that did emerge there represented a more modest undertaking. Commencing shortly after the introduction of printing, it was most often based on a simple collaboration between author and printer.[76] The author would serve as his own editor and copyreader; the printer would manufacture the book and publicize it in the newspaper he usually issued as his main business. Economically it was a simple operation, achievable at minimal cost, just like the production of a newspaper: a printing device, a low-paid typesetter, and a modest quantity of newsprint were all that was needed. The majority of all books published in pre-1948 Palestine

65

were produced this way, primarily in the presses of *bayt al-maqdis, dar al-aytam*, the Franciscan mission press; *al-matba'ah al-tijariyyah, al-matba'ah al-'asriyyah*, and *matba'at al-'arab* in Jerusalem; *matba'at filastin al-jadidah* in Jaffa; *matba'at al-zahrah* in Haifa; and *al-matba'ah al-wataniyyah* in Acre.[77] A variation of this kind of enterprise appeared after the First World War and became more common from the early 1940s onward: a partnership between writers and bookstore owners, with the initiative for publication often coming from the latter. This kind of operation involved some of the country's more resourceful booksellers, who had their own printing facilities or collaborated with a nearby press. They would team up with authors, print their texts, advertise them in journals, and sell them in their own store and other bookshops (this and other roles played by bookstores in Palestine will be examined in the next chapter).

Nonperiodical publications in Palestine were of several kinds. A considerable portion of them comprised political and religious tracts, directly inspired by the tense current events and thus often polemical. They bore such telling titles as "Bleeding Palestine," "The Atrocities of the English," and "A Voice from the Palestine Graves." Another category was school textbooks, primarily in history, Arabic language, and the natural sciences, which Palestinian educators authored from the mid-1930s onward to replace imported texts. The rest, a small proportion of the modest total, were original and translated works of various types. They included literary pieces—novels, plays, and poetry—an output for which certain writers won local eminence, among them Khalil al-Sakakini, Khalil Baydas, Sayf al-Din al-Irani, 'Arif al-'Azzuni, Iskandar al-Khuri al-Baytjali, and Ishaq Musa al-Husayni. There were also occasional studies on social issues, history, and geography (works by 'Arif al-'Arif, 'Izzat Darwazah, Khalil Tawtah, and Ihsan Nimr are the better known in this category); political thought; some works in the sciences, including popular science; and a handful of utilitarian pieces, such as cookbooks.[78]

A full record of Arabic books published in mandatory Palestine is yet to be put together. Meanwhile, we have some partial lists and certain quantitative assessments that give us a fairly reliable clue about the scope of the venture. The general census of 1931 explored this question, among others, for the years 1923–1931 (the British had to rely for that on partial data supplied by the Jewish National and University Library in Jerusalem). The findings, reportedly complete from 1927 onward and possibly incomplete for the earlier years, indicated a total of 96 Arabic publications during this period, of which 57 (ca. 60%) were defined as pamphlets (i.e., comprising

5–48 pages). The rest—5 books annually on average—included 9 school textbooks, 8 items in politics, 8 in literature, 5 in law, 3 in theology, 2 in philosophy, and 4 in other miscellaneous fields. This was a humble yield by any standard. For comparison, the Jewish community in Palestine recorded an output of 1,120 books and an even greater number of pamphlets during the same period.[79]

In the mid-1940s, in a gloomy essay on the state of Arab culture, Palestinian writer and journalist Ishaq Musa al-Husayni presented the results of another probe into the matter, his own. In the 26 years between 1919 and 1944, he found a total of 209 Arabic books published in Palestine—an annual average of 8—including a large segment of school texts. For comparison, he noted, 349 books in Hebrew were published by the country's Jews in a single year, 1933–1934.[80] Husayni also presented a year-by-year breakdown, and there is some discrepancy between his data and other testimonies for some of the years,[81] possibly because he used a more rigorous definition of "book" (as distinct from a pamphlet). This creates the impression that he minimized his figures so as to substantiate his pessimistic analysis. Still, even if Husayni underestimated the actual number, realistically it could not have been much higher. Appraisals by contemporary Jewish observers in Palestine, who monitored developments in the Arab community, spoke of 250–300 printed Arabic publications for the entire mandate period, an estimate in tune with Husayni's.[82] A more recent study of literary translation in Palestine showed that between 1908 and 1948, a total of 42 books translated from other languages into Arabic were published in the country: 6 before 1920, 11 in the 1920s, 16 in the 1930s, and 9 in the 1940s.[83] Such data are similarly consonant, by and large, with the previous assessments.

In October 1946, an exhibition was held in Jerusalem of books published by Palestinian authors in and out of the country from the late nineteenth century onward. The event was organized by the Committee of Arab Culture in Palestine (*lajnat al-thaqafah al-'arabiyyah fi filastin*), an ad hoc forum of men-of-letters and public figures who also issued a catalogue of these publications. The catalogue comprised a total of 650 entries in Arabic and 103 in English, French, and German that had appeared throughout the period—a mélange of items on every topic, from school texts to poetry, from health manuals to missionary reports. The list featured books, booklets, and pamphlets, as well as casual pieces such as printouts of broadcast programs and incidental periodical articles. Since the data available to them was partial, the editors chose not to sum it up statistically. They related, for example, how writer Khalil Baydas, when first approached regarding his record of publications, remembered having authored a total of 13 books; reexamining his library, however, he realized that he had actually written 44.[84] But even without being comprehensive, the list—like the other assessments quoted here—does give us a general sense of the nature and scale of the endeavor. In essence it corroborates the other evaluations.

Of all the works published by Palestinians anywhere during the hundred or so years prior to 1946, 372 are mentioned in that catalogue as having been issued in the country itself: 326 in Arabic and 46 in other languages. Of the items for which the place of publication is given, 188 (151 in Arabic and 37 in other languages) were published outside Palestine, primarily in Egypt (69) and Lebanon (50).[85] With a friendlier publishing environment and a livelier consumer market, Egypt and Lebanon attracted Palestinian authors, who often preferred to turn to them even when residing in Palestine. Thus, Khalil Baydas, who had some of his books printed domestically, also published works in Beirut during the 1910s and in Cairo during the 1920s; ʿAbdallah Mukhlis published in Beirut and Damascus in the 1920s and 1930s; Qadri Hafiz Tuqan had his books published in Cairo in the 1930s and 1940s; and so also did Ishaq Musa al-Husayni, Iskandar al-Khuri al-Baytjali, and others in the 1940s. In the 1946 list, the year of publication is given for 292 of the items produced domestically; of these, 10 came out before 1900; 37 between 1900 and 1920; 34 in the 1920s; 93 in the 1930s, and 118 in the 1940s. The items whose year of production is known represent an average of c. 6 items annually from 1900 onward, a rate that would increase only marginally if pieces with an unknown year of publication were added. These figures are, yet again, consonant with previous assessments.

One last survey should be mentioned, based on a more systematic effort to produce a record of pre-1948 Palestinian publication. It has been recently conducted by Rasim Jbarah, an Israeli Arab from Tayyibah and for three decades the curator of Arabic at the library of Tel Aviv University. Jbarah has accumulated a bibliography (at present still in draft form) containing details on 962 Arabic books and pamphlets printed in Palestine from 1847 to 1948.[86] The place of publication is indicated for 939 of them, and the names of publishers or printers are given for 764. The list includes 81 items appearing before 1900, 38 from 1900–1910, 39 from 1911–1920, 236 from 1921–1930 (a remarkable leap following the First World War), 291 from 1931–1940, 238 from 1941–1948, and 39 for which no year of publication is mentioned. Jbarah's bibliography thus contains more than twice the number of entries appearing in the 1946 catalogue. Many of the items are literary works, political manifestoes, or school texts. But the author, seeking to be as comprehensive as possible (though by no means claiming completeness), has also included numerous entries of a technical nature, such as school brochures and exhibition catalogues, as well as ephemeral pieces such as odd transcripts of leaders' speeches. Counting only the items published from 1900 onward, the annual average would amount to 18 publications of every nature—books, pamphlets, catalogues, and the like. Even in its fuller form, then, this record of publications represents—in Jbarah's own words—"a very meager yield, unfortunately."[87]

What this list—and all the other available data—does not tell us is the number of copies printed for each title. We may assume that in this, as in the number of titles, production was modest. One knowledgeable observer has estimated that the standard print run for works published in Palestine during the mandate was "a few hundred copies" per item, apparently a realistic assessment. He also added that rarely was a book published in more than a single edition.[88] "We know of no author in this country—save for those who write school books—whose work was so successful as to merit a second printing," Ishaq Musa al-Husayni noted in dismay. "Moreover, we know of no author who has returned the expenses he spent on his book."[89] In the literary scene of mandatory Palestine, itself rather small, the share of domestic book production may thus be said to have been slight, even marginal.

Texts in the Public Domain

Public places nowadays confront us with myriad written messages. Cityscapes feature street names and traffic signs, shop and office name plates, billboard announcements, flashing and mobile advertisements, political banners, placards and graffiti, price tags in shop windows and inside the shops, instruction plates on parking meters, journals in newsstands, messages on people's T-shirts, and so on. They offer directions, provide guidelines for conduct, alert us to changes, promote business, and pronounce views. Typically Western in origin, they have become universal; typically an urban feature, they now exist everywhere, in the countryside and remote villages, on highways as well as byways. Such textual signs represent a broader reliance on written messages as an essential tool of everyday life, from operating a domestic appliance to boarding the right plane. Those employing written messages assume that the public to which they are addressed can decode them, an assumption whose soundness is confirmed daily by the constant spreading of the phenomenon. In earlier times, fewer such signs were needed; and in smaller and more intimate places their appearance has remained sparser. Their increasing presence, then, is a mark of declining intimacy borne by familiarity—or, of growing alienation—in the expanding units of human cohabitation. Written signs do not necessarily alleviate estrangement, and one may argue that they even contribute to it. But they provide signposts by which these alienated systems function and even thrive.[90]

What was the situation in this respect in Palestine a century ago? Photographs taken there from the mid-nineteenth century onward carry us into town streets and village alleys, laying before our eye scenes of their surroundings. They should be examined with caution because photographers of the Holy Land were likely motivated by objectives other than accurately documenting the realities there.[91] The availability of a sizeable bulk of pictures from the late nineteenth and early twentieth centuries, however, seems to compensate to some extent for such shortcomings. Photographs taken around the turn of the century reveal two basic and striking facts: a marked paucity of written signs in public places; and a predominance, almost exclusivity, of foreign languages in the few signs that did exist. Signs were concentrated in certain busy spots, such as oft-visited holy places. Only in later years would they appear in sites such as marketplaces, streets, shops, and public buildings.

Pictures taken between 1870 and 1914 outside Jaffa Gate in Jerusalem—a busy area and one of the country's most photographed spots—show an imposing board reading "Cooks Tourist Office Inside Jaffa Gate." It must have been installed there sometime in the 1870s (it is absent from a picture taken in 1870). Other signs appeared on two adjacent shops, "A. Fast, Restaurateur" and "Tabak Depot," and there was a sign directing people to "Lloyd Hotel von Fast." The only visible Arabic script in the neighborhood was the stone inscription on the gate by the sixteenth-century builder of the wall, Sultan Suleyman the Magnificent.[92] The Cooks tourist office was indeed located inside the gate, marked by a big board bearing the company's name and another sign that promised "Tickets to All Parts of the World."[93] Inside the gate, a host of other names were displayed in an eye-catching way: "Deutsche Palaestina Bank," "Assad C. Kayat," "Magasin Oriental, Andre Terzis & Fils," "Grand New Hotel," "Central Hotel," "Dentiste," and more, all in Latin script.[94] Other spots in the vicinity had comparable signs in French, German, and Italian.[95] Pictures from the town of Jaffa around the same period reveal similar views. Thus the Jewish "Hotel Cohen" announced itself with a board in English and Hebrew only, while no other written sign on that market street was visible; and stores on Bustrus street,

Outside Jaffa Gate, Jerusalem, 1898.

From Jacob M. Landau, *Eretz yisrael bi-yemey 'Abdul Hamid* (Jerusalem: Carta, 1979).
© Jacob M. Landau. Courtesy of Carta Publishers, Jerusalem.

the main business artery, bore signs that were almost exclusively in Latin script.[96] In all of these, Arabic appeared rarely; when it did, it was only where the more prominent text was in other languages.[97]

Clearly, then, the use of written messages in public places was alien to Palestine. Even its use in foreign languages was relatively recent, dating from the last third of the nineteenth century, when foreign agencies and businesses began to appear in the country. Palestinian Arabs before the twentieth century rarely relied on writing in public places for orientation, advertisement, or making a statement of any kind. There were obvious exceptions: stone inscriptions on public structures, ordered by rulers to eternalize their names and acts (indeed, much of their effect stemmed from their very exceptional presence); textual ornaments on mosque walls and other holy places, carrying spiritual messages; and tombstone inscriptions in cemeteries. There was little else. Functional writing for daily needs was all but unknown.

This rarity of written signs in public was hardly unique to Palestine. It was

Jerusalem, view from Jaffa Gate into the Old City, 1898.

From Ely Schiller, *Tsilumey yerushalayim ve-eretz yisrael ha-rishonim*
(Jerusalem: Ariel, 1980). © Ariel Publishing. Courtesy of Ely Schiller, Ariel Publishing Ltd.

a common reality all over the region prior to the late nineteenth century (as any visitor to Arab countries even in recent years can attest, it has been slow to change even subsequently in places other than urban centers). A seeming sense of intimacy accounted for that to an extent: familiar with their close and seldom changing surroundings, local residents needed no written aids to guide them. Widespread illiteracy was another obvious factor, for written signs would be useless if most people could not make them out (though, of course, the absence of signs and illiteracy relate to each other like chicken and egg). And there seems to have been yet another reason for the absence of written signs, specific to this particular culture: the traditional reluctance to use Arabic in its written form promiscuously to such mundane ends, a propensity that had earlier hindered the introduction of printing into the region.[98] Pre-twentieth-century Arab towns reflected a basic concept of

Jerusalem, street scene in the Old City (Jaffa Gate vicinity), around 1900.

Photograph by Felix Bonfils, from the collection of the Israeli Museum of
Photography at Tel-Hai Industrial Park. © The Israeli Museum of Photography,
courtesy of the museum.

spatial order that obviated the use of writing. Thoroughfares, streets, even
alleys, sometimes did have names, but these names were a matter of common knowledge (and strangers could always inquire about them). Nor was
it customary for a tinsmith or grocer to announce their trade in this way.
The location of their business was usually known to the relevant customers
or otherwise discernible without writing.

Once an adequate compass, the old intimacy ceased to suffice when the
environment itself began to change more dynamically. The change started
with the arrival of foreigners, who came to Palestine as tourists, missionaries, or tradesmen, sometimes settling in the country and opening businesses
and offices there. Newcomers in an alien land, they resorted to the credible
devices of written signs for guidance and trade promotion, thus introducing their alien concept of public space into the country. Zionist immigrants
arriving from Europe similarly subscribed to the habit of relying on such
signs, which they displayed in Yiddish and Hebrew in their new urban
neighborhoods. The presence of foreigners in turn prompted the more enterprising local merchants to imitate the practice and boards advertising

their businesses in English and French began to pop up in the commercial centers. It did not take long for Arabic to appear in like manner, at first as an ornamental addition and later as an increasingly useful device. Here and there it was visible as early as the turn of the century; a famous early instance was the board affixed above the Khalidiyyah front door around 1900, alerting the public to its existence in both French ("Bibliothèque Haldieh") and Arabic (*al-maktabah al-khalidiyyah*), to which was proudly added: "*fiha kutub qayyimah*" (valuable books inside).[99] A novel institution was thus among the first to introduce a novel practice, along with some stores and new commercial ventures.[100]

The British, who imposed their rule on the country after the war, brought with them a colonial order for the public domain. Intent on applying a general order as they understood it, they installed written signs systematically all over the country—naming streets and public buildings, indicating directions on highways, and marking Arab and Jewish settlements in English, Arabic, and Hebrew. This large-scale organized effort by the government went a considerable way in altering the scenery and "textualizing" the public domain. Zionist institutions and businesses also began using Arabic in their written signs, especially in mixed cities such as Jerusalem and Haifa, and the Tel Aviv sections adjacent to Jaffa. Palestinian Arabs followed suit from the early 1920s, with shops and individual professionals proclaiming their trade to urban passers-by with boards placed above store doors, plaques at the entrance to office buildings, and names imprinted on shop windowpanes and walls. Names of persons and families owning the businesses always figured prominently in these, a proud assertion of presence and possession.[101] Large billboard advertisements also began to appear in central urban locations, such as the imposing "Drink Lipton Tea" (*ishrabu shay libtun*), which hovered over the Jaffa central square in the 1930s.[102]

The shift to relying on written messages could be seen in a variety of other forms as well. One of these, more transient in nature but equally eye-catching, was cloth banners hung over city streets or on buildings and stores, and carried on festive occasions and during marches and demonstrations. Banners were already appearing in the early 1920s; one such banner, on the house in Haifa where the 1920 Palestinian "national congress" was held, read "*filastin 'arabiyyah*" (Palestine is Arab) and "*hafizu 'ala al-masjid al-Aqsa*" (Protect al-Aqsa mosque),[103] thus expressing a passionate call in a modern mode. Toward the end of that decade banners became frequent enough to upset the authorities, prompting them to ban the practice: a notice by the Jerusalem municipality strictly prohibited "the publication of announcements imprinted on cloth and displayed in public roads in this city, for any purpose."[104] On the whole, Arabic boards and banners were relatively few in Palestine—fewer than their Hebrew parallels in the country's Jewish areas. But their presence, in marked departure from past habit, was expanding and continuously modifying the view that met the eye.

A more conspicuous feature of this changing landscape was written proclamations, which in the twentieth century became a lively medium of public exchange. For governments in Europe, printed posters and proclamations had long served as a useful control device; for others, they had been effective means of protest that had scored many achievements.[105] In the region itself, the use of written proclamations went back at least to the late eighteenth century (whether or not the Ottomans used them earlier is a matter for further exploration). The French, who invaded Egypt in the summer of 1798, disseminated printed leaflets, copies of which "were affixed in crossroads and alleys, on mosque doors," and "on walls in the marketplace."[106] It is unknown, again, whether the local authorities resorted to this practice after the departure of the alien forces; if they did, it was not a very common practice. Then, starting in 1880, written notices became tools in the hands of opposition groups in Lebanon and Syria. They clandestinely published placards and circulated handbills attacking Sultan 'Abd al-Hamid for his tyranny, just as Protestant reformists in France had done three centuries earlier.[107] As for Palestine, the first testimony encountered in the present research is from 1914, when the Ottomans declared general mobilization (*seferberlik*) upon the outbreak of the war, printing announcements (*manshurat*) in large red letters and attaching them to walls in towns and villages.[108] As the war developed, the authorities opened a propaganda office near Jaffa Gate in Jerusalem, which published pictures from the battlefield and—as a local resident later related—"proclamations were affixed to the office doors, announcing the horrendous casualties inflicted on the Russians, English and French."[109] In early 1917, British planes dropped printed circulars on Palestinian locations in an effort to enlist local support for Sharif Husayn's Arab revolt in the Hijaz.[110] Once in control of the country, the British army used the device of bulletin boards to publicize their notices to the population.[111]

The use of placards and handbills by the government and others became commonplace after the war. The government employed printed posters as a matter of course to address the public, disseminate information, and impart instructions. It also used leaflets to similar ends and, where access was difficult, resorted to dropping them from planes, mostly over the countryside, thereby bringing the printed word to places where it was only infrequently seen. Such leaflets sometimes ended up being publicized in other ways. "When the British dropped proclamations from the air during the 1936 revolt," related Butrus Dalleh, from Kafr Yasif, "children would gather and bring them to my father, who had a shop at the center of the village. He would affix them to the shop's door, so the clients could read them."[112] Written notes of every kind also became a major tool in the hands of groups and individuals for promulgating political views, attacking those who failed to subscribe to them, and stirring public action within and across the country's different communities. Sometimes handwritten but more often typewritten or printed, such notes were attached to house walls and fences, electricity poles, mosque and shop doors, and even tombstones in cemeteries in the towns and villages. They were signed by a variety of organizations and ad hoc groupings, such as "the supreme command of the revolt in Palestine and Trans-Jordan," "Arab students of Jerusalem," "the Black Hand Band of Haifa," and "Arab physicians and pharmacists." They were addressed "to the noble Arab nation," "to the Arabs of Palestine," "to the Jerusalem youth," "to the artisans," "to the butchers and shopkeepers," and so on, signed by better or less known individuals or circulating un- signed, and dealing with the hot issues of the day in a passionate way. For example, a 20 × 30 cm. note, handwritten and error-ridden, was signed by a "patriotic writer" (*katib watani*) and affixed to a tombstone in the Jeru- salem Muslim cemetery in 1921. It prompted "the youth of Jerusalem" to wake up and, like their brethren in Jaffa and Haifa, massacre the Zionists. A 10 × 20 cm. leaflet on behalf of "an Arab group of craftsmen in Jerusalem," circulating in the city in September 1929, was addressed to Arab business owners (*ashab al-'amal*). Evoking patriotism, it called on them to get rid of all Jewish employees and replace them with Arab ones, reinforcing the call with a Qur'anic anti-Jewish citation.[113] Palestine, a British intelligence report noted, "is exceptional in the Middle East territories as being a good ground for the distribution of pamphlets."[114] More than a channel for pro- nouncing views, such notices made up a real battle arena among rivals, with messages triggering countermessages and thus constantly enriching the textual surroundings.

Previously poor in written features, the streets of Jerusalem and Jaffa, Haifa and Nazareth, became replete with printed messages of many shades. In various ways this shift epitomized the broader process of text prolif- eration in Palestine. Typically an urban phenomenon, such written mes- sages were as permanent as bus-stop signs or as short-lived as political collar

A proclamation distributed in Haifa by the newly formed "Black Hand Band" in December 1929. It called upon "every Arab man and woman" to boycott the Zionists and avoid selling land to them, and threatened to punish those who disobeyed.

badges. Some were perpetually changing, as were newspapers in the hands of street hawkers. Others literally passed through people's hands: money bills, bus and theater tickets, postage stamps, official notes and documents, and more. Again, we ought to keep in mind the novelty and hence limited scope of these changes prior to the mid-twentieth century: a quick glimpse at the sight of a European city at the same time would readily reveal a scene infinitely more colorful and dynamic than those of Jaffa and Haifa. In the present study, however, the more relevant yardstick is the comparison with the local point of departure. A person who fell asleep in the Jerusalem of, say, 1910, and awoke two decades later would have been baffled by a sight profoundly different from his own familiar vicinity. So would a Palestinian villager coming to the city at any time during our period. By that measure, the change in Palestine was indeed momentous.

It is hard to overstate the importance of this expanding visibility of writings. Prominent in every manner, written messages in cities enunciated to those who could decipher them and to others alike that their cosmos was changing in a profound way. One's capacity to function properly under these changing circumstances increasingly depended on one's command of the new rules, a competence which, in turn, was obtainable through education. It was becoming vital for finding one's way around, both literally and metaphorically. Without it, a person might not necessarily be lost in the changed habitat; but he would be handicapped and incessantly dependent on the help of others. Enhancing the appeal of reading skills, the growing presence of written messages also allowed those with imperfect proficiency to practice and improve, and those with better proficiency to retain it. Beyond reflecting the society's state of literacy, then, written signs in the open also boosted it.

Essentially a spontaneous phenomenon, written messages in public places mushroomed uncontrolled, unremittingly impinging, almost imposing themselves on whoever was present. As against this, books and journals required special channels of dissemination to reach their target. These channels had to be developed along with the publications themselves. Exploring them is the subject of the next chapter.

CHAPTER 3

Texts Accessed and Afforded

Conduits of Dissemination

Until the late nineteenth century, an educated Arab who wanted to acquire a book could do so in one of several ways. He could approach a book dealer, if one was to be found in his own town or nearby, who would sell him the desired item or find it for him. Certain cities in the region had book markets with clusters of shops trading in written texts (it is unknown whether there was such a place in Palestine itself). There were also roving dealers who moved between provinces and countries, hauling written treasures across the lands of Islam. Another way of getting possession of a book was by copying it from an exemplar available in a local mosque or private library. In many places this was a common practice, and libraries were equipped to assist those wishing to engage in copying, often providing the necessary paper and ink. Yet another option, when one did not have the skill or time to undertake the exacting task of copying by oneself, was to hire a professional copyist (*nassakh*) to perform the job for a fee.[1] Finally, once books in Islamic languages were printed in Europe—from the early sixteenth century onward—one could order them from there if one had the necessary funds. All of these ways to increase a collection were both slow and costly. But slow pace and high cost were in line with the low level of demand and consumption. On the whole, books were regarded as expensive, prestigious objects. In nineteenth-century Palestine they concerned a very small circle of men of wealth and education.

The abrupt acceleration in text production, which the introduction of printing spurred in the region after the mid-nineteenth century, upset the traditional balance between the making of books and demand for them.

The presses put out written works quicker, cheaper, and in far bigger quantities than had hitherto been conceivable, a flow the market was little prepared to absorb. This included books, a familiar item in a new dress, and periodical publications, a complete novelty. Books were more complex products—harder to make, buy, and read—and their public assimilation was a slow process. Newspapers were a different matter: here the capacity for enhanced production coincided with a growing demand for the kind of knowledge they carried, and the printing industry readily met this demand. Both kinds of publications required channels for public circulation, the likes of which had been neither developed nor needed hitherto. The flood triggered the emergence of new conduits.

We shall begin with periodical publications and their distribution. Given the earlier success of newspapers in Egypt and Lebanon, enterprising writers in Palestine sensibly assessed that their country too was a potential market for similar products, a market that had to be awakened and activated. Once newspapers began to appear, the common way of attracting a prospective audience to them was by sending free copies of the first few issues to would-be customers who had not asked for them, spreading as wide a net as possible. The recipients would thus be turned into indebted subscribers unless they took the trouble of returning the copies immediately. Familiar throughout the region, this was a problematic practice that caused much consternation to senders and recipients alike. But it seems to have been effective and contributed to the emergence of a circle of consumers wherever applied.[2] Until close to the end of the nineteenth century, papers in the Arab Ottoman provinces circulated almost exclusively through mail subscription; street sales would come later. Palestinian intellectuals were among those who accessed the early press of the region through such channels, and journals for which they had subscribed—first abroad, then locally—were brought to their doors by the postal services.

Eager to boost distribution, journal owners from the neighboring countries appointed agents (*wakil*, pl. *wukala'*) to act on their behalf in the region's cities and provinces. These were usually people who had previously traded in written texts, sometimes themselves men-of-letters. Their new task included selling subscriptions, distributing the journals to the customers, promoting advertising, and collecting fees. Papers usually announced the names of their representatives as a service to the readers, as well as to show off their geographical reach. A network of such agents spread throughout the region. For example, the Beirut-based *Hadiqat al-Akhbar*, one of the earliest Arab newspapers, announced the names of agents in six different places from Cairo to Baghdad as early as 1858, and the Egyptian *al-Ahram* boasted no less than 23 of them, similarly spread, from its inception in 1876.[3] Towns in Palestine had quite a few such agents acting for papers abroad during the later part of the nineteenth century. By the 1870s, there were at least 5 of them in Jaffa, at least 5 in Acre, 3 or more in Jerusalem, and a few others in Haifa, Nazareth, Nablus, Gaza, and Shafa 'Amr, representing journals from Istanbul, Beirut, and Alexandria.[4] The role which these intermediaries between publisher and reader played in literary developments remains to be explored; it may have been more considerable than one would tend to assume. Newspaper agents continued to fulfill similar tasks in twentieth-century Palestine, both for foreign publications and for the local press that emerged after 1908.

When bookstores began to open in Palestine just before the First World War (see below), they became natural depots for the sale of journals and newspapers as well. This mirrored a shift in the public role of periodicals, coming out of the private mailboxes of elite subscribers into the urban stores and marketplace, and subsequently newsstands and street hawkers. In Egypt, with its more experienced press and bigger readership, newspapers were already selling on the streets around the turn of the century, by vendors or by "barefoot newspaper boys in their blue or white robes and grubby turbans," who would "detect the people's thirst for them as swiftly as lightning."[5] In Palestine, city newsstands seem to have appeared before the war,[6] while hawkers (*ba'ah mutajawwilun*, literally, "roving sellers") apparently came only later, with the proliferation of journals and the postwar rise in demand. Here, too, newspapers employed urchins. "I used to sit on the stairs of the printing shop with children from the shack neighborhood (*al-awlad al-'ara'ishiyyah*)," related "Abu Bandali," who had worked for the Jaffa-based *Filastin* since 1922. "We had hired them for selling the paper in the markets. After rehearsing their [promotional] phrases, they would run out on the streets selling it. This was the first time for Palestinian newspapers to be sold in the markets."[7] Moving all over the city announcing headlines and highlights, they played the role previously performed by the city crier—establishing the presence of information orally in the public domain.[8] Disseminating printed items, they also helped to entrench written texts as inseparable features of the urban public scene. Newspapers were brought to the homes of subscribers—those who could afford to pay the lump sum for this convenient service once a year or every six months—until the end of the mandate. But they were also readily seen everywhere in the streets and squares of the bigger towns.

In the cities where newspapers were printed it was, thus, fairly easy to find them, and it became still easier with time. Away from the publication centers, however, circulation was slower and at times problematic, mainly due to poor roads. In the years before the First World War and immediately thereafter, related Niqula Ziyadah, a member of a humble family from Jenin and a teenager at the time, "newspapers were published in Jaffa, Haifa, and Jerusalem, but only rarely did they reach Jenin [then a rural town with some 4,000 people]. When they did, they went to a very limited number of the town's residents. We, the simple and small people, had nothing to do with the newspapers sent to Qasim Bek ʿAbd al-Hadi or to Mister Fahmi al ʿAbushi [Jenin's leading notables]."[9] Newspaper publication extended later on to a number of smaller towns, such as Bethlehem and Tulkarm (though not Jenin), where products of a more local nature circulated in modest numbers. The country's leading papers, above all those from Jaffa, also continued to arrive and be read in these towns and elsewhere, the pace of their arrival being dictated by the quality of transportation. Villages along the country's main arteries usually enjoyed a more or less regular supply of the few newspaper copies they needed, which came to them by bus or, if the distance permitted, by donkey. The more remote places received them slowly and irregularly until the end of the period.

Printed books, produced outside the country until 1908, were ordered directly from abroad by the few who took interest in them. Journals and newspapers throughout the region promoted the sale of books from very early on in the history of the Arab press, carrying ads that lured prospective buyers and referring them to the books' authors and printers. Thus, to pick a random instance from back in the 1860s, al-Jawa'ib—a weekly paper appearing in the Ottoman capital—announced the sale of a book in Arabic that dealt with Napoleon's invasion of Egypt and Syria and that had been printed in Beirut. A flowery, 19-line-long notice on the paper's front page depicted the book's many virtues and urged members of the educated class to order it from a shop in Alexandria. Al-Jawa'ib is reported to have had a very wide circulation, from Morocco to Najd and beyond, and an ad like this would give the promoted item the widest possible exposure among those who would be interested in it.[10] Arabic papers regularly advertised books in this manner, and some of them—the Egyptian al-Hilal is a prominent example—had book review columns that also provided details on prices and publisher names. The potential customers in Palestine targeted by such ads purchased books via this modern means, which supplemented the more traditional acquisition from local dealers. The practice was carried over into the twentieth century and continued during the entire period explored here, even as other ways of obtaining books were developed.

Old-style book dealers may have been operating in some places in Palestine in the nineteenth century. On the whole, however, given the limited demand, this could hardly have been a thriving trade. A survey of shops in the Jerusalem of the late 1860s, conducted by a contemporary foreign observer, found only 2 booksellers among the 1,932 businesses he recorded, a Jew and an Armenian.[11] Another observer reports a bookstore operating in Nablus at the end of the century, apparently a humble business,[12] and it is possible that by that time there were a few others, most likely small dealerships of the traditional style. Local traders also catered to the demand for tourist handbooks—obviously in foreign languages—for the growing number of visitors to the Holy Land. Thus, Bulus Meo's souvenir shop near Jaffa Gate in Jerusalem carried, in addition to "olive, wood, and pearl" artifacts, also "tourist guidebooks," according to its front door sign (which appeared on so many photographs of that vicinity before 1900).[13] More such businesses may have opened elsewhere in the city, and possibly also in the town of Jaffa, the country's main port of entry. Sometime before the First World War, the brothers Bulus and Wadiʿ Saʿid launched their Palestine Educational Company (*maktabat filastin al-ʿilmiyyah*) in Jerusalem, a venture with a somewhat broader interest that would become one of the country's biggest enterprises in the trade after the war.[14] Another bookshop seems to have opened in Haifa in mid-1914, but the war soon forced its owners to close it.[15] The scope of these initiatives was small at that stage. If they reflected a nascent demand, it must have been very modest.[16]

The changes following the war encouraged the blossoming of the bookshop, known in Arabic as *maktabah* (pl. *maktabat* or *makatib*). The name was derived from a root whose essential sense was writing. Initially denoting "a library," the term also referred more loosely to other related notions, such as a study room or a bookcase. As a name for a new kind of endeavor, it was likewise loose, implying the gamut of activities in which these businesses engaged. In the Palestinian experience, a *maktabah* was above all a stationery shop, but also a book dealership, sometimes a book-lending shop, and at times a depot for book production, binding, and publishing. Most of the *maktabat* in Palestine sold writing and office supplies, and some of them also carried imported books and whatever existed of local ones. Some concentrated particularly on school textbooks. Many of them sold local and foreign journals and newspapers, commonly serving as agents for one or another of them. In the later part of the period, some such businesses produced their own notebooks, promotional calendars, and diaries.[17] Thus, the Jerusalem shop of the Sa'id brothers, expanding its trade after the war and opening a second branch in Jaffa (and later also in Cairo and Alexandria), purported to carry "all scholarly and cultural books in Arabic and foreign languages, writing materials, school and business supplies." It also distributed current periodicals and sold gramophones as well as Arabic, English, and Hebrew typewriters.[18] *Al-maktabah al-wataniyyah* of the Bahri brothers in Haifa sold schoolbooks, works on science and history in Arabic, English, and French, and writing materials. It also produced a periodical, the literary monthly *Zahrat al-Jamil* (later *al-Zahrah*), edited by the owners; offered printing and binding services; and turned a section of the store into a free public reading room.[19] 'Isa al-Sifri's *maktabat filastin al-jadidah* in Jaffa, acting as a bookshop, also ran a bookbinding operation.[20] And the Tahir brothers' *maktabah* in the same city sold books and periodicals in Arabic and English, pens and paper, gifts, toys, and household aids.[21] *Maktabah,* then, was a versatile institution, and most shops of this kind addressed several types of needs simultaneously, a practice called for by the gradual transition to an age of reading and writing. Promoting books from the early 1920s onward, commercial ads of local and foreign publishers, dealers, and later also local printers, regularly referred potential buyers to "all Palestinian bookstores" for attaining them.[22] Some of these institutions, acquiring printing equipment or teaming up with printing shops, would turn themselves into modest publishing houses beginning in the early 1940s.

We may take a closer look at one of these enterprises. Fawzi Yusuf of *maktabat al-andalus*—we have already encountered him as the energetic entrepreneur who imported Egyptian printed works—published two autobiographies laying out his 50-year experience in the Jerusalem book trade.[23] As a young man out of school in the early 1930s, Yusuf engaged in journalism for a while and then started a small bookbinding plant. In the winter of 1935, to "fulfill an old dream," he opened a *maktabah* in the Old City's tanner's market. By that time a few such businesses had already been operating in the city. Yusuf rented the small place for 18 Palestinian pounds a month, renovated it, and started his trade. At first limiting his business mainly to writing materials, Yusuf sensed that running it on such a limited scale would not take him very far. He toured around schools, social clubs, and other bookstores, searching for joint commercial ventures. Detecting a rising demand for books, he worked out an arrangement with a Cairo dealer that allowed him to import Egyptian school texts and literary works. Yusuf gradually intensified his trips to Egypt, and within three years after starting his business had set up his own branch in Cairo, which permitted him to upgrade his import services. It also helped him expand his connections in Egypt itself, and he was appointed as the Jerusalem agent for the prestigious Egyptian literary journal *al-Risalah*. Yusuf's *maktabat al-andalus* prospered. In the late 1930s it regularly brought in Egyptian publications, selling them through other shops whose owners acted as his agents for the purpose, in Jaffa, Haifa, Ramlah, Nazareth, and elsewhere. Among his customers were prominent Palestinian personalities and officials, by his account, and numerous students bought their textbooks and writing materials from him. On the eve of the Second World War, the shop was among the first to introduce yet another service: it began lending books to subscribing readers for a monthly payment of 8 qirsh—not a trifling sum, as we shall see later on. For that fee, Yusuf recalled, the customer "could take any book he desired and read it; when returning it he could take another."

The war cut the supply of books from Egypt and forced Yusuf to close down his Cairo office in 1941. Still optimistic and resourceful, he now collaborated with Palestinian educators in preparing local editions of schoolbooks. Importing his own paper, he arranged for the books to be printed in the well-known *bayt al-maqdis* press near Jaffa Gate. This was a typical instance of a foray into rudimentary publishing born out of necessity. Yusuf personally walked from school to school, trying to sell his products, and even managed to persuade the Department of Education to endorse them as standard texts. He also designed a variety of original paper products with his shop's logo, scoring a commercial success that helped his business stay above water during the years of austerity. Once the war was over, *maktabat al-andalus* could resume its book dealings in full swing. By now it had acquired experience in production and was in a position to become a small-size publisher of school and children's books.

Fawzi Yusuf's business career, a glowing success story by his own testimony, must also have had its low points and difficulties. Of these he tells us much less, but it is easy to sense from his story that the country's circumstances often made life in this trade an arduous struggle. His enterprise seems to have been typical, in more ways than one, of other businesses that sprang up in interwar Palestine. The centrality of selling imported products, the combination of trading in printed books and writing materials, the marketing of school texts along with other works—all were novelties of the post-Ottoman era which *maktabat al-andalus* shared with other book trad-

Ta'rika Filastin, by 'Umar al-Salih al-Barghuthi and Khalil Tawtah (Jerusalem 1923).
A 300-page "History of Palestine" from biblical times to the mandate. As the title page
indicates, "its publication was the initiative of (*'ana bi-nashrihi*) Bulus and Wadi' Sa'id,
owners of *maktabat filastin al-'ilmiyyah,*" who had it printed in *bayt al-maqdis* press—an
early instance of bookseller-printer collaboration.

ers. These were all marks of a transition to literacy evolving from below. The
more creative booksellers gradually turned their businesses into embryonic
publishing houses, moving to book production toward the end of the period. Most active among these, along with Yusuf's shop, were *al-maktabah
al-'asriyyah* and *maktabat al-tahir ikhwan* in Jaffa (the former producing
20 books or more during the 1940s, the latter at least 16) and apparently also
maktabat filastin al-'ilmiyyah of the veteran Sa'id brothers in Jerusalem.[24]
Many of the books and pamphlets appearing in the country during the later
years of the mandate—a humble yield, as we have seen—were not only
distributed but also manufactured by these shops. These, and several other
book dealers, adopted Yusuf's idea of the late 1930s and introduced lending
arrangements for a periodic fee.[25]

The expansion of education, inflow of foreign publications, local journalistic enterprises, and nascent literary endeavor were thus matched by
evolving circulation channels that competed with each other in a healthy

commercial atmosphere. In 1945, a "union of Arab bookstore owners in Palestine" (*ittihad niqabat ashab al-maktabat al-ʿarabiyyah bi-filastin*) was established, with headquarters in Jaffa. No fewer than 51 businesses joined the union, altogether an impressive net, from Haifa (8), Jaffa (6), Jerusalem (5), Nablus (5), Acre (4), Gaza (3), Nazareth (3), Hebron (3), Beisan (3), Beersheba (2), Tulkarm (2), Safad (2), Tiberias (1), Ramlah (1), Lydda (1), Majdal-Gaza (1), and Samakh (1); several others declined to join.[26] Obviously, they did not all operate on the same scale. Some, especially in the bigger towns, were larger and more successful, while smaller businesses, mostly in the remote locations, often depended on supplies from their more prosperous counterparts. All shops, big and small, reached out to the public with merchandise that was a mark of the new era.

Buying One's Own Book

Books and journals, imported and local, were out there for sale, from publishers, booksellers, and hawkers. But were they affordable, and to whom? As we examine the economic angle of the process, we should bear in mind that economic factors represented one out of several determinants influencing access to printed texts. Other considerations were sometimes as important, or more so. Still, affordability was undoubtedly a major factor in shaping the pace of text diffusion as well as the modes in which it occurred. Scrutinizing the relevant figures is not one of the more gratifying parts of this study; but it is necessary for getting a notion of what was a vital aspect of the story.

A sensible approach to the question of affordability is by juxtaposing data of two kinds: the prices of publications and the income levels across the society's different sections, of which the disposable portion—beyond the most basic needs—should be estimated. The former is fairly simple to establish, but the latter is more difficult. In the case of pre-1948 Palestine, we can make only some very general observations on the matter.

We know little about the prices people from the Ottoman provinces paid for publications they ordered from Europe, though we may safely assume that these, like so many other imported goods, were quite expensive by Middle Eastern standards. They were exclusive items that only few could afford. Prices of books and journals produced in the region itself, however, are readily available since they often appear on the publications themselves and in contemporary ads. Rates for such items varied fairly widely even in the nineteenth century. They were usually quoted in qirsh (pl. qurush), of which there were 100 in the Ottoman pound.[27] During the last third of that

century, literary works including novels and poetry in popular editions—
apparently thin paperback booklets—sold in Egypt and Lebanon for 4–
8 qurush apiece and occasionally for less. School texts were advertised at
5–12 qurush per copy. There were also more costly items, such as hardcover
history books that sold for 25–50 qurush, and dictionaries, whose price was
still higher: Wartabet's famous Arabic-English dictionary cost 60 qurush in
Egypt in 1889; Faris al-Shidyaq's philological study, *al-Jasus 'ala al-qamus,*
was offered for 23 francs, or c. 100 qurush; and Butrus al-Bustani's celebrated modern dictionary, *Muhit al-muhit,* in two exquisitely bound volumes, sold for no less than 250.[28] Customers from Palestine, some distance
from the sources of publication, had to add postage fees to these expenses,
ranging from 1 to 4 qurush per delivery. When books began to be printed
in Palestine itself after 1908, the publisher of the Haifa literary monthly
al-Nafa'is al-'Asriyyah offered for sale such locally made items, mostly
modest-size pamphlets that featured translated stories, for the equivalent of
4–8 qurush apiece, but there were also works, seemingly more massive, that
sold for 12–20 qurush.[29]

Subscribing to newspapers and journals published in the neighboring
countries—the standard way of getting them—was, on the whole, more
expensive than buying books, as it required committing to the fees for six
months or a year. Of the papers that circulated in Palestine, an annual subscription for the Lebanese biweekly *al-Jinan* and the Egyptian monthly
al-Muqtataf cost 100 qurush each in the 1880s; for the monthly *al-Hilal*
80 qurush in the following decade, and for the Syrian monthly *al-Muqtabas*
c. 60 qurush on the eve of the First World War. Semiweekly newspapers
cost from 75 qurush (*Lisan al-Hal,* Beirut, 1877) to 130 (*al-Qahirah,* Cairo,
1885). Once daily newspapers appeared in the neighborhood, they sold for
170 qurush (*al-Muqattam,* Cairo, 1889) and up to 225 qurush (*al-Ahram,*
Alexandria, 1881). When periodicals began to be published in Palestine itself,
their prices were somewhat lower than those for the imported publications:
Filastin, a weekly newspaper at first, charged 10 francs, or c. 40 qurush,
for an annual subscription on the eve of the First World War; *al-Nafa'is
al-'Asriyyah,* a literary monthly, charged 30.

The cost of books and journals both in and around Palestine rose somewhat after the war, and the price range remained broad. In the 1920s, readers of Palestinian newspapers could see ads urging them to buy a Cairo-
printed 650-page book that featured 50 illustrations for 20 qurush, and
an illuminated English-Arabic dictionary for 75.[30] The postwar *al-Nafa'is*
(now operating from Jerusalem) advertised the sale of books and book-

lets of different sizes, priced at c. 15 qurush on average, including items that cost as little as 5 qurush or as much as 25, many of them imported from Egypt. School texts ranged from 8 to 25 qurush.[31] Prices continued to rise slowly, and by the mid-1940s the cost of 40–60 qurush for a book had become common in Palestine. There were cheaper items that sold for 10 qurush or less, and imported booklets from the popular Egyptian series *Iqra'* sold at 6 qurush each.[32] Subscription rates for foreign journals likewise mounted: the Egyptian monthly *al-Majallah al-Jadidah* charged 80 qurush per year in 1929, making it, according to its owner, "the least expensive journal around." Annual fees for the Egyptian *al-Muqtataf, al-Hilal, al-Manar, al-Risalah,* and *al-Thaqafah,* as well as for the Lebanese *al-Adib,* all of which had clients in Palestine, ranged from 80 to 150 qurush in the 1930s and 1940s, depending on size and frequency of publication. The Egyptian daily newspaper *al-Muqattam* (1939) charged 260 qurush; *al-Ahram* (1934) charged 300. Locally, again, subscription for the Jerusalem literary monthly *al-Nafa'is* went up from 30 to 60 qurush after the First World War. Palestinian newspapers charged 100 qurush per year in the earlier part of the period (*al-Quds al-Sharif,* 1920; *Filastin,* 1924; *al-Karmil* and *al-Ittihad al-'Arabi,* 1925; *al-Yarmuk,* 1926), but the cost climbed once the press became daily, to 125 qurush in the case of *Filastin* (in late 1929) and 150 for *al-Hayat* (1931) and *al-Difa'* (1934). It would reach as high as 450 qurush in the 1940s (*al-Difa',* 1947). Another development, however, had important implications for the affordability of printed texts during this part of the period: single newspaper copies, unavailable before the First World War, were now on sale, usually at 0.5 qurush (5 mills) apiece, occasionally a little more.

Who, then, could afford to buy these products? We have information on the resources available to different sections of Palestinian society and on the cost of living in both Ottoman and mandatory times; naturally, we know more about the latter period. The data that exist, however, are often less than adequate for establishing disposable income for any given group or time during this period. Estimates are bound to be shaky, not merely because the notion of disposable income itself depends on subjective variables, but also because during the period under consideration, there was much fluctuation in the size and composition of income groups. Appraising affordability would be especially tricky with regard to the middle sectors, those who were neither very wealthy nor very poor and whose revenue from work could make them potential buyers under certain circumstances.

Let us start with the obvious. It goes without saying that the country's affluent families, those making up the uppermost socioeconomic layer, were always capable of purchasing printed products and much more. This was the group whose members, in Palestine as in the neighboring provinces, were in a position to build their own book collections; subscribe to Egyptian, Lebanese, and foreign journals; and buy textbooks for their children, usually without difficulty. Those whose names appeared on the lists of subscribers for Butrus al-Bustani's encyclopedia in the 1870s and 1880s (see Chapter 2, "Impact of the Neighborhood") could only come from this class. The Khalidis of Jerusalem, owners of illustrious book treasures, were prominent representatives of this aristocracy in the nineteenth century, as were those who, once a literary journal appeared in Palestine in 1908, granted their relatives and friends a gift of a year's subscription for it.[33] Members of this class also constituted a prime segment, perhaps the majority, of local journal and newspaper subscribers under the mandate. One document that came down to us, a detailed register of subscribers to a Jerusalem paper in the mid-1930s and a rather uncommon piece of evidence as such, reads like a guest list for a fancy elite event in Palestine: Husayni, Nashashibi, Dajani, ʿAlami, Khalidi, Darwazah, ʿAbd al-Hadi, Khatib, Tamimi, Tuqan, Zuʿaytar, Rimawi, ʿAnabtawi, Masri, Shawa, Bsaysu, ʿArif, and so on—making up the urban elite of Jerusalem, Jaffa, Nablus, Hebron, Gaza, and other towns.[34] It is equally obvious that Palestine had, at the other end of its socioeconomic structure, a sizeable poor class whose members were bound to remain out of the pool of buyers, in both the nineteenth and twentieth centuries. These were groups that struggled to survive on subsistence budgets, for whom purchasing books and newspapers was clearly out of the question. They comprised the mass of the village population—until the end of the period the great majority of all Palestinian Arabs—with some exceptions among the rural leadership. Also included in this category were the lower sectors in the cities, notably those engaged in unskilled labor, of which many were recent migrants from the countryside.

Between the wealthy and the poor were groups, mostly urban, whose material condition sometimes permitted the allocation of funds to printed goods. In the later years of the Ottoman era, their number must have been very small. The average per capita income in the Fertile Crescent provinces around 1900 has been estimated at c. 800–1,000 Ottoman qurush annually, or 2.5–3 qurush daily. One qurush was adequate for buying an adult's daily needs in basic food, and a person would thus have to earn several-fold the average income per day in order to feed a family. Put differently, for the price of a small book—say, 10 qurush—one could buy food for an entire family for one day—or, more graphically, a package consisting of 1 kilogram of meat, 1 kilogram of wheat, 1 kilogram of rice, and 2 kilograms of sugar. An annual newspaper subscription cost as much as a family's average needs in food for several weeks.[35] Only those with considerably higher income than the average could spend money on items other than such basics. In Palestine, the normal wage of an unskilled urban laborer—in construction or services—was c. 7 qurush daily around 1900, rising to c. 15 just before the First World War. Even the latter, higher, sum would scarcely buy more than the very bare necessities. It would leave such breadwinners, along with the overwhelming mass of the rural population, outside the pool of potential book or journal buyers. As against this, skilled workers such as masons, carpenters, and craftsmen reportedly were earning 15 qurush at the turn of the century, and their pay reached 30 qurush per day, or more, during the next decade.[36] With this level of income, such (predominantly urban) workers in the more lucrative jobs were in a position to join the wealthy in purchasing a journal once in a while, or even a book.

The circumstances slowly improved after the war. The country's economy grew at an accelerated pace between 1920 and 1948,[37] as did the average income of both unskilled and, more pertinently, skilled workers. The former earned 8–10 qurush daily in the early 1930s, 25–40 in the mid-1940s; the latter, 25–40 qurush daily in the early 1930s, 40–65 in the mid-1940s.[38] Meanwhile, the cost of living witnessed a general trend of decline throughout the 1920s and 1930s, which meant decreasing retail prices of basic commodities in real terms and hence, in principle, more disposable income (this trend was reversed in the 1940s when, under the impact of the Second World War, both income and prices increased).[39] As we have seen, the cost of books rose by only a small margin during this period, and inexpensive printed products of every kind were on offer at all times. Newspaper prices remained basically unchanged throughout the period, and thus were decreasing in real terms. Equally important, from the outset of the mandate the sale of single newspaper copies on the street became common, making their purchase without the massive commitment of subscription a ready option. For the price of a small book—again, we may take a modest 10-qurush item as an instance—one could buy 20 eggs, or 23 kilograms of white flour, back in 1922; in 1938 the same sum would buy as many as 34 eggs or as much as 35 kilograms of flour. The 0.5 qurush one would have to pay for a single newspaper copy was equivalent to the cost of 350 grams of local cheese or 1,300 grams of milk in 1938, as against a mere 250 and 600 grams, respectively, in 1922.[40] All of these changes combined to form a material environment more convenient for buying goods beyond the basics, including printed publications. We may cautiously assume that those with more-or-less permanent employment, and hence with income above the very basic rate earned by the unskilled, were able to buy copies of daily newspapers, sometimes even regularly, as well as schoolbooks and other printed texts. Among them were waged workers in the public and private sectors and skilled laborers in the better-paying jobs.

Testimonies of non-elite urbanites and villagers who bought books and periodicals during the mandate confirm that this practice was spreading. Jabra Ibrahim Jabra, an elementary school student in Bethlehem in the 1920s, was the son of a laborer who could not afford the 15 qurush needed to buy a second pair of shoes. The father used to put on his only pair on Sundays, so as not to wear them out too fast. Nor could the family afford the half-qurush needed to buy their child a pencil and a notebook for school. Yet, Jabra tells us, when his older brother went out to do odd jobs in the summer, he was able to save money from his meager teenager income and buy books (often secondhand) enough to fill a "treasure box"—from popular detective pamphlets, to *Robinson Crusoe,* to a pocket dictionary.[41] The child, of course, did not have to live out of his income, but the money he earned did serve to balance the family's budget. Driven by a passion for books, he managed to lay aside some of his income and spend it on his hobby. Jabra also tells us about Musa the stonecutter who, though illiterate, used to buy newspapers periodically and have children on the street read them for him. A stonecutter's wage at the time was 20–35 qurush, and Musa, who had a family to feed, was still able to allocate the half-qurush for a single copy of *Filastin* once in a while.[42]

This last personal story is quite remarkable. Here was a man whose education and economic capabilities were limited, yet his craving for information made him devise ways to overcome both handicaps. He was successful on both counts. Musa and Jabra's older brother embodied a new social trend: people of lowly origin, lured by the printed word and the immense richness behind it, who were prepared to go a long way to obtain it despite their limited resources. A trickle at first, the phenomenon was visibly expanding, boosted by the favorable upturn in buying power. It was the increase in the number of buyers from this class that largely accounted for the growth in the country's book trade. To an even greater extent, this increase was responsible for the circulation level of many thousands that the Palestinian press had reached by the second half of the mandate.

Back to the overall picture: on the whole, the expanding book trade and growing newspaper circulation affected a minority of all Palestinians.

The majority was left out of the market of buyers, to a large extent due to poverty. That majority was predominantly—though by no means exclusively—rural. Only a small number of newspaper copies circulated in the countryside, and even by the 1940s it was rare to find more than two or three copies from the same day in the same village. Copies of books were still rarer there. Obviously, the reasons for this were several, but indigence was surely a major factor. This was repeatedly echoed in responses by villagers interviewed for this study, when asked about buying newspapers during the mandate: "Newspapers? Who could afford them?" would be the immediate answer, almost invariably. The same was true of the urban lower class of unskilled, low-income laborers like Jabra's father. Constricting the consumer market, poverty was a major obstacle to the diffusion of printed publications. It also had an adverse impact on the development of the local text industry, to which buyers mattered more than readers. As we shall see, however, Palestinians found ways to circumvent the obstacle, especially where this was most vital: in getting the news. While the buyers' market remained small, ways of accessing printed texts other than by buying them flourished.

Accessing without Buying: Libraries, Clubs, Reading Rooms

Books and journals gradually became available free of charge or for a slight fee in public places: in libraries, book-lending shops, and reading rooms of social and cultural clubs. Such places, all but nonexistent in the country before 1900, were in a dynamic swing of expansion half a century later. They were initially modeled on institutions recently set up in Egypt and Lebanon, which, in turn, had been inspired by European precedents. These new channels made access to the written word relatively easy.

Public libraries were meant to be open to all, regardless of social status and economic background. Reading ability and adherence to some rules of conduct were, in principle, all that was needed in order to benefit from their riches. Libraries offered their visitors the comfort of browsing in their reading rooms and often also borrowing books for reading at home, usually for a fee. In western Europe, such institutions had flourished in the eighteenth century; by the beginning of the nineteenth, England, France, and Germany each had hundreds of them.[43] Their counterparts in the Arabic-speaking countries were the centuries-old reading places associated with religious institutions, many of which had existed before across the lands of Islam. By the late nineteenth century, the foreign example had stimulated the emergence of more modern reading facilities in the region, notably the Khedivial library (later *Dar al-Kutub*) in Cairo, founded by Khedive Isma'il in 1870, and the Zahiriyyah in Damascus (1881). In Palestine, there were no such places before 1900. Old-style libraries had reportedly flourished there during the Ayyubid, Mamluk, and early Ottoman periods, but had gradually declined during the later Ottoman era. A few of them, in Jerusalem and certain other towns, still existed at the end of the nineteenth century, as we have seen, and continued to be open to the public intermittently during the first half of the twentieth century. Most accounts depict them as physically debased places; if people visited them for the purpose of reading or copying, their number must have been minuscule. The copying of manuscripts, which printing gradually rendered redundant, dwindled down to a state of curiosity. As reading facilities, too, the attraction of mosque libraries remained small and limited mostly to religious scholars and their pupils.

A notable exception in this scene was the al-Aqsa mosque library in Jerusalem, a classic sample of an old-style institution. Al-Aqsa's uniquely revered status had traditionally brought it endowments of private book collections and book gifts. From the late nineteenth century onward, the intellectual horizons of many future donors were shifting, something that was reflected in the changing contents of their libraries, which came to include items new in both substance and format. Such gifts revitalized al-Aqsa's traditional collection with modern items. Alongside the old works, the library thus came to comprise pieces, often printed, on hitherto "alien" matters, such as European history and politics, translated belles lettres, modern science, and, remarkably, volumes of imported and local journals.[44] For a while lying in disorder and largely inaccessible during the early years of the century, the collection was reorganized and put at the public's disposal in 1922 as *dar kutub al-masjid al-aqsa*. The Higher Islamic Legal Council declared it to be a public library and assigned a special facility to it, which included a reading room. It was first housed in Qubbat al-Nahwiyyah (in the southwestern corner of the Dome of the Rock compound), from where it was moved to the Is'ardiyyah *madrasah* (at the north border of the Haram) in 1927, after the place had been profoundly renovated. Comprising a variety of traditional and modern topics, its stock of titles reportedly reached c. 3,000 items within a year of its opening, increasing to 11,000 by midcentury.[45] Literate people unable to buy printed works could now consult those that had been bequeathed to al-Aqsa.

The Khalidiyyah, just a short walking distance away, had opened more than two decades before al-Aqsa. At that time, the opening of an autonomous public library in Jerusalem unrelated to a place of religious learning was a novelty. The Khalidis introduced their undertaking as a proud mark of the scholarship that had long underlay their prominent local status.[46] Thanks to this initiative, they asserted, members of the educated public could from now on acquaint themselves both with the classic legacy and with the most recent fruits of the human mind. To their intellectual cohorts, the opening of such a place implied a new link in the chain of exciting modern literary activities that had preoccupied them for some time through self-immersion in the *nahdah*. It is important, however, to note what the opening of the Khalidiyyah did not signify: it did not come as a response to any public demand for this kind of service. Such a demand would evolve much later. While the country's small educated elite had become accustomed to engaging in literary matters, the great bulk of the public had not, and had yet to be brought into this circle. The Khalidis created a convenient access to literary treasures and modern printed works previously available only to members of their own family. Rather than responding to a public call, it was a call upon the public—or rather upon its educated segment—to come and explore.

The Khalidiyyah was by far the most serious private endeavor of its kind. The introductory statement in the library's catalogue, published upon its inauguration, laid out the rationale underlying the initiative. The virtues of knowledge were innumerable, it noted, and the quest for it was an essential human need, something that required "ample consultation of many important books." This, in turn, called for the existence of a public library (*maktabah ʿumumiyyah*) in every town, which should include books of every kind, sacred and temporal. The Khalidis were therefore opening "a wide room" and placing in it a big quantity of books from their ancestors' collection and from their own, thereby "turning the said room into a public house of learning (*dar ʿulum ʿumumiyyah*)." The library was to be open to "any person desiring to read (*man yarghab al-mutalaʿah min ayy fard kan*)," and a reliable caretaker was appointed to run its affairs. For the sake of the public good, however, books were not to circulate out of the building.[47] The enterprise was indeed impressive. Along with manuscripts, many of them rare and precious, were modern books and bound volumes of the leading Arabic periodicals of the time. There were also current issues of imported journals and newspapers. Reading conditions were comfortable, with a large table that had tilted sides for supporting books and ample light coming through large windows in the walls and ceiling. The collection itself grew constantly during the decades following its opening, from a little over

2,000 volumes at first to 4,000 in 1917 and 7,000 in 1936 (a figure apparently representing an upper limit dictated by the available storage space).[48] Whether or not the library indeed became an attractive locus for "persons desiring to read" is a question of much importance for our discussion, and will concern us in another chapter.

The Khalidis also expressed a wish: that the notables in every big town set up "a public library as good as this one or better."[49] This wish, however, would remain just that until after the end of the mandate. No similar facility opened in the country during the following decades. There were libraries of foreign religious organizations, some of them older than the Khalidiyyah. Some, mostly in Jerusalem—the libraries of St. Anne Catholic Seminar, and the Dominican, Franciscan, and Greek convents—were open to the public (at least to the male public) by the turn of the century. A few of them boasted collections comprising thousands of volumes, for the most part in foreign languages but also in Arabic—reportedly including some distinctly secular works[50]—as well as reading quarters of the comfortable standards known in their lands of origin. The evidence at hand does not permit a proper assessment of the role these places played in changing the country's reading scene; but given the alien image they usually projected, that role may well have been rather modest, limited as it was to the small, urban, educated elite. There were also a few urban school libraries, apparently a dozen or so, most of which only opened in the 1940s.[51] "Attaching special importance to independent reading (*al-mutala'ah al-hurrah*)," as one of them announced, they built up a collection, usually several hundred books, so their students could "read in their leisure time."[52] Sometimes they purported to serve not just the students but also other "lovers of reading,"[53] and were in principle open to the public at large. Judged by the paucity of their mention in memoirs and other sources, however, these places too must have been very modest both in scope and in their contribution to the community.

Another channel by which the nascent demand for printed knowledge was met was reading rooms of cultural clubs and associations. In other parts of the region such places had emerged sometime earlier. In Europe they had a long tradition, with roots going back to the seventeenth or eighteenth century, when they had similarly appeared in response to an awakening desire for reading. It would be worthwhile to pause for a moment and glimpse at these earlier models, before moving on to consider the Palestinian variations.

Reading fora in western Europe, bearing different names and operating under diverse rules, were basically of two kinds: bourgeois societies (*Lesegesellschaften, cabinets littéraire*), designed as social-cultural clubs, with carefully selected membership and well-equipped premises where books were read and literary subjects discussed; and commercial reading rooms (*Leihbibliotheken, chambres de lecture*), where people of wider classes read books and journals for a monthly fee and sometimes could borrow them for reading at home. Both types offered their customers the advantage of shared and hence affordable acquisition of printed texts. The former also provided a framework for discussing the material with fellow members of the same social class and interest. Reading societies of the more aristocratic type began to spring up in Europe in the seventeenth century, often starting as an initiative to get joint subscriptions for periodical publications. They evolved into centers of sociability whose quarters included reading halls for books and journals as well as rooms for other activities, such as game playing, smoking, and drinking. By the onset of the nineteenth century, there were hundreds of them in the towns of Germany, with membership amounting to tens of thousands, and similar associations appeared in other countries of western Europe. In many places they lasted throughout the nineteenth century and even into the twentieth. Their numbers and span of life changed with place and time, as did the balance between reading and other activities pursued in them. The other type of institution, popular reading rooms, appeared somewhat later and likewise flourished in the nineteenth century. They played a major role in exposing wider circles of the society—those left out of the more refined reading clubs—to the routine consumption of books.[54] Both types served as models to be adopted in the Arabic-speaking countries.

In the Arab provinces of the Ottoman Empire, clubs devoted to reading, as part of a broader enlightenment venture, began to appear around the middle of the nineteenth century. "We have borrowed [the idea] from the Europeans, just as we have taken from them . . . all kinds of other projects of collective working for the common good," observed the Lebanese-Egyptian writer Jurji Zaydan, himself a member of one such club in the late nineteenth century.[55] Scientific and literary societies were typical products of the cultural *nahdah*. One of the earliest clubs, and certainly the most famous, was the Syrian Society (*al-jam'iyyah al-suriyyah*), founded in Beirut in 1847 by a group of missionaries and local Christian intellectuals, "in consequence of the urgent solicitation of intelligent natives, chiefly young men, desirous of knowledge." Its members used to meet periodically, listen to lectures, and engage in scholarly discussions.[56] Before too long it was followed by a host of associations (*jamʿiyyat*) with various cultural, social, and political agendas, formed by members of the educated elite and graduates of the modern institutions of learning. One objective common to many of them was collecting books and journals that were put in libraries and reading rooms (*ghuraf qiraʾah* or *ghuraf mutalaʿah*) on their premises for their members to read or peruse. The library of the Syrian Society, for example, contained no fewer than 756 books within a year of its foundation, including as many as 229 printed books in foreign languages. It reportedly functioned as a lending library for members, open once a week.[57]

Alongside these societies, private reading rooms popped up in the towns of Egypt and Lebanon during the last third of the nineteenth century. Like their European forebears, they thrived on the growing desire for news and views and the need to share expenses. In Alexandria, a "public office (*maktab*) for the reading of cultural books of all kinds, as well as Arabic, Turkish and European newspapers" was opened in 1876. In the same year, a journalist and businessman from Beirut who believed that "public libraries are one of the greatest devices that contribute to the betterment of society," announced the opening of "a place in the city that would include . . . a well-organized hall, where Arabic and foreign books and newspapers will be available for browsing and reading." Similarly, some time later a group of intellectuals, comprising teachers and graduates of the Syrian Protestant College in Beirut, opened a reading room in that city, in which they placed "the best books that elevate and enlighten the mind," along with Arabic and other periodicals. It became a meeting place for a "group of reading lovers of all factions."[58] The centrality of newspapers in these activities and the ongoing political uncertainty subsequently turned many of the reading centers into political clubs, which would continue to operate along similar lines throughout the region during the first half of the twentieth century.

As was the case in western Europe, Lebanon, and Egypt, literary societies in Palestine first appeared as an elite phenomenon. Their activity is reported toward the end of the nineteenth century, stirred by both local and foreign initiative. We know little about them beyond their names and sometimes the names of their most prominent members. A precursor, the Jerusalem Literary Society (*jamʿiyyat al-quds al-adabiyyah*), was founded in 1849 by the British consul to that city and devoted itself to literary and scientific exploration of the Holy Land. For the elite of the local community, however, this kind of activity was still an alien idea at that stage, and the society's membership consisted exclusively of foreign diplomats and missionaries.[59] Societies of the local educated class would emerge only several decades later, reportedly in Jerusalem, Jaffa, and Acre, of which the one most frequently mentioned in the sources is *jamʿiyyat al-aadab al-zahirah* (society of shining literature) of Jerusalem. It was apparently formed in 1898 by Daʾud Saydawi, a banker, and comprised mostly young Christian Arab men. Among them were people who would become cultural and educational leaders, including Khalil al-Sakakini, ʿIsa al-ʿIsa, Bandali al-Jawzi, Faraj Farajallah, Eftim Mushabbak, Shibli al-Jamal, and Alfonse Alonzo. The group, we are told, used to convene periodically for "cultural evenings" of lectures and discussion. They had no regular place for their activities and met in private homes, presumably for fear of the Ottoman police.[60] This and similar groups that may have operated in other towns are not known to have had their own libraries, or even permanent quarters. They were modest antecedents of associations that would spring up in the towns of Palestine after the First World War with greater vigor.

No public reading rooms similar to those in Beirut and Alexandria seem to have existed in Palestine prior to the war. Text production and a reading audience were both still in their inception at that stage and there was little use for such facilities. The first reading rooms in the country may well have been those opened, for instrumental purposes, by the propaganda unit of the British army, which had conquered the country in 1917–1918. Set up in Jerusalem, Jaffa, Ramallah, Bethlehem, Bayt Jala, and perhaps elsewhere, these places had little to do with intellectual curiosity or passion for reading. Rather, they were meant to address, on British terms, the familiar wartime hunger for news. The rooms were furnished selectively with reading materials, including British daily reports on the front situation, newspapers, and books. "The various reading rooms . . . are all well frequented," an intelligence officer reported from Palestine in May 1918; "in the central reading room [in Jerusalem] any morning types of all races, religions and sects may be seen looking at the newspapers." A report from Jaffa observed that "owing to the tact of the [reading room] director, an Egyptian Sheikh, it has become quite a meeting place where conversation is indulged in over cups of coffee."[61] Such activity, naturally intense in a time of instability, declined once the war came to an end.

From 1919 onward, societies of different stripes proliferated in Palestine, lending color to the country's public life. They defined themselves variably as *jamʿiyyah* (association), *halqah* (circle), or, most commonly, *nadi* (club, a term applied both to the forum of members and to their meeting place). Sometimes they were professedly elitist, as was the "literary circle" (*halqat al-adab*) in Haifa, a Palestinian variety of a *cabinet littéraire,* which reportedly admitted only authors, writers, and poets to its ranks. Others were designed specifically for such groups as young women, "railway officials and other educated men," or members of one religious community or another.[62] Christians were, on the whole, better organized than Muslims in that, often leaning on support from missionary and other foreign-based organizations. Many of these clubs had their own quarters, in which they conducted social, cultural, and sports activities, from lectures by visiting writers to football contests. Against the backdrop of increasing public tension and friction, some of them turned into centers of political action, becoming a breeding ground for the leading political groupings in mandatory Palestine. 'Adnan Abu Ghazaleh, a former member of one such club who subsequently studied the phenomenon, has noted that these associations existed all over Palestine during the mandate. No fewer than 30 of them were operating, and by the 1940s there was at least one in each town of 10,000 residents or more. At that stage, he has observed, every educated Palestinian was a member of one club or another[63]—a somewhat optimistic if not entirely implausible assessment.

Though a fascinating aspect of the country's sociocultural and political scene, detail on the activities of these associations and clubs must be left out of the present study. Of relevance to our discussion is the fact that their premises often included libraries and reading rooms, with printed materials that were available to their members. By far the most prominent of these was the library of the Jerusalem YMCA, which began sometime in the 1920s, moving to its sumptuous new headquarter upon its inauguration in 1933. Its collection, initially comprising some 3,000 volumes, increased to as many as 25,000 by the 1940s, the vast majority of them in European languages.[64] Similar though much smaller libraries operated during the mandate in the urban clubs, with the bigger cities housing several of them each. To pick an example, the library of the St. Anthony club in Jaffa had a stock of a few hundred books in the 1940s, about a quarter of them in Arabic and the rest in European languages. "There was no public library in the city," related Fakhri Jdai, the society librarian and a member of the Jaffa upper class until 1948; "for reading, people were affiliated with clubs. There were many of them in Jaffa. They would come, leaf through the newspapers and journals available there and borrow books for reading at home."[65] The YMCA, St. Anthony's, and, similarly, some of the other better-off associations operated as exclusive social clubs, normally charging membership fees. Their libraries and reading rooms carried books and periodicals in Arabic and in other languages, and they allowed their members to peruse them there or borrow books for reading at home.

There were also clubs of a more popular nature, whose affiliates were mostly lower-class people and youth, among them people with little or no education. Their activities included mainly social meetings, games, and sports, but also educational activities such as evening reading classes for the illiterate. Their quarters sometimes had a section designed as a *makta-bah*—a space for reading and browsing of such printed items as were at hand and where a stock of books was sometimes present. For example, a note reporting the opening of a new cultural club in Hebron, in January 1919—designed to enhance "friendship, amity and unity" among the people—indicated that the club's premises included a reading room (*ghurfah li'l-mutala'ah*) as well as halls for music, games, and dining.[66] In Nazareth, an Islamic youth society was formed in 1925 with a noble cause: teaching the illiterate in an evening school, guiding them to stay away from drinking and laziness and "training them in reading useful books, newspapers and journals."[67] In Jaffa around the same time, the Christian Youth Club operated a game room and a library, where public lectures were periodically offered. So did the Islamic Youth Club in that city.[68] And in Acre of the 1930s and 1940s, the Usamah bin Zayid sports and cultural club had, in addition to a basketball field and a table-tennis hall, "a *maktabah* for the use of its members."[69] These were usually modest facilities with small book collections, based primarily on book donations and little else, of which members were sometimes allowed to borrow for reading at home. But the more common service these places offered as channels for diffusing printed materials was in making journals and newspapers available to members and other visitors, who could peruse them in the reading rooms when they could not buy them for themselves.

Yet another option for those with more passion for books than an ability to buy them was the private lending library. The idea was simple, and advantageous to reader and shopkeeper alike: a small periodic fee would buy the customer access to all the printed treasures in the store, while the owner would profit from renting the same items repeatedly. It was a convenient arrangement that had thrived in western Europe during the eighteenth century and part of the nineteenth.[70] There, the subsequent proliferation of inexpensive books and journals had forced most private lending libraries to close down toward the end of the nineteenth century, when the Palestine variation of it was still in the future. A shop lending books for a fee is reported to have operated in Nablus around the end of that century by ʿIzzat Darwazah, then an inquisitive youngster and a client.[71] This, however, must have been rather exceptional for the time. Another instance, after the First World War, involved a somewhat different arrangement. In 1923, a Haifa bookstore called *al-maktabah al-wataniyyah* equipped one of its rooms with Arabic and foreign newspapers, journals, and books and turned it into a "free-of-charge reading club (*nadi mutalaʿah majani*)" for all "readers and literature lovers."[72] The owner, Jamil al-Bahri, an intellectual and journal editor, may have sought to contribute to public enlightenment; or, just as likely, to attract buyers to his shop. Available sources, however, are silent about its subsequent operation, and one tends to assume that the venture met with little public response. In the next decade we again hear of a lending shop, Fawzi Yusuf's *maktabat al-andalus* in Jerusalem, which introduced this option in the late 1930s, among other initiatives, as we have seen. But as a more popular arrangement, it evolved in Palestine only in the 1940s. We have reports from Jaffa, Haifa, and Nazareth—and the practice may well have obtained in other towns—of stationery-cum-bookstores that invited the public to subscribe to their "lending library" (*maktabat al-iʿarah*), adding yet another public service to their already diverse activities.[73]

Public and lending libraries, clubs, and reading rooms were all urban phenomena. In the villages there was not much demand for such modern services, and the physical conditions were not conducive to their development. Perhaps the closest rural parallel to these urban services was an arrangement initiated by the mandate authorities after organized education had begun to spread into the countryside. The Department of Education introduced "circulating libraries": boxes with a few volumes that were brought by car or donkey to a village, left in the local school for several weeks, and then moved to the next place. The books were essentially intended for schoolchildren—the segment of the rural community that was acquiring reading skills and that had the time for such pursuits. But here and there graduates and others who could read took advantage of this arrangement. In a few places the Department of Education helped schools set up modest book collections of their own. Such collections were "small but useful," recalled a resident of Shafa ʿAmr who had graduated from the local school in the late 1930s: "we relied on [our local library] heavily."[74] On the whole, this was a marginal activity with marginal effect: the many who were interviewed for this study from rural places throughout the country either had difficulty recalling the appearance of books in their villages through such channels or treated it as an insignificant curiosity. By contrast, newspapers—the lifeline of vital intelligence—were regarded as useful and relevant, and the eager village communities found effective ways to access them, as we shall now see.

Accessing without Buying: Open Public Places

It was in the open public domain that the largest number of people accessed the contents of written messages. This was true both before and after the turn of the century. Printed texts, primarily newspapers and political proclamations, reached places of common gathering and presented attractive knowledge that could be consumed there privately or collectively.

In cities, the most popular of these places, and certainly the most colorful, was the café. In the Middle East this was an institution with a centuries-old tradition of circulating news, exchanging views, and enjoying entertainment, where everything from political rumors to ancient legends was communicated, with or without the presence of written texts.[75] The café was a purely male institution; women were excluded, and their access to the information circulating inside depended on men's readiness to share it with them at home. When the press entered the region, places of such public gathering soon turned into locations of collective newspaper reading. The match was perfect: coffee and tea were proven stimulants for reading and for the discussion it often prompted; and the presence of journals, in turn, increased the appeal of the place and assured an inflow of customers. Owners of cafés redoubled the allure of their businesses by buying or subscribing to a range of papers. Patrons, for their part, enjoyed the fact that for the trifling fee of a cup of tea or coffee, they could read or listen to the reading of several papers. Foreign visitors to the cities of the region were struck by the rampant phenomenon of newspaper reading in cafés and repeatedly reported it with amazement in their accounts. "They learnt this habit as well as the café habit from France," a British visitor to Cairo suggested in 1911 (a flimsy assumption on both counts).[76] Egypt indeed seems to have been the country where this habit was most popular, and observers got the sense that "no city [had] a more active café life than Cairo."[77] But it was also widespread in other places. In Istanbul and the Turkish-speaking parts of the empire, the marriage between café and reading resulted in a hybrid institution, the *kıraathane*, literally, "reading house," and in reality "*mi-salon de lecture à l'européenne et mi-cafés orientaux.*"[78]

Palestine was no exception in this. Social and political activity in cafés was reported in the towns of Palestine at least from the early nineteenth century. Some of these places were "dark and disgusting, their straw chairs short, their tables low and filthy," and their customers coming from the lower social classes. Others, better equipped and cleaner, served the "educated middle class."[79] Loci of leisurely pastime in quiet days, they would turn into centers of passionate gatherings when public troubles loomed. An account of one such session, convened in a Jaffa café amidst excited encounters with Zionist and British foes, illustrates this routine:

> The meeting took place on February 10th [1923] at 4 P.M. About 800–900 people were present. It is believed that the most active organisers of this meeting were Scheikh Abdel-Kader El Musaffer from Jerusalem and Yhia Woffa, the Secretary of the Jaffa Moslem-Christian Association. Omar Eff. Bittar asked the said Scheikh Abdel-Kader to hold a speech. The Scheikh spoke in a very excited manner for about two hours. During that speech he weeped [sic] himself and made the present weep. The audience was extremely excited. He said: ". . . Brothers, know that this country is our country and the country of our fathers. Nobody will be able to break us down . . ." [Other local notables also spoke] on the same subject and nearly in a similar manner . . . There is full reason to believe that the impression made on the audience by the speeches etc. was far greater and stronger than one could get out from [sic] all the above said, taking into consideration the state of mind created by this meeting.[80]

News sheet reading became a common feature of the country's café life on the eve of the First World War. Iliyas Hamati, then a teenager employed by the *maqha al-bahr* (sea café) in Acre, remembered it as a "gathering place of the educated, who used to read the *Filastin* newspaper."[81] Once the war broke out, journals became less accessible, due to censorship and other problems.[82] But with the thirst for information growing, getting together in cafés for circulating news and views on the unfolding events only intensified. The conquering British army relied on this common local habit for spreading their propaganda and even opened new coffeehouses especially for the purpose, in which, one intelligence officer reported, "all the telegrams and newspapers" were placed.[83] From the early 1920s onward, cafés were often depicted as locations where, alongside more traditional activities, newspapers were being read. One famous such place was *maqha al-mukhtar* of Sayyid 'Isa al-Tubbah, which opened near Jaffa Gate in Jerusalem in 1918. It became an activity center for some of the leading men of letters in the city, headed by Khalil al-Sakakini, who nicknamed the place *maqha al-sa'alik* (baggers' café). In that place, where discussions were held

A Café in Tulkarm, 1936. Note the written notice on the front door.
© The Central Zionist Archive, Jerusalem. Courtesy of the Central Zionist Archive.

and social and political problems resolved, "there was always a large number of newspapers and periodicals," including "the various papers of the week, both local and foreign."[84] In Lydda in early 1920, local leaders were reported to be "reading the papers out in the cafés and telling the public about the heroic deeds of their brethren in Syria and their war with the French."[85] Journal publishers sometimes complained about people "who try to get the paper from friends who had already read it, or to read it in a café" rather than buy their own copy, thereby depriving the owner of "a meager profit, indeed less than half the cost of shoe-polishing."[86] Coffeehouses and the press cohabited in a kind of symbiosis: when the editor and reporters were sitting in a café engaging in a discussion, the content of their exchanges occasionally found its way to the next issue. Reportedly, some pieces were actually written on the spot.[87]

Not all coffeehouses became sites of such cultural activity. In some, the spirit was distinctly remote from the more "educated and cultured" surroundings of social clubs.[88] Cafés were occasionally criticized as institutions of "waste, idleness and stupidity." Before entering these places, the editor of *al-Karmil* charged—having visited some coffee shops in Haifa and Acre—the "café maniacs (*marda al-maqahi*)" should think of "the time they waste, the damage they cause to their own interests, and the loss of their hard-earned resources. [They should also consider] what they could have gained had they spent this time on reading useful books and learning practical matters."[89] This censure was voiced in 1922, when daily newspapers were still in the future in Palestine and journal reading in coffeehouses was a limited phenomenon. As the political atmosphere turned warmer and the press shifted to a daily pace, public reading became more widespread and cafés took on a more respectable image as sites of news circulation. They offered a comfortable solution to the common dilemma of curiosity being greater than the ability to buy the papers. Later, when radio was introduced in the country, coffeehouses—their clientele of news consumers already in place—naturally became the scene of collective listening by the many for whom buying their own receivers was but a remote dream.

Printed texts became available in other open sites as well. Certain written products were specifically designed for consumption in the open. Official announcements, clandestine placards, political leaflets, commercial advertisements, personal notices of every kind—affixed to billboards, house fences, mosque and church doors, trees, electricity poles—were meant to be read *in loco*. To an extent, this also became true of newspapers, which evolved as commodities to be consumed outdoors no less than at home or in a club. They came to be advertised visually and vocally, displayed and sold in the open, and eventually read in the street, in shops, in the marketplace, and in the village gathering sites. The German archaeologist Peter Thomsen, who visited Syria and Palestine in 1914, noticed "people eagerly reading newspapers in the streets, the railway stations, the houses and shops" of their towns.[90] And Jabra Ibrahim Jabra, describing the sale of periodicals in the Bethlehem market of the late 1920s, similarly related how his older brother used to "trick the vendors into allowing him to read whatever articles of the journals he chose before their few copies were sold out."[91]

While in cities the channels of open access formed a varied scene, in the rural areas the situation was simpler. Most villages had one central public institution, the *madafah* (Palestinian popular pronunciation *madafeh*, literally, "a hosting place"), also known as *diwan* (gathering hall), where most of the communal business was managed. In some places it was owned by the family of the Mukhtar; in others, it was the collective property of the entire village. Where a village was divided into different or rival factions, several such institutions sometimes existed side by side, all fulfilling basically the same social and cultural functions. The *madafah* was the beating heart of the village. It served as a gathering spot where news was reported and public issues deliberated; a place for celebration and mourning; a guesthouse for putting up visitors, official and other; and a cultural center where men would be entertained by listening to stories while sipping coffee and smoking.[92] Like city cafés, the village *madafah* was a male institution (indeed in some places it was more commonly referred to as *bayt al-rijal*, "men's house").[93] In some villages there were variations to this meeting site. In ʿArʿarah (in the Jenin district) the big mulberry tree at the village center was the usual place for summer evening gatherings.[94] In Tarshihah (in the upper Galilee), people used to convene in the barbershop or grocery store, small places whose owners expanded them as meeting sites by adding chairs on the adjacent grounds around them.[95] And in Masmiyyat Hurani, men were convening "on *masatib* (outdoor stone benches) or under the *sidrah* (Christ's Thorn) tree" to similar ends.[96] Women, always excluded, sometimes formed their own assemblies in private homes, in which, in addition to listening to stories, they also circulated information.[97]

When printed materials began to arrive, the customary gathering sites were the obvious places for passing them on. As in the past, information was transmitted collectively; illiteracy, poverty, and tradition accounted for this. It was an effective way of accessing printed information. In some locations this may have begun in the later part of the nineteenth century: evidence suggests that imported journals most likely read in this way arrived in at least one rural community in the Galilee as early as the 1880s.[98] In 1913, the editor of *Filastin* reported his decision to deliver free copies of his paper to every village in the Jaffa district with 100 souls or more, so as to "teach the peasants their rights." The papers—apparently one copy per village—were sent to the Mukhtars, who would put them at the disposal of the public in the usual meeting places.[99] As we shall see, sessions of public newspaper reading became customary in villages in the 1920s and grew increasingly common in the 1930s, especially during the troubled late years of that decade. More printed items that reached the rural regions in those stormy years, such as government leaflets and rebel handbills, were likewise collectively accessed. In a few of the villages, mainly the bigger ones, coffeehouses began to open during the interwar years, quickly assuming the role of public communal centers. Upon their opening, most of the collective functions, including the reading of papers and whatever else was at hand, were transferred there.[100]

Enhanced production in and around Palestine and growing demand at home were thus met by the advent of new mechanisms for bringing the commodity to the customers. Some of these were indeed old conduits adapted for the new tasks. Such, for example, was the book dealership, a traditional trade that seemed to have died out in Palestine and then been reincarnated in a modern form. Such also was the odd literate person in a village, traditionally the community's reader when the need arose, who was now assigned a task markedly more intensive than before. Other channels represented complete innovations: street newsstands, newspaper hawkers, club libraries, reading rooms, and book-lending shops. These modern circulation routes, accommodated or newly introduced, were marks of a cultural transition. In mandatory Palestine, as in other Arab societies at the time, the most pressing popular demand for printed items was for printed news. In addition to shaping the nature of the text industry and its market, this last fact also determined the routes of access to these products. Information sheets were not only easier to make and cheaper to buy than other printed products; they could also be accessed, more practically, in open places that required no particular status, membership, or affiliation. As against this, demand for books grew rather slowly, and the conduits devised to make them available evolved at a commensurately slow pace. The modes in which the public made use of these channels will be considered in the remainder of the book.

CHAPTER 4

Individual Reading

✦

Musa the stonecutter was a simple, illiterate manual laborer in Bethlehem of the early 1930s. Highly curious about political matters, he was eager to acquire reading skills, the key to a world of news and views. He eventually found the way, enlisting a high school student as his tutor. The boy, later a celebrated novelist, tells us Musa's fascinating story:

He said to me one day: "Do you know . . . what the wish of my life is?"

And before I had a chance to guess, he added: "To learn how to read . . ."

I said: "So, why don't you learn how to read?"

He said: "I am afraid they would say about me: after he became old he joined the *kuttab*."

I said: "First, you are still young. Second, I am ready to teach you, if you accept me [as your guide]."

He could not believe my words and asked: "Really? Do you think you can teach me how to read a newspaper at least?"

I said: "Let's try. And let's begin from today. Where is your newspaper?"

From that day on I began to teach him how to read, using, in addition to the newspaper, also his son's primer, authored by Khalil al-Sakakini . . . As we were making some progress in reading and I asked him to study at night, he began to express fatigue and said: "You know . . . I return [home] exhausted after dressing stones all day, with no energy left in me to focus on anything. Besides, you know, my eyes are not in the best of shape."

I accepted and lowered my expectations, and he was content with his acquired ability to read the major headlines of his favorite newspaper. He would sometimes try to read the editorial as best he could, grasping it in his own way, perhaps more by inference and reading between the lines than by comprehending the meaning of whole sentences. But the important thing was that he now read the newspaper. He read it to himself or to his family, without relying on help from the others.[1]

Musa's personal experience may not have represented a widespread phenomenon at the time. Still, his story typified the country's entry into the world of written texts in more ways than one. During the first half of the twentieth century, reading in Palestine expanded considerably. An elitist pursuit at first, it was gradually becoming a popular routine. A series of momentous developments, borne out of the Arab-British-Zionist tangle, largely accounted for this trend: the Mufti's rise to national leadership in the 1920s, the 1928–1929 disturbances, the 1936–1939 revolt, the 1937 partition plan, the 1939 White Paper, the end of the Second World War—each further reinforced the habit of leaning on printed knowledge. But it was more than the daily news that was on demand. Information less urgent in nature, a means to riding the mounting wave of modernization, was also increasingly sought from written sources. Reading emerged as a vital skill: for obtaining up-to-date intelligence, communicating with the authorities, finding solid employment, navigating in the city. The rising importance of this proficiency became a social criterion, setting those capable of accessing written messages apart from and above the rest. As the gap between these two categories became manifest, many of the unskilled looked for ways of bridging the gap or at least minimizing its effect. As so often happens, the flow of printed information enhanced the demand for it, and popular appetite, in turn, boosted production. Underlying these circular processes was the country's intensive political drama, the main drive in this metamorphosis.

The remainder of the book will be devoted to examining these lively developments in the public assimilation of written texts. The changes had a quantitative side, of course, the ever-elusive dimension that will be attended to in due course. But perhaps more instructive were the varied modes in which these changes evolved, a functional diversity that was a quintessential aspect of the process. The increasing presence of publications, the growing hunger for their contents, and the training in reading offered by the schools combined to broaden the circle of readers. But appetite soon proved bigger than reading skills, prompting people to find other ways of accessing the coveted information. They did so, most commonly, by relying collectively on the skills of individual readers. The different modes in which reading was practiced in Palestine will be considered here, most profitably, under two distinct headings: individual or private reading, which will be treated in the present chapter after a brief discussion of some historic antecedents; and its complement, collective or public reading, the focus of the next.

Individual Reading: Past Legacy

Historians exploring the changing manners in which people read in different times and places often refer to a historic process of transformation: from a practice involving reader and audience in a vocal-aural experience to one of individual, visual, silent reading. For a long time it was commonly agreed that the shift from one mode to the next was determined primarily by a change in the availability of written texts. The scarcity of books at first forced people to share them: a pastor reading out to a group of believers, or an educated person reading to members of his family, were doing so largely due to the dearth of writings. Illiteracy, of course, was another reason for this practice; but illiteracy itself resulted, at least in part, from the paucity of books. In this concept, Johannes Gutenberg's invention was naturally the single most revolutionary development in the process. Printing made possible the fast diffusion of books, inspired and greatly facilitated the spread of education, and thus put more written texts in the hands of more people capable of using them. With written texts readily available and reading skills widespread, people could do away with the dependence on collective fora for accessing the texts.

Further research, however, while not underrating the importance of printing, has shown that the shift from old to new was a more complex and multiphased process. One phase was the change from vocal to visual assimilation of writings by individuals reading to themselves. It has been persuasively shown that silent reading was known in times immemorial—there are testimonies of it going back to ancient Greece and the fifth century BCE.[2] At that time, however, it was an exception, the standard being vocal reading with the texts spelled out. This last standard was abandoned in a process of which an American scholar, Paul Saenger, has recently offered an intriguing analysis. Saenger has suggested that reading aloud was once necessary because the form of writing itself—the shape of letters, of words, and of the whole page—was difficult to decipher for anybody not highly proficient in it. The main problem was the absence of spaces between the words, which were normally written in uninterrupted sequence (*scriptura continua*). Vocalization assisted in comprehending the text by helping to verify its correct reading. Changes in writing style, especially, again, the introduction of spaces between words, along with simplification of the grammatical structure of sentences, made reading markedly easier than it had been previously. Permitting a swift visual recognition of words and a quick perception of intent, this change made it possible to dispose of oralization and perform reading silently. The process, Saenger has noted, seems to have begun in the British Isles during the seventh century CE, and by the eleventh century it was already common throughout northern Europe, from where it continued to spread further. Silent reading gradually ceased to be an exclusive domain of a few well-trained scholars and became the popular norm, a momentous historic development. This change, then, had taken place centuries before the invention of printing.[3] Placing the revolution in reading before the revolution in book production, Saenger's thesis is now widely accepted in the field. We shall come across him again in due course.

Another phase in the evolution of reading, according to the now-accepted wisdom, was the shift from group practice, most commonly in a reader/listeners format, to individual practice. This change occurred in western Europe at a much later time, mostly during the eighteenth century and especially in its second half. In between the former shift from vocal to silent reading and this last one, the production of written texts had been industrialized following the advent of printing. The invention of movable letters was a historic milestone between the two major changes in reading modes; it also, of course, facilitated the later change by permitting the proliferation of printed works and the subsequent emergence of mass written products such as periodicals, almanacs, and chapbooks. The effect of that technological invention was soon felt in many areas, but more progress in education and sociocultural organization was needed in order to lend it its full public impact. A considerable leap forward occurred in western Europe in the eighteenth century, reflected in the rapid spread of institutions such as lending libraries, reading clubs, and literary societies. This, in turn, led to a dramatic growth in both production and consumption of books, as well as newspapers and magazines, that reached unprecedented scope and variety. Having previously shifted from vocality to silence, reading was now transforming from a collective to an individual act. The latter process was so significant that some scholars have come to regard it as a second "revolution" in the history of reading in the West.[4]

More recently, scholars' attention has been drawn to other, hitherto little noticed, modes of reading. Largely a result of rapid technological advances, the appearance of these new modes may well represent yet another turning point in the history of the practice. In a study of New York City prior to the Civil War, David Henkin has examined what he terms "city reading": the visual and mental absorption of the innumerable written signs that make up a modern city setting—bulletin board notices, shop name plates, mammoth ad banners, newspaper racks, even money bills and theater tickets. Perpetually transforming the cityscape, such products have created an environment where writing serves as an increasingly vital device of orientation and communication. In this environment, people use written messages to find their way, align their conduct with public norms, learn about changes in the vicinity, and run their affairs as sellers and buyers. Reading in these circumstances is quite unlike that in the older modes. Distinct from a deliberate review of longer writings that require concentration, it consists of fleeting glimpses in lighter and shorter messages that confront those present in endless ways. The use of writing in open places and the growing public reliance on it evolved not subsequent to but simultaneously with the trend of individualization in reading noted above. In a certain way it represented a converse tendency: as against the previous process of a shift to a greater privacy, in the new phenomenon reading was coming out into the public domain. What is true of antebellum New York is, of course, also true of urban (and, to a lesser extent, rural) surroundings anywhere. It is a universal phenomenon, although its pace and development differ from one place to another. Clearly a modern trend, it is perhaps two centuries old in the bigger Western cities, less than that elsewhere. A direct sequel to it is now beginning to show in the dazzling impact on reading style of later technological inventions, especially of the most recent electronic media, from desktop to palm.[5]

Reading in twentieth-century Palestine will be examined here in view of the Western experience. We will, however, leave out one significant part of this story: the shift from vocalized to visual mode by individuals reading to themselves—the earlier phase of change in the European example. The focus of our story is different. We are primarily concerned with a community's rapid transformation from a negligible use of writings to massive reliance on them and with the mechanisms it devised for facilitating it. In principle, the development of reading in twentieth-century Palestine is analogous to that which occurred during the post-Gutenberg phase in the West. In both societies, shifts in reading patterns resulted from the industrialization of text production, the emergence of various distribution channels, and the spread of education. But there was an essential difference between them. In Palestine the process was far more condensed, if not to say rushed: printing, a periodical press industry, various distribution apparatuses, mass modern education—all arrived at the same time. This intensive change within a short period caused reading to expand concurrently in all of its forms, private and public, individual and collective. As for the other facet of the story—the change from vocalized to silent reading—it is a question whose focus is different enough from that of the present case to merit a separate study.[6]

Two terms, *mutala'ah* and *qira'ah,* commonly serve in Arabic to denote the act of reading, each suggesting a certain manner of the practice. The two are often used interchangeably and there is considerable overlap in their semantic ranges, but each also has specific connotations that are not shared by the other. *Mutala'ah* is derived from a root which, in this third stem form, means viewing, looking at, inspecting, perusing, or—in William Lane's *Arabic-English Lexicon* definition—"consider[ing] with the eyes." Employed in connection with a written text, it normally implies individual visual reading, often with a sense of reflection. Accordingly, it also suggests the physical presence of a written text. Standard attributes of *mutala'ah* are individuality and silence, where one is reading to oneself using one's own eyes. Another mark of it is a measure of concentration: *mutala'ah* usually implies close attention to that which is being read, as distinct from the quick glancing at a brief message or sign, such as a newspaper headline or a billboard ad. One other characteristic, solitude, often goes with this definition, but is not absolutely essential: one can practice *mutala'ah* in company, next to other people who are likewise engaged in reading or in other activities.

The other term, *qira'ah,* may be employed in the same sense as *mutala'ah.* But it also carries additional meanings, of speaking, calling, summoning, or declaiming. In Islamic history this noun, and the verb from which it is derived, have commonly served for recitation of the Qur'an (whose name is from the same root) and for reading texts of other kinds, aloud or otherwise. *Qira'ah* is thus a looser notion than *mutala'ah:* a person may be engaged in *qira'ah* while reading quietly to himself, reading aloud to an audience, or reciting vocally from memory without the actual presence of a written text. When the two terms are juxtaposed to depict two distinct activities, the distinction implied is between silent individual reading and reading that is spoken and sometimes collective. The latter kind will be considered in the next chapter.

In Islamic tradition, texts that were central in the community's life became valid only when spelled out orally. Vocal recitation from the Holy Book, the basic prayer source of every believer, was a major duty in practicing the faith. Though written, the Qur'an was meant to be recited aloud; it became a living message only when spoken out and heard. Such a clear preference for oral over silent reading also applied to other writings: learned men, in charge of preserving the community's spiritual legacy and passing it on, had the duty of memorizing tradition (*hadith*)—sayings and deeds ascribed to the Prophet and other pious men—and conveying it vocally. Here, too, the text assumed its authority only when spoken aloud; it was properly transmitted when heard. Other important, mostly doctrinal texts were likewise supposed to be read, learned, and communicated orally, and there were clear injunctions against dealing with them in private.[7]

Does all this mean that written texts and their private/solitary handling had inferior status in Islamic religious tradition? Not quite. As Franz Rosenthal has told us, these principles represented no more than a "pretended belief in the superiority of oral transmission." It was "pretended," for at a very early phase, apparently around the beginning of Islam's second century, Islamic scholars succumbed to the need for using writing due to the constantly increasing volume of traditions that had to be passed on. Written texts came to be highly valued since, as Rosenthal has suggested, it was recognized that "all knowledge would disappear without books."[8] "What is memorized flies away," said an eminent thirteenth-century scholar; "what is written down remains."[9] Books were thus regarded as indispensable implements in the retention and transmission of the legacy. It is known that even ancient Arabic poetry, perhaps the epitome of oral Arab texts, was communicated in writing, not only orally, as were the Qur'an and *hadith,* let alone Islamic law and other fields of knowledge. More than a backup device for the preservation of wisdom and assisting in memorization, written texts were also used as instruments for teaching and learning. Knowledge imparted orally was committed to notes by the listeners, students, and others, and then copied and made into books; the jurists of Islam devised rules for their care and copying. In fact, so many books were produced and copied that sometimes the need arose to get rid of some of them.[10] Nor did the traditional duty to vocalize certain sacred texts preclude solitary, quiet reading of everything else. Indeed, the fact that teachers had to warn their disciples repeatedly against approaching these special writings privately would suggest that individual reading was very much alive,[11] possibly a standard habit among students, scholars, and others. It may thus be assumed that in Arab societies, just as in Europe, the manner of handling and communicating texts was for the most part determined by practical—rather than religious—considerations, such as text availability, text quality, and the reader's proficiency.

The modes in which books were actually read throughout Arab and Islamic history still await a systematic exploration. If conducted imaginatively, it may yield results as instructive as those produced for premodern Europe. Meanwhile, the sources suggest that solitary reading in the privacy of one's home was a common act at a fairly early stage in Islamic history. The ninth-century author and poet Ibn ʿAbd Rabbihi, for example, praises the virtues of solitary reading: "What a good companion a book is when you happen to be alone with it. You can find consolation with it, even if those whom you loved have betrayed you."[12] Similarly Jahiz, the great scholar of the same century, who was known for his love of books, commended the book as "the companion (*jalis*) who never bores you and associate who never tires you . . . Books remain at your service at night as well as during the day, in travel and while staying at home."[13] Scenes of Muslim scholars sitting at home with their private book collections and notes, reading, writing, or copying in silence and solitude are depicted here and there in the sources. Thus, it is related of al-Fath ibn Khaqan, who had a splendid library in Baghdad in the ninth century, that he always carried a book with him either in his sleeve or in the lagging of his boot. Whenever he had a spare moment, he would take it out and read, "even when he went to the lavatory," the most solitary of places. Jahiz himself, an avid reader, was said to have regularly heaped up all the books he needed for his scholarship around him in his study. He died, appropriately enough, when a pile of books fell on him.[14]

For centuries, individual Muslim scholars had been buying books when they could, building their private collections. They had also been borrowing books from mosque libraries and from each other, a time-honored custom that was warmly recommended by the community's leaders as conducive to the spread of knowledge.[15] It was thus told of Shafiʿi, the great eighth-century jurist, that "he used to take books of Malik from . . . [a colleague's private library], every day two volumes (*juz'ayn*), and they would remain with him that day and night. Then he would arrive in the morning, having already finished with them. So he would return them and take two more."[16] Bought or borrowed, books were read and copied at home. Literacy and affordability usually limited the scope of the reading circle to the educated elite. Members of that class, especially in the cities, also enjoyed such advantages as convenient reading quarters at home and sufficient space for storing a collection, which made the pursuit the more pleasant. But individual reading also occurred in public places. The sources tell us about mosque libraries over the centuries across the lands of Islam that were used to such ends. Many of them had stocks of manuscripts, catalogues, and study rooms that were well lit and equipped with comfortable seating, most often mattresses and cushions lined against the walls. Where no such special section existed, people would use the open space of the mosque itself to read and study. Libraries also offered free paper and writing tools for those seeking to copy texts. Sometimes they lent books; the borrower had to be a scholar of good standing and a reliable man.[17]

In an oft-quoted passage, Yusuf Eche ('Ishsh) has reconstructed the reading practice that obtained in medieval Muslim libraries. These standards, he has noted, are "still observed today [1967] in certain old libraries" in the region. The reader comes to the place and requests the catalogue from the librarian, or directly asks for the book he needs. The librarian brings the requested book and gives it to the reader, who may also ask for paper and ink in order to take notes.

> The reader then finds a seating place on the ground—as is customary in the East—sometimes on a cushion and, in most cases, near a wall against which he would lean. Sometimes he puts the book on his legs, crossed *à l'orientale;* at other times he lays it on a small wooden table in front of him. When he is done, he returns it to the librarian and asks for another, or quits, leaving behind no written record [of his visit]. Such a routine for consulting [texts] seems, in the main, to have been applied to book copying as well.[18]

Mutalaʿah in Twentieth-Century Palestine: The Comfort of Home

The amount of writings circulating in Palestine prior to the advent of local production was small. Outside the few mosque libraries, books and journals did not readily present themselves in the country; they had to be ordered from abroad. Men of the educated elite who were eager to read and able to afford the investment would buy them and normally read them at home. Trained in handling writings of the old kind, they now applied their skills to new types of texts. This was also the social group that had the required material conditions for reading privately, with homes that provided the appropriate physical implements and the necessary leisure time. When journals began to appear in Palestine, it became fashionable among members of this class to buy each other subscriptions as gifts. The lists of donors and recipients of such presents, published periodically in *al-Nafa'is al-'Asriyyah,* the leading literary journal of the time, made up a typical cross section of this educated and well-off class.[19] The formulation of ads for books that appeared in that journal likewise betrayed the elitist nature of this activity: its editor used to address customers with appellations that bore undertones of exclusivity, such as *jumhur al-udaba'* (class of men-of-letters) and *muhibbiyy al-mutala'ah* (reading lovers).[20] The sources do not tell us whether these men-of-letters and reading lovers were proficient enough to read privately or independently. Quite likely, there was diversity among them in this respect, with some of them better trained than others for individual *mutala'ah.* Those less qualified for it might have had to share the experience with more educated colleagues or members of the family.

It goes without saying that possession of books did not necessarily mean reading. People purchased and collected texts for reasons other than the urge to explore their contents. They did so in order to increase their prestige, which the very ownership of books often imparted; out of reverence for manuscripts, especially those regarded as particularly holy; or simply out of a collector's passion, an impulse that has driven people anywhere to accumulate items of every imaginable kind.[21] Written works were thus found in the homes of illiterate people, and book collections of the educated contained titles in languages their owners could not read.[22] And just as possession in itself did not mean reading, so reading at home did not necessarily indicate ownership of written texts. As we have seen, people could borrow books and journals from friends, club libraries, and private lending shops for reading at home, thereby continuing the practice of borrowing written works from mosque libraries. (In Palestine, this last practice seems to have been abandoned before the twentieth century, or at least declined to negligible proportions.)[23]

Bought, borrowed, subscribed to, or received as gifts from educated colleagues, written works in late Ottoman Palestine were read mostly in the homes of the affluent, which were spacious and furnished for comfort. It was in such commodious private residences that Palestine's early literary societies held their meetings around the turn of the century (see Chapter 3). For members of these families, the practice continued throughout the period as a matter of course. Numerous such houses in Jerusalem, Jaffa, Haifa, Nablus, and other cities still carry the markings of their pre-1948 luxury. They sometimes included a special study that served for keeping the collected books, reading, and writing, which was usually equipped with a desk and various other convenient fittings.[24] Other sections of the house are also reported to have been used for this activity: the family living room, the balcony, front- and backyard, and, for children, their own quarters. Direct references in the written sources to actual reading are unsurprisingly few, yet they—along with many oral testimonies—allow us to picture the residents of these lavish homes engaging in this practice, reading the books and periodicals they had acquired or borrowed, either alone or in company. To quote an example, Serene Husseini-Shahid, a member of one such aristocratic family in Jerusalem and a teenager in the 1930s, noted how she used to read while guarding her younger siblings. "Often as I watched," she said, "I sat on the verandah reading books which I borrowed from the Arab Women's Society, where I had a subscription"[25]—a personal experience whose elitist nature is evident in every detail.

The cultural changes in the late Ottoman decades permitted members of other social sectors across the region to engage in reading, for the first time. Essays in Arabic periodicals at the beginning of the twentieth century, laying out the benefits of reading and offering elementary guidance on how best to exercise it, reflected the novelty of the practice. *Mutala'ah* was "like an adventure journey, allowing man to see the country from one end to the other while still sitting under the roof of his own home," one writer explained in the Egyptian monthly *al-Muqtataf* (which was also delivered in Palestine) in 1906. One should approach this activity "with a fit body, a healthy mind and a ready soul." This would assure that the reader (*mutali'*) reaps fruits of good taste and pretty shape, returning from his journey gratified with that which he has seen and enlightened with that which he has learned."[26] Another article, entitled *al-mutala'ah al-mufidah* (Beneficial Reading), proposed to enlighten newcomers on the differences between useful and useless reading and provided them with some tips: do not read too much, so as not to tire yourself; read only valuable books, journals, and newspapers; and review the books you read critically in your personal diary.[27] Similar rudimentary directives to fresh readers also appeared in local publications. In two consecutive articles, published in *Filastin* in 1911 under the title *shay' fi'l-mutala'ah* (Something about Reading), author Habib Khuri Ayyub elucidates the uses of reading and the habits one should adopt while engaging in it. One ought to read selectively, he says, for "the hundreds of works and thousands of newspapers and fantasy writings" which the presses pour out daily might be harmful. Also, one ought to take advantage of the practical benefits offered by reading: it is an error and a waste of time to sail across oceans and travel to the end of the earth for months in search of news and reports obtainable in an hour through reading. "A useful book, if properly read for a month, is more beneficial than staying in a high-level environment for an entire year."[28] An essay of similar style and argumentation appeared in the journal of the Jerusalem Teachers' Seminar in 1922, still marking the novelty of the custom.[29] For the elite of seasoned readers such guidance was obviously redundant. For those entering the world of reading for the first time it might have come in handy.

By the onset of the twentieth century, members of the Palestine non-elite classes had begun to join the old elite in this activity. First among them were Christian Arabs, who were more enterprising than their Muslim neighbors in acquiring education. "I have in my room but a desk, a rug and two beds with their bedding," Khalil al-Sakakini reported from Jeru-salem on the eve of the First World War.[30] Sakakini, a Greek-Orthodox of humble socioeconomic background, would later become one of the coun-try's most eminent educators. Recording the early years before the war in his personal diary—Sakakini was in his early thirties at the time—he often depicted himself working privately at his desk, reading and writing in these modest physical conditions, with a *nargilah* (water pipe) and coffee always mentioned as part of the setting. "I washed and exercised, and after break-fast I sat at my desk, smoked my *nargilah* and proofread the drafts for *al-Asma'i* journal," ran a typical entry from 1908.[31] Such solitary reading was sometimes performed in locations other than one's private residence, under similar conditions. 'Ajjaj Nuwayhid, later to become a prominent writer and intellectual leader, described a like experience in 1921 while he was stay-ing in a room in Jerusalem. Having bought a certain book in English and brought it to his room, he asked the landlady to fill up the lantern with gas "so it could last from evening to morning," then sat in his bed and browsed through the book. Impressed with its contents, he decided to translate it into Arabic, something he accomplished sitting at his desk in the same modest room for the next 100 days:

> At eight o'clock [A.M.] I would be at my desk, as if I were working for an official department. I would rectify the translation of the previous day, then start translating my daily quota: three pages, no more, no less. I did not set a time for ending [the day's] work. It could end at three o'clock, or at four at the latest. Then I would go to meet my friends, mostly in Bristol café ... At night I would return to my chamber and re-read the new three pages while

in bed, correcting that which required correction. I would sleep and wake up in the morning to resume the very same routine.[32]

The spread of education created more readers; the proliferation of printing created more homes with books and journals. Niqula Ziyadah, an exceptionally inquisitive youngster in the early years of the century, was perhaps a typical representative of this new trend. He related how, moved by a burning passion to read, he would not miss an opportunity to obtain books for reading at home. At the age of 14, visiting a Coptic monastery in Jerusalem, he borrowed books from a local priest and read them at his home in Jenin. Around that time (1922) he began his studies at the teachers' seminar (*dar al-mu'allimin*) in Jerusalem, which had a lending library for the students. Out of the 400 volumes in its collection, Ziyadah recalled, he left none unread or at least un-borrowed during his three years of study. "I cannot describe the happiness that would overwhelm me upon entering the room where the bookcases were placed, during the borrowing-and-returning periods scheduled for us by teacher George Khamis," he noted in his memoirs. "I do not quite know whether my emotion was that of a person entering a shrine of prayer or of he who enters a place of eating. In any case, I was looking for food, but not of the material kind."[33]

Those more gifted and better trained were capable of fully independent reading. Other members of the household relied on those whose skills turned the home into a place of reading. A wide range of reading modes, from silent-visual to vocal, came to take place under the same roof. Children, the generation that benefited from the new schooling system, often performed this role for their seniors. Sayf al-Din al-Zu'bi, a high school student in Nazareth in the 1920s, recalled how in the long winter nights his parents "used to make fire, bite on chestnuts, and I would read." To a relative visiting the house who was fond of Arab epic stories, the young Sayf al-Din would read for long hours under the "dim light of a gas lamp."[34] Writer Jabra Ibrahim Jabra, a young boy in Bethlehem in the same years, related how his teenage older brother managed to save funds out of his employment income, which he would then use for buying books. He kept his books in a box that thus became "full of magic," and the two brothers would read from them regularly in the small room they shared. The young Jabra went one day to visit a classmate at his home and found him "sitting on the floor with a book in his hands in front of his father, who was urging him to read."[35] And Tadrus Effendi Furayh, from Haifa, seemingly of the same social stratum and a novice to reading, sent a letter to the editor of a scientific journal in Egypt inquiring about the risks of reading in domestic conditions. "I have a great passion for reading, but cannot find enough time for it during the day," he explained. "Is reading under the light of a gas lamp harmful to the eyes? And what is the average number of hours for exercising it without harming one's vision?"[36]

A plain room with simple furniture, books in a box, the dim light of a gas lamp, sitting on the floor—all were marks of modest residential quarters that were slowly becoming the scene of exposure to the written word. Buying new books and subscribing to foreign publications remained prohibitively costly throughout much of the period, and hence available to few. But single copies of newspapers and magazines and the chapbook-like paperback story pamphlets that circulated in the country were increasingly affordable. Elementary and high school teachers, middle class by definition, are reported by their students to have owned books in the 1930s and 1940s. "The library of the teacher, who happened to be [my friend] Jamil's brother, was full of books," recalled Hanna Abu Hanna, a pupil in the Nazareth School for Boys in the early 1930s, so he and his friend used to "borrow and return regularly."[37] Niqula Ziyadah, himself a teacher in Acre in the 1920s and 1930s, reported a similar practice, as did former students in the Kafr Yasif high school.[38] Others borrowed books from the odd literate man in the village or neighborhood who had them in his possession. 'Abd al-Hamid Abu Laban, a teenager with a curious mind in Kafr Zakariyyah (near Hebron) of the early 1940s, was first acquainted with non–school texts by borrowing them from Khalil Zaqtan, one of the two village intellectuals in whose home books could be found.[39] And Ihsan 'Abbas, from 'Ayn Ghazzal (near Haifa), related how he and his friends used to spend their summer breaks during their high school years in the mid-1930s:

> We would . . . read [books] that were not a part of our school curriculum. Shaykh Muhammad Muflah Sa'd would return from Egypt with books that had exquisite binding. So, we would go to the *diwan* (guesthouse) of the Sa'd family, each of us choosing a book, and we would spend a long time reading them. That was how these friends of mine came to make up the tiny educated group in the village.[40]

The remarkably curious Jabra brothers, Abu Hanna's teacher, Ziyadah and his professional colleagues in other places, Abu Laban, 'Abbas and his friends—all persons with a passion for reading—were able to purchase books by cutting back on their expenses or borrowing them from others, bringing them home and reading them there. Schoolchildren prepared their homework under the same conditions, making their first steps in the world of texts. And newspapers, which sold in the country in growing numbers, reached homes through organized distribution or were bought on the street (as in the case of Musa, the stonecutter) and read in the house.

One other characteristic of individual reading distinguished it from the collective mode that will be considered later on. While both private and collective reading were employed in quenching the thirst for information, obtainable mostly from newspapers, private reading also meant another kind of pursuit: delving into books and other serious texts in a more re-flective manner. It was primarily through individual reading that people familiarized themselves with the leading literary and scientific journals, the writings of prominent Egyptian and Lebanese authors, the translated works of Europeans, pieces of intellectual discourse published locally and—for those with proper training—the wealth of literature in foreign languages. Those who became capable of independent reading, beyond sharing the practical information available to the rest of society through many chan-nels, also tasted the more profound printed works that had hitherto been an elite domain.

How many people in Palestine of 1900 read privately at home, and how much bigger was their number half a century later? By now it will be clear that questions of this nature cannot be answered with any mea-sure of certainty. Moreover, the quantitative view is nowhere dimmer than in the sphere of home reading, for reasons that are all too obvious. Even where rich records on various facets of reading do exist—for example, on the functioning of lending libraries, the number of reading-room users, or the precise circulation of certain journals (such as we have for nineteenth-century France; see introduction), the scope of reading at home, never re-corded systematically, remains a matter of conjecture. The scanty, largely descriptive evidence we have for Palestine, apparently as good as we are likely to get, allows us to make only two basic assumptions with some as-surance: that the overall number was extremely small at the outset, and that it gradually increased as the century unfolded. Such assumptions are a far cry from a quantified assessment of any value. But any attempt to be more specific would be foolhardy.

This said, a more impressionistic observation might be ventured regard-ing nonquantitative aspects of the change. Reading at home was slowly coming out of the realm of the privileged into the broader zone of the salaried and working classes, from the preserve of learned intellectuals to the common world of the young. More homes that had never before seen printed materials under their roofs were now becoming loci of books and reading. And members of social groups previously accustomed to attaining knowledge of many kinds by listening to oral transmitters were being equipped for obtaining it independently, in the comfort of their residence. Personal testimonies on this experience and, more generally, what we know about the vigorous progress in education and the broadening presence of printed writings in Palestine, clearly suggest that the trend was widening. A variation of this independent reading was the exposure of uneducated people to books and journals at home through reading by literate members of their family—not quite the same as reading in person yet clearly an experience apart from the collective and vocal practice in open public places. With this last phenomenon taken into account, we may assume that, by the end of the mandate, the number of Palestinian Arabs who were accessing texts in a domestic setting was perhaps several-fold bigger than that in 1900.

Private Reading in Public

Private reading of books and journals also took place outside the privacy of one's home, in the libraries and reading rooms that emerged in the country after 1900. People turned to these facilities because they offered physical conditions more convenient than the home and, more significant, a richer variety of printed materials. Individual reading could also take place in any other public location, of course—in a café, for example, or in the marketplace. But reading in such open sites was more typically a collective experience and is thus better discussed in the next chapter.

Some clues about the norms by which books were to be consulted in libraries can be found in a famous photograph taken inside the Khalidiyyah shortly after its opening at the turn of the century. The picture features 10 men, among them Tahir al-Jaza'iri (founder of the Zahiriyyah library in Damascus and an instrumental figure in setting up the Khalidiyyah), as well as Raghib al-Khalidi and other members of the Khalidi family. Half of the men are seated around a wooden reading table; the rest are standing. Four men are holding books in their hands or have them on the table in front of them, pretending to be reading, their lips sealed. Obviously, they were all posing for the photo opportunity (a festive—and rather cumbersome—operation at the time) so as to create an image of serious scholar-

The Khalidi library at its inauguration. Sitting in the middle is Raghib al-Khalidi, with Tahir al-Jaza'iri to his left. From Walid Khalidi, *Before Their Diaspora: A Photographic History of the Palestinians, 1876–1948,* 2nd ed. (Washington, DC, 1991).

Courtesy of the Institute for Palestine Studies.

ship.[41] But it would make sense to assume that the way in which they posed was meant to portray what would be considered appropriate etiquette for this kind of place. If so, it teaches us that the Khalidiyyah reading room was designed for silent, visual perusal by several people sharing the same table, along the tradition of classical Islamic libraries, as we have seen. This is also confirmed by a list of rules that was put together for regulating library use which was prominently posted in the reading room, apparently from the very beginning. The directives stated that "readers must not engage in excessive conversation, shouting, or argument so as not to distract those who are reading or copying." It was also stipulated that "those using the library may do so only to read and conduct research. While they are within the library or in its courtyard, they must not pursue personal matters." Needless to say, "smoking of cigarettes and water-pipes inside the reading room of the library [is] strictly forbidden, regardless of who is concerned."[42] Foreign institutions in Palestine and the more aristocratic social clubs sought to cultivate similar standards in their libraries. Thus in the Jerusalem YMCA reading room, a lavishly furnished and amply lit hall, silence was a strict requirement from the start.[43] We thus know that such norms of considerate behavior were deemed desirable, although the extent to which they were actually enforced is unknown.

We ought to return, once again, to the question of numbers: how many people used these libraries? Is our knowledge on public library and club reading in Palestine any better than that on home reading? Let us examine an instance that might cast light on this question and the limitations involved. Discussing the public libraries of al-Aqsa and the Khalidiyyah at the beginning of the twentieth century, Rashid Khalidi has suggested that imported journals, which were available at both the Khalidiyyah and al-Aqsa, "were accessible to a wide range of readers."[44] How wide was the range, and were the accessible sources actually accessed? Khalidi, who had a chance to inspect the Khalidiyyah's visitors register, got the impression that "all manner of local and foreign scholars, and many ordinary people, availed themselves of its facilities, particularly in its first few decades of operation."[45] Lawrence Conrad, who has studied the Khalidiyyah collection extensively, similarly suggests that the library "received many visitors and readers," the most famous of whom he names in his study.[46] Neither Khalidi nor Conrad would commit himself to a quantitative estimate, and for good reasons. Conrad, who, like Khalidi, had an opportunity to review the visitors' record, notes that it hardly formed a systematic account. Users were registered in it haphazardly, and the names did not necessarily represent actual readers. Some may have merely come as visiting spectators, popping in to be impressed with the library's modern organization, which was of a kind unseen in the country before: books standing upright on the shelves rather than lying horizontally, labeled book spines, a special safe for the most precious items, a printed catalogue, and so on. Conrad noticed that after the 1930s, the register contained only one entry, in 1952—a mark of the decline in the library's stature, in its record keeping, or in both.[47] The register, then, was a flimsy document of little use as a mirror of reality. As noted by Eche in his description of Islamic libraries, these institutions traditionally operated without keeping records of users. One would thus tend to suspect that nobody ever intended to keep an orderly register for the Khalidiyyah. Nothing more organized than this is known to have existed in the country's other reading places, either.

We may take a look at some other odd fragments of evidence that concern the readership of another library, that of the al-Aqsa mosque. The library attracted a mixed array of visitors, from traditional 'ulama' to secularly oriented writers and thinkers. There were also students who would use its resources for their homework. A casual report by the library director, published in a Jaffa newspaper in January 1924, noted that in the previous November the number of "visitors" (*za'irin*) to al-Aqsa library had reached 63—not a big crowd, especially given the uncertain meaning of the term "visitors." In the following month, the report noted, the number leaped up to 294, including both "visitors to al-Aqsa library" and "those who frequented (*mutaraddidin 'ala*) its reading room."[48] This last figure, again, could represent active users or, just as well, groups of visiting spectators. This statement is both isolated and ambiguous. Another such piece of data, a report published in the same year by the Higher Islamic Legal Council, similarly noted that during that year the number of those who "frequented the reading rooms (*al-mutaraddidin 'ala qa'at al-mutala'ah*)" had "exceeded three thousand people, most of them scholars, school-students and teachers." In addition, there were some 150 "visitors."[49] Summarizing an entire year of activity, this last report was basically in tune with the previous figures.

Such bits and pieces clearly come short of providing a solid picture, but they may not be utterly useless. Indeed, they give us a rough indication of scale: essentially a handful of daily users and visitors to al-Aqsa in the early 1920s, with 2–3 a day in one of the two months mentioned, c. 10 in the other and, again, about 10 for a daily average in the annual assessment. Assuming that only some of these were actual readers, this could be fairly described as modest activity in what was then the leading library in one of the country's leading cities. Other testimonies leave us with a similar impression. The Jerusalem YMCA had a membership of some 200 people on the eve of the First World War, increasing gradually thereafter to about 1,000 by the late 1940s. Roughly half of these were local residents—Christians, Muslims, and Jews; the other half were diplomats, missionaries, and other foreigners. Similarly, the Jaffa branch of the British Council had a total membership of 173 in 1943, only a part of them local Arabs. Of the few hundred local members of these clubs, only a segment, unknown in size, made use of their libraries. This was certainly not a big mass of customers.[50]

More can perhaps be inferred from the actual size of these reading places. The YMCA reading hall (which has remained basically unchanged to this day) was 10 by 8 meters, with 4 tables and a total of 24 seats. It was spacious and comfortable enough for a few club members but hardly designed for a massive public of readers. The physical measures of the Khalidiyyah reading area were still smaller: 4.5 by 6.5 meters—the size of an average living room—with a single table in the middle that could accommodate some 10–12 users at a time. Tall bookcases and shelves along the walls left little room for more users.[51] The physical size of al-Aqsa library, in both of its locations during this period (Qubbat al-Nahwiyyah and the Is'ardiyyah *madrasah*), was basically of the same scale, as was that of the Islamic library in Jaffa and of all other reading facilities.[52] Such limits of space, unchanged throughout the period, would suggest a realistic frame for the possible level of activity. "The day for this magnificent library [the Khalidiyyah] to turn into a house of reading and study" will come only "when it has been relocated to a spacious place, supplied with the necessary equipment and furnished for comfort," the editor of a Jerusalem newspaper sensibly observed in 1922. "Only then will people come over in big numbers to acquire knowledge."[53] No such changes occurred in this library or in any of the other reading places until the end of the mandate.

Taken as a whole, these clues seem to suggest that private reading in Palestinian libraries remained a limited phenomenon during the period studied here. It may well have been more restricted than reading at home, and we may cautiously assume that on no given day before 1948 were there more than, at most, several scores of readers using these facilities countrywide. Historically, public libraries, associated with mosques (or churches), had been accessed for consulting traditional texts, a narrow scholarly rather than popular pursuit. The libraries and reading rooms founded in twentieth-century Palestine were different in their setting, in the nature of their collections, and even in the assumed objectives of reading. That the novelty was slow to attract a public response—besides reflecting the still-limited level of education—may have had something to do with the society's generally conservative outlook and suspicion toward innovations. Some of the new places designed for this kind of activity, such as the Khalidiyyah and the facilities of the finer Christian social clubs, including the YMCA, projected an elitist image that served as a subtle social filter, inviting a rather select public. The small-scale activity in these libraries was consonant with the intimate size of their reading space. Of those who frequented the more celebrated clubs, many came from comfortable homes and could take advantage of the option to borrow books and read them there, rather than on the site, using the reading room mainly for browsing journals and newspapers.

Reading rooms of the more popular clubs normally featured a less austere environment. As we have seen, in many of them the *maktabah* was a part of a facility that also included such sections as a game room and sports grounds, a setting less conducive to contemplative *mutala'ah*. To pick an example, the Gaza youth club in the mid-1920s had at its disposal "a single room where meetings, reading, administration, as well as playing cards and backgammon, all took place concurrently"—a state of affairs that, as one reporter lamented, "profoundly undermined" its activities.[54] But notwithstanding their modest facilities, these places attracted visitors in constantly growing numbers. The bulk of these were youth and low- to middle-class workers, who would arrive for other activities and occasionally come by the *maktabah* to browse the newspapers and recent journals, chat with friends, and perhaps borrow a book. A report by an observer who visited the Islamic Sports Club in Jaffa in 1929 reflected this kind of routine. The writer related how he and his friends were sitting in a city café along with "the indolent, who waste their time in vein talk." Having become weary, they decided to move "from the café, which hosts all classes and types of people," to the club, "where one can find well-educated and cultured youth (*al-shabab al-muhadhdhab al-muthaqqaf*)." They found the site of the club to be spacious, with a big hall, four large rooms, and three smaller ones. Youth were cheerfully playing dominoes and backgammon in one room, and a drama team was rehearsing an act in another.

> I saw the library room (*ghurfat al-maktabah*), and realized that it contained a great many Arabic newspapers and journals. There was also a large bookcase full of modern, valuable books. In the middle of the room stood a big table, at which young people were seated, reading and talking to each other. When one of them would find an anecdote or a new idea in what he read, he would tell his friends about it; they would laugh at the former and seriously discuss the latter.[55]

The Jaffa club offered a variety of activities, intellectual and otherwise, to the "well-educated, cultured youth." The account does not comment on the quantity and nature of the books on the shelves, beyond labeling them "modern" and "valuable." But these apparently mattered less than the availability of newspapers and periodicals. To young people still attending school and to graduates of the educational system, the presence of journals, the leisurely atmosphere, and the companionship of friends may have provided the most suitable setting for reading. To literate middle-class members, the club's *maktabah* was attractive for its comfortable browsing opportunities and its selection of dailies and magazines. The club also accommodated visitors of a lesser cultural background, among them people unable to read, who would come for the other activities. Clearly, where illiterates and proficient readers were sharing the same space and vocal conversation was standard, reading meant not an absorbed delving into serious books but rather a light perusal of periodicals. It would not be risky to assume that this last mode was more prevalent in public reading places of mandatory Palestine than the quiet practice that was confined to a few refined institutions. Once again, we may speculate that the overall number of *maktabah* readers in these popular clubs reached several hundred during the later years of the period, as against a few scores in the more polished places. Consisting of lighter and usually vocal browsing, however, this activity was private only in a very loose sense, and often not at all. Indeed, in many cases it could be squarely described as collective reading. But most often—a typical mark of a transition phase—it was on the borderline between these two modes.

Two general assumptions were offered toward the end of the previous section: that the overall number of private readers in the Palestine of 1900 was tiny and that it went up subsequently, though by an unknown margin. We may perhaps add a third, equally plausible hypothesis: that the number of those entering the circle of independent readers represented a small minority of the society even at the end of the period. This was certainly so in what concerned the reading of books and serious journals. Functional literacy of the kind that would permit ready access to written texts of every kind, though spreading, remained confined to a small section of the population, mostly urbanites and younger people; and economic constraints further limited the number of those with the necessary skills who were able to acquire books. As we shall see in the next chapter, however, this hardly meant that the rest of society remained in the dark.

CHAPTER 5

Collective Reading

Arabic-speaking societies and Third World communities in general have sometimes been portrayed as typically "oral." The tag is intended to distinguish them from societies in the West, whose culture, especially in modern times, has been characterized as "literacy" oriented. Thus Walter Ong, once a guru of "orality and literacy" theories, spoke in 1967 of "the still functionally oral-aural Arab cultures." He related the story of an Arab student of engineering who, though educated, was an illustrative "product of a verbo-motor society, an oral-aural personality." When this man was faced with a challenge of building a bridge, Ong observed,

> Every fiber of his being made him want to respond to the situation by verbalization—he wanted to speak of what so-and-so had said in the past about building a bridge, of great battles fought over bridges, of the usefulness of bridges to men, and so on. A bridge, like everything else, had its most glorious existence in the universe of discourse. The idea of withdrawing into himself and starting out with surveying and drilling . . . struck the typical Arab student as antisocial, a prostitution of intellect, infrahuman and bestial.[1]

According to this argument, Arabs were not only intrinsically inclined to excessive verbalization; they were also prone to "oral-aural" communication—as distinct, so Ong seems to imply, from written modes of expression—and that tendency represented an inherent if not unchangeable cultural quality in them. Such a sweeping attribution of traits to whole societies is, of course, ever problematic; and Ong may well have sinned by oversimplifying an intricate case. It is true that Islam, the faith of the great majority of Arabs, has traditionally attached particular importance to the spoken word, memorization, and recitation, especially in relation to certain sacred texts, as already noted. It is also true that oral modes permeated the circulation of information and ideas in Arab societies until very recently, and that this characteristic went together with illiteracy, which the dependence on oral means at once reflected and encouraged. In addition, there is little doubt that in following such practices in modern times, these societies increasingly differed from their European counterparts, in which oral modes of communication had been outstripped by other mechanisms. At the same time, however, it is equally true that Arabic-speaking societies had a rich tradition of written scholarship, book production, library building, and a written discourse in many fields over the generations. The concept of the Arab inherent "orality" is thus somewhat shaky, and its value in explaining the recent Arab reliance on the spoken word dubious.

Leaving aside such flat labels as offered by Ong, it is quite clear that in pre-twentieth-century Arab societies, illiteracy, the paucity of written texts, and the centrality of religious rituals performed vocally combined to make oral forms of communication predominant. Most often the circulation of messages of any kind was conducted without the actual presence of a written text. At other times, writings were at hand and read or cited by one individual to an audience. A time-honored norm, it served the society satisfactorily to the extent of rendering any other means—including printing—rather superfluous. By the onset of the modern phase, as written information began to arrive in unprecedented quantities, the old channels, long proven effective, were in place to contain the flood. At first there was no alternative anyway. But the massive inflow of information in print was followed by the arrival of organized education, whose fruits—always taking a generation or two to ripen—would put into the society's hands more tools for handling the wealth of written texts. In the interim, between the late nineteenth and mid-twentieth century, they were circulated largely by way of the old, familiar conduits.

The Old, Familiar Conduits

Oral transmission of messages—from religious injunctions through current news to popular legends—was a practice which Arab societies had long shared with Europe. Text-based oral communication was widely employed in the West in conveying old and new types of knowledge until quite recently. As late as the first half of the nineteenth century, reading of news and commentary by an educated person to a crowd of illiterate listeners was still common in London and Paris, let alone smaller towns and villages in the two countries. This was also the case among the lower urban classes and certainly the rural population of the German states at the time. Such crowds would gather for reading books and journals in cafés, taverns, the streets, and private homes. In nineteenth-century England, workers in industrial plants undertook to do extra duties in order to release one of their numbers so he could read out loud for them during work, for entertainment.[2] Similarly, and more famously, employees of the cigar industry in Cuba during the same time used to pay one of the workers for reading newspapers and novels to them during work. When Cubans migrated to the United States and established cigar factories there, they also renewed the workplace lector function, something that lasted at least until the 1920s.[3] In Russia, with its old practice of literate people reading to others, a new kind of calling appeared toward the end of the nineteenth century, following the emergence of the press: professional newspaper readers, who would perform the job for a fee to changing audiences, sometimes making a living out of it.[4] And in Hungary—and apparently elsewhere in eastern Europe—a tradition of storytelling as a collective cultural event continued into the twentieth century, in which the gatherings were also used to convey other kinds of information to those unable to read.[5] By the onset of the twentieth century, however, all such practices had been relegated to the margins of the grand scene of communication, and independent reading had become the norm in the West.

In the Muslim experience—as well as in that of Christianity—the archetypal occasion of oral communication was the session of vocalized praying in the house of praying. Reciting the Holy Book meant turning the written, lifeless letters into a vocal message that far transcended the apparent contents of the words. The quality of a reader's voice—the rhythm, the resonance of speech in the praying hall, the concerted response by the praying crowd—were central to this reality no less than the text itself. To borrow, once again, Ong's terminology from another discussion, the Qur'an was thereby turned from a material piece of writing into an "event." The event could occur only when the text was recited aloud, in an intimately familiar way, the only sure way to establish the believer's contact with God. Performed in a group, the experience was particularly intense. One did not have to be literate or to make out the sense of each word uttered in order to share it; memorization and then recitation sufficed for evoking this auditory reality, with its profound spiritual effect. Throughout history, groups of men gathered in mosques in a solemn atmosphere and listened to the Imam and *khatib* speak with authority. Imparting not only religious but also other messages vocally, these leaders extended the experience of prayer to additional domains. In the Friday noon prayer, the typical occasion for such gatherings, public announcements of many kinds that had been received from the higher authorities, often in writing, were transmitted to an attentive audience, sometimes with the preacher's commentary. Here too, the message consisted of the written text itself and the vivid experience of its reception through the ears. The event in the mosque, of course, had its counterpart in the praying houses of non-Muslim minorities within the Arab community.[6]

In Islamic institutions of learning, Hadith, *fiqh,* and certain other fields of traditional knowledge were likewise imparted through methods involving dictation (*imla'*) by a shaykh, listening (*sama'*), and reading aloud to the mentor (the verb here is *qara'a 'ala,* literally, "to read [aloud] to," and, metaphorically, "studying under someone's guidance"). Students in *madrasah*s were exhorted "not only to read correctly the black lines of the text," but also "the white parts" between the lines—the implied accentuation and hidden meanings—"in accordance with the oral transmission stored in the memory of the master" and communicated vocally in the class.[7] Testimonies from Mamluk Egypt and Syria, for example, indicate that in certain fields of knowledge individual learning from books was regarded not only as inferior to group learning but also as outright condemnable. Readers who consulted books silently and in private were said to be committing "one of the most scandalous acts (*min adarr al-mafasid*)."[8] It was believed that the right way to assimilate such texts was by reading them aloud with peers while bearing in mind the shaykh's example. Students were thus encouraged to study in groups after class hours and "drill each other." This group practice would allow the shaykh's authority to be implicitly present even in his absence.[9] The notion that a proper assimilation of the text required its vocal recitation so as to check it against the mentor's version prompted scholars to urge their trainees to raise their voices while practicing. This would also help the memory, it was claimed, for "what the ear hears becomes firmly established in the heart." Consequently, reading or learning was sometimes reported to be a vocal act involving audible pronunciation of the writing, which, to an outsider, would sound like a kind of "buzzing" (*hamhamah*).[10]

Sessions of public reading of Islamic traditions and stories about pious men, popular in medieval times and later, represented a similar phenomenon. Religious texts were presented to groups of listeners who would assimilate the stories and retain them in their memories. Those who attended a session would get a diploma (*ijazah*) attesting to their participation and certifying them as authorized transmitters of the recited texts.[11] There were also less formal occasions, in which religiously edifying stories loosely associated with written texts were recounted by popular tellers (*qass*, pl. *qussas*) or "preachers" (*waʿiz*, pl. *wuʿʿaz*) to attentive audiences. Begun as early as the first century of Islam, this practice became a common phenomenon of much social significance, as Jonathan Berkey has recently shown in an insightful study.[12] In events of these kinds, the listeners would often include educated people who would be able to read for themselves. But this last skill was of little relevance to the multilayer experience for which they had convened, based as it was on an authorized handling of the story. Direct evidence on public reading of Hadith and the deeds of pious men in Palestine itself is yet to come to light. On the other hand, we hardly need direct testimonies to confirm the experience of routine gatherings in the country's mosques, or churches, traditional locations of oral activity since time immemorial.

Nonreligious messages such as news and official announcements also circulated through oral channels. The most common occasion of receiving such notices outside the prayer house was while listening to the town or village crier, the *munadi* (literally, "announcer"). The *munadi* was an official functionary employed by the local authorities for publicizing the messages arriving from the central or provincial government, for example, on taxation, mobilization, administrative changes, and dates of official visits; and for announcing local news, for example, on food and water supply, deaths in the community, and upcoming events. *Munadi*s were employed under the Ottomans all over the empire, including Palestine.[13] Fulfilling a task with long-proven efficacy, this public messenger was a crucial figure in the community's life. "Hasan Bek the governor and Asʿad the *munadi* were, in my view and that of others, the two most prominent men in Jenin," noted Niqula Ziyadah, a child in that town before the First World War.[14] Public announcers would continue to perform the same duty in Palestine's towns and villages until well after the middle of the twentieth century, bearing different titles in different times and places. Apart from *munadi*, they were variably called *natur*, literally, "warden" or "keeper" (the common appellation in villages, where they also had other duties, most frequently servicing in the local guesthouse); or *dallal*, "auctioneer" (from a root meaning "to indicate, demonstrate, or announce").[15]

Before loudspeakers and radio, this plain human voice was a major source of public information on any matter that the authorities deemed fit to announce. The main requirement was a vigorous voice; reading ability was not absolutely necessary. He would come to the usual places and locate himself on an elevated or otherwise visible spot. Calling for people's attention, he would use a standard formula known to all, alerting the public to the event. Often he would start by making mention of the Prophet (*"Ya ahl al-balad, sallu 'ala 'l-nabiy!"*—Oh people of the town/village, pray for the Prophet!), intended to lend importance to the notice itself.[16] Once the message had been delivered, the announcement would be likewise sealed with a standard formula, requiring those present to notify the rest of the community (*wa'l-hadir yu'allim al-gha'ib*), thereby assuring broader circulation by the same means. People often hired the services of the local *munadi* to publicize private events or lost-and-found. Hanna Abu Hanna vividly remembered the announcer's performance in the Nazareth of the 1930s and 1940s. Once the man's voice was heard on the street, Abu Hanna recalled, his mother would send him out, ordering him to listen and get the message:

> Abu Zahrah the *dallal* would stand there, his right hand on his ear, his palm rounded around it as is done by the chanter or camel-driver . . . He would stretch his neck so his voice could reach far, and with his left hand would lean on a stick, following the custom of ancient orators . . . Abu Zahrah was slim and short, with a big head and mighty voice. You could almost see his voice chord as the veins in his neck contracted while he sent his words rolling in the streets . . . "Oh, he who saw, Oh he who found, Abu Zayid's green she-ass! She has a burn on her right side and her left eyelid is blurred, sagging and tearful. Whoever saw her or has knowledge of her whereabouts should notify Abu Zayid. A reward is guaranteed, and God would give [the finder] no sorrow. Those present should notify those who are not." Abu Zahrah would move around the neighborhood, his voice reverberating everywhere. Most of those gathering around him were children, who would then take the news home and to anyone interested in hearing the details.[17]

To break the drab monotony of everyday life, people would turn to yet another kind of collective oral experience: listening to storytellers. This custom existed in practically every culture, accounting for the survival of much of the folk tradition for centuries, long before printing as well as subsequently. In many places in Europe this tradition continued straight into the twentieth century. Nothing embodied oral culture more typically than public sessions of listening to stories. They involved the teller—*hakawati, rawi,* or *qass,* normally a person with an excellent memory for retaining the

many details of the stories, high verbal and expressive ability, and prefer-
ably also a theatrical gift—and an audience hungry for entertainment.[18] In
Arab tradition, several famous epics (*sirah*, pl. *siyar*) had circulated through
the generations, all relating the heroic deeds and adventures of legendary
personalities. These epics also existed in writing, at least since the ʿAbbasid
period, and printed editions of them appeared in the nineteenth century,[19]
but oral transmission, told or sung, remained an essential aspect of this
form. In addition to the *sirah*, a variety of folktales and legends (*qissah,
riwayah, hikayah, usturah, khurafah*) were often told, some of them local,
others known more widely. This popular institution was unrelated to the
ruling establishment or the spiritual leadership, which can be seen in the
fact that both the state and the ʿulama' were often wary of this form and
tried to suppress it[20]—but with little success.

Sessions of listening to stories took place in public locations—in town
cafés, street corners, and village gathering places, from Fez to Baghdad.
They were also conducted in private parties in homes of the affluent. Such
events continued to be held in many places well into the second half of
the twentieth century (in Damascus they have been reported at its end).[21]
They could take place at any time of the day, but were primarily evening
and night events. The teller was at the center, presenting the text with the
right narrative and the rich intonation to the best of his talent, sometimes
physically acting out the story. Written or printed texts might or might not
be present.[22] The audience comprised people of different classes, mostly
though not exclusively illiterate or semi-literate. While the backbone of
the event was the passing on of the story from the teller to his listeners, in
effect the whole experience was interactive. The audience would normally
encourage the teller, directing him to tell favorite tales or focus on favorite
episodes; sometimes the listeners would vividly identify with the heroes and
respond emotionally to the unfolding plot. As in the practice of the *munadi*, storytelling sessions usually opened in a standard pattern, mentioning
God or the Prophet, and terminated likewise.[23]

In Palestine of the twentieth century, as elsewhere, listening to storytellers was a popular pastime. It occurred in towns and villages, most typically in the long winter evenings and Ramadan nights. In many villages
the custom persisted until very recently. Such sessions were designed for
men; women would sometimes meet separately, normally in the home of
one of them, to hear stories usually different in kind from those shared by
the men.[24] Reminiscing on mandatory Jaffa, a former resident of the city

recalled storytelling sessions in the town's cafés, whose patrons were "mostly owners of small businesses and fishermen":

> The role of the *hakawati* or *rawi* would begin after dinner. He would position himself on an elevated bench, and the listening crowd would gather around him to hear popular stories, such as about Abu Zayid al-Hilali, al-Zir Salim, 'Antarah bin Shaddad, Sayf bin dhi Yazan and the rest of them. His voice would rise and subside, his manual gestures and excitement would increase in accordance with the course of related events. Curiously, the audience would split into parties siding with [the different] heroes and passionate arguments would take place between them—one party siding with al-Zir Salim, another with 'Antarah, and so on.[25]

Stories were also told in private homes, and it was common for children who had received some education to read stories out of books to the elders. Ibrahim al-Dabbagh read 'Antar stories and legends from the One Thousand and One Nights to his two grandfathers in the late Ottoman period.[26] Muhammad 'Izzat Darwazah, Niqulah Khuri, Sayf al-Din al-Zu'bi, and, no doubt, many others also told stories to older members of their families when they were youths.[27]

The Imam, *khatib, munadi,* and *hakawati* were all sources of vocally produced or reproduced texts. They offered religious, spiritual, and political guidance; up-to-date intelligence; and cultural recreation. As we have already seen, in education too oral transmission played a central and sometimes exclusive role. The common reliance on such expedients evidently reflected widespread illiteracy. But one wonders whether such practices did not, at the same time, contribute to its perpetuation. Inasmuch as these methods effectively addressed society's needs, the motivation to seek alternative channels for attaining the same ends was limited, or minimal. It may well be that, once such alternative channels presented themselves with the introduction of printed products, rooted habits and the comfortable serviceability of the old mechanisms acted to check their assimilation. It would be difficult to prove this assumption, but it is perhaps worth bearing it in mind.

Vocal Reading: Bridging across Illiteracy

Adherence to old methods, then, may have limited the society's receptiveness to the printed word. Yet the very existence of these traditional channels also facilitated the circulation of the new written knowledge flowing in from many directions. One obvious location where the old modes were applied to new needs was the private home, in which individual and collective reading came to be practiced side by side. Traditionally, intelligence gathered from outside the house by some of its members—from official announcements to neighborhood gossip—was conveyed orally to the rest of the family. Usually it was the men of the family, the father and adult boys, who would bring in news from the street, market, mosque, or church and share it orally with the others. From the early twentieth century on, knowledge collected in these public places increasingly had its origins in printed texts. Brought home, it was imparted in the familiar manner as a matter of course. But there was a novelty here: young children came to replace, or join, their seniors as family informers, employing skills they alone had acquired. While the ritual of communicating news and views orally at home remained basically the same as before, the mode of the practice was changing as youngsters were sharing the role of conveying enlightenment with their fathers and older brothers. Newspapers, handbills, and even books came to supplement the more traditional sources of information, turning the private residence into an intimate locus of group reading.

But it was, more typically, in public places that the familiar, collective modes were used for circulating the contents of written information. City cafés and markets, the village *madafah* and grocery shops, remained places of vocal group reading, where the skills of one individual served to enlighten a gathering, now with knowledge of a new type.

Nothing mirrored this shift more vividly than the use, in printed products, of a language fit for oral-aural communication. The phenomenon is universally familiar: medieval European authors, intending for their writings to reach the audience vocally, often called upon them to "lend ears" to the message or "listen" to a tale, formulas that remained in use long after the popularization of visual reading. As one observer has recently noted, our language today is still replete with these frozen expressions that echo ancient practice, such as, "I've heard from so-and-so," in the sense of "I've received a letter" from him; or, "this text doesn't sound right," meaning "it isn't well written."[28] A few examples may illustrate this phenomenon in Palestine, which was very common during the transition period in publications designed for oral circulation, such as newspapers and printed proclamations. In the opening article of the Jerusalem weekly newspaper *al-Ahlam,* from 1908, the editor addresses his readers/ listeners:

I can hear you, oh gentlemen, saying to me (*taqulu li*): "tell us (*ihki lana*) about the opening of this paper of yours and preach to us in your popular Arabic, with its delightful words, marvelous ideas and delicate expressions" . . . I hear and obey (sam'an wa-ta'atan), oh gentlemen, oh honorable, oh you who for me are of noble ranks . . . [And a few lines later:] Lend me your ears, oh you who is calling out, and hear the answer to your question from me.[29]

Another paper, launched in the same year, thus ended its inaugural essay: "I have phrased my thoughts in my statement, offering it to the people, so they can hear it, add to it their own views and convey it to others. This way, ideas can be exchanged."[30] A passionate 1923 essay on the poor state of Arab culture ended with the words "*wa'l-salam 'ala man sama'a fa-wa'a*" (Peace be upon him who listens and heeds).[31] A daily paper in 1929 carried an article under the title "Our brethren everywhere—listen (*isma'u*) to what they are saying about us."[32] And one more example, from much later: "*man lahu aadhan li'l-sam' fa-liyasma'*!!" (He who has ears for hearing, let him hear!!), closing an equally animated newspaper article in 1944.[33] Other devices from the same rhetoric arsenal included repetition for emphasis, rhetorical questions, and exclamatory expressions, as well as rhyming, which made sense mainly in an oral usage. "Is this impudence? Is this a lack of culture? Is this stubbornness?"—thus opened an article on Zionist demands in a 1929 issue of a daily paper, entitled "A New Status Quo around the Wailing Wall!!!" And a response: "Certainly not! It's much worse than that!" and so on.[34] Political and other essays in the press of the period abound with such usage, taken from the vocabulary of oral dialogue. Other verbal indications attest to the continuity of vocal modes into the era of written discourse. An essay in an early issues of the Jerusalem newspaper *Mir'at al-Sharq*, addressed, as the title announced, "To the peasant" (*ila al-fallah*), started with a story that took place "once upon a time (*yawm^{an}*)." Comprising two paragraphs of the article's four, the story was about a peasant and his sons, with a lesson regarding the importance of clinging to the land and the virtue of hard work. The style of the narrative was of the kind one would hear in storytelling occasions, especially for youth. Having established a context in the long-familiar style, the writer than proceeded to call upon peasants to apply the lesson on their own land.[35]

The reliance on oral means for transmitting knowledge of a new type and scope was assumed smoothly as soon as such knowledge appeared in the region. The phenomenon of educated men reading newspapers or street placards to groups of listeners was frequently reported from neighboring provinces in the last decades of the Ottoman era as well as later. Such accounts carry lively descriptions of occasions in which papers were read and discussed by merchants and buyers in the marketplace, people sitting in cafés or walking in the street, crowds gathered around teenaged newspaper hawkers, who would decipher the writing for them.[36] Direct evidence on this practice in Palestine during the early years of the period is scarcer—there were few printed texts around—but suffices to confirm that it was known there following the emergence of the press, if not before. Such was a report by one observer, dated 1911, about "educated people in the villages (for example, teachers and spiritual leaders) who can read a little. They sometimes read out to their neighbors a paper they happened to obtain."[37] The delivery of copies of *Filastin* to village heads in order to enlighten the *fallahin*, reported in 1913,[38] similarly implied the existence of the practice in the rural areas. So did a complaint by the owner of the weekly *al-Quds*, in the same year, that every issue of his paper was "reaching another fifty people," to his understandable consternation.[39] The British, who conquered the country in 1917–1918, saw urgency in spreading their propaganda to the local population, since the war was not yet over and harmful rumors were percolating and circulating there. They needed a well-controlled transmission network and organized it with military efficacy. Paid readers were hired, armed with bulletins and other "suitable literature," and sent to the cafés and public gathering places in the towns and villages, where they would be "reading and explaining the news." The tactic was deemed useful: "the people here being backward and mostly illiterate, this appears the best way of interesting them."[40]

The old communication channels, which the British army competently exploited, continued thereafter to serve Palestinian society in various ways. With the hunger for news growing faster than the spread of education, the sight of literate, mostly young readers enlightening a circle of unlearned listeners quickly became familiar in urban as well as rural places. In Bethlehem of the 1920s, men used to gather in the backyard of the Church of Resurrection during Sunday prayers and "discuss public issues and the Palestinian problem in particular." One of them, a simple laborer, would usually "buy the paper on that morning and hand it to any of the kids who appeared to be literate, and [the kid] would read for him the headlines and some passages, with emphasis on editorials."[41] In Nazareth in the following decade, a child would "read the newspaper to some older illiterates, who would hand him a copy and listen attentively; sometimes he came across

"Reading newspapers aloud at night in a Stamboul café," a cartoon from *The Graphic* (London), 17 November 1877, front page. Those present seem to be listening attentively, in a relaxed but earnest atmosphere.

incomprehensible words, but in general he grasped the sense of the item."[42] And a somewhat different variation of the practice was recorded in the later mandate period—a routine of "newspaper-reading breaks" in workplaces, where papers were often read out collectively.[43]

The sources, including numerous informants who were interviewed for this study, confirm that such collective reading was known all over Palestine. But it was markedly more common in rural places than in the towns. The lower level of literacy in the villages made them more dependent on communal circulation of information, and the centrality of public gathering in village life made sessions of group reading a more natural habit than it was in the cities. Numerous accounts reflect the phenomenon of collective vocal reading in rural Palestine, suggesting that the practice obtained in the great majority of the villages. Increasingly politicized and eager to stay on top of events, villagers would meet daily in the usual places, where the learned among them would perform the same duties they had in the past, now by reading out newspapers, handbills, or any text that had reached the place. Meetings occurred daily, normally at the end of the working day. A single copy would suffice to enlighten the whole community. "When someone traveled to the town, he would always bring with him a newspaper," a man from Qaqun reported in a typical instance. "The elderly, who could not read, would then sit around the one who could, and listen to him [read] about the political situation, especially the news of the [1936—

1939] rebels."[44] The increasing severity of political developments during the later years of the mandate, with their direct impact on the country-side, entailed a passion for news as intense as it was in the cities. During the Palestine revolt of the late 1930s, Hajj Hasan Salim Abu ʿAql related, men gathered every evening at the village center in ʿArʿarah, where one of them, reputed as an expert coffee maker, would prepare the bittersweet drink for everybody. The village teacher, Shaykh Ahmad al-Barqawi, would read the newspaper of the day, after which a discussion of the events and their practical implications would always take place. The forum was designed for adult men only; Abu ʿAql, merely 16 at the time, could hang around and listen from a distance but not attend.[45] In Kafr Yasif, Abu Jiryis (Hanna Daʾud) regularly bought newspapers, which were brought to him by bus from nearby Acre. He would at first peruse the pa-per privately at home, noting the highlights to himself, and then go to the village café—which had operated there since 1924—and selectively read from it to the people, adding his own commentary.[46] In Bituniyya, near Jerusalem, a youngster educated in the city's Anglican St. George School used to perform a similar service for a group of attentive visitors to the vil-lage café in the 1930s: "Ibrahim . . . was a coffee house regular who took to demonstrating his learning by reading aloud from a Jerusalem newspaper to other, mostly illiterate regulars. They would gather around him while he conducted his recital, spicing whatever he read with snide comments as he went along and occasionally making up stories completely."[47] And one more example, from Masmiyyat Hurani (al-Masmiyyah al-Saghirah)—a small rural settlement in the Gaza district, with some 500 souls in the mid-1940s: there, the whole village was enlightened by two youngsters educated in the city, who would routinely read out the newspapers to the others. "The arrival of the two learned youth, with the acumen they had obtained in the towns—the centers of national action, of leadership and of political clubs—stirred a new spirit in the village," one member of the community recalled.

In the *madafah*, on the stone benches where people would gather in the eve-nings, or under the *sidrah* tree, the newspaper came to be read aloud and in a proper style. In addition to his command of the language, Nafidh [one of the two youths] also had an attractive voice for reading and a gift for accentuat-ing the words so as to harmonize sound and meaning in a comprehensible way. With the presence of a reader with such skills, who was perfectly quali-fied to add the needed interpretation to the obscure texts the paper carried, the circle of listeners broadened daily. People began to discuss public affairs, and their minds opened to worlds hitherto unknown to them.[48]

These channels of conveyance proved as effective as ever. British officials, ever sensitive to the impact of the press, got the impression that "newspapers do not lose their force in the process" of being orally transmitted. On the contrary, "the Arab fellahin [peasants] and villagers [of Palestine] are . . . probably more politically-minded than many of the people in Europe" (an accurate observation on a community whose wits had been sharpened by endless historic challenges).[49] The British knew they could rely on these age-old conduits when, during the violent encounters of the late 1930s, they used planes to drop printed leaflets in the countryside, addressed "*ila al-fallahin*" (to the peasants)[50]—the largely unlearned crowd that was well trained in handling written messages. Even as the number of the educated in the villages increased, the practice of getting updated through oral channels persisted. It was sometimes regarded as an inherent feature, likely to last forever. Thus, in the early 1930s, Khalil Sakakini, then inspector of Arabic in the Department of Education, established "reading and writing squads" in villages of the Ramallah region, whose members "should be trained in reading newspapers and useful books to the villagers and write their letters for them, and [everything else] they needed. From among these squads "will emerge the future readers and writers of the village," Sakakini envisioned.[51]

The disparity in this regard between town and country had another, curious, aspect. As literacy expanded and education came to be associated with social and political success, reading skills loomed as a prestigious asset and their absence as a handicap one would feel uncomfortable to admit. This new social perception of learning first appeared in the cities, where exposing one's inadequacy in reading was increasingly seen as a problem. People are reported to have carried a newspaper conspicuously in their hand or under their arm as proof of their learnedness. The middle-aged stonecutter from Bethlehem, who learned how to read from a child, had a habit of buying a paper while he was still illiterate. He used "to fold the paper lengthwise, shoving it into the pocket of the jacket [which he wore] above his *qunbaz,* so that its upper end with the paper's name *Filastin* could be seen conspicuously . . . 'I carry the newspaper so as to make people believe I am a newspaper reader. Imagine!'" he confided to the child who would become his teacher.[52] Such instances, though not inconceivable, were far less likely to occur in the villages, where illiteracy was standard rather than a weakness to be ashamed of.

Seeking to overcome both illiteracy and poverty in transmitting written texts when their inflow intensified, the society relied on traditional expedients with a marked degree of success. Accustomed to gathering in prayer houses, flocking around the *munadi*, and grouping next to storytellers for listening to messages of every kind, people continued to get together in order to be informed. The standard rule of *munadi* sessions—"those who are present should notify the rest"—guaranteed circulation to the far end of the community and to the last relevant member of the household. We shall never know the true number of the people exposed to information through such practices. But we may safely assume that written information, especially that concerning current affairs, whether arriving from above (sometimes literally from the sky) or from clandestine bodies below, reached nearly every part of Palestinian society. People did not have to wait for the full elimination of illiteracy to be enlightened. When radio was introduced during the last decade or so of the period—this "magic instrument that can speak, recite the Qur'an, convey the news, and sing"[53]—it fulfilled the same function of enlightening the uneducated, and listening to it took place in a very similar manner. A single receiver in the neighborhood café, in the Mukhtar's house, or in the *madafah* would perpetuate the role of these places as sites of collective listening. Still, reading in the more traditional style, by an educated person actually present, did not cease. It persisted, in villages more than in towns, along with public radio listening. These mechanisms would give way to mass (though not quite universal) command of reading skills long after the end of period explored here.

Collective modes of reading served to overcome insufficient education and indigence. As we shall see, however, the lack of skills or funds was not the only drive for resorting to such measures.

Vocal Reading: The Extra Benefit of the Collective Experience

A scene from a black-and-white Egyptian movie:[54] in a police station, a sergeant is seated at his desk, browsing through some papers, as someone enters the room and lays a report in front of him. The sergeant rises from his seat, summons a policeman from the next room, and orders him to read out the report, while he himself stands in an authoritative posture behind his desk, listening to the message. Starting at the beginning of the document, the policeman soon gets lost in the jumble of introductory remarks, while the sergeant repeatedly urges him to move on and get to the point. Eventually losing his patience, the sergeant grabs the report from the reader's hand and skims through it on his own, murmuring as he reads. He quickly obtains what he needs to know and proceeds to act upon it.

Why would the sergeant ask another man to read the text for him if he could do so himself in the first place? Watching this episode, the spectator may at first assume that the sergeant was illiterate, forgetting for a moment that he was attending to other papers earlier in the scene. But the unfolding plot soon proves this impression to be false. How, then, is it to be rationalized? People to whom this scene was described, among them Egyptians and Palestinians, explicated it mostly by focusing on the need to display authority: the sergeant was exercising his privilege to demand and receive service from his junior in rank; and the movie director included the episode to establish that the sergeant was smarter than a bottom-of-the-ladder official. This seems to be a sensible explanation. But a more illuminating one was also suggested: having the message read aloud by another person would make it easy for the sergeant to grasp its sense—more than if he had to read it with his own eyes. That would be so because, by vocalizing the text, the reader would be saving his listener the effort of "translating" the written signs into a living message, thereby allowing him to concentrate on its contents. This last analysis touches directly upon the phenomenon that concerns us in this part of the chapter: the intricate relationship between visual and vocalized texts and its practical implications.

Like the Egyptian sergeant, Palestinians trained in reading participated as listeners on occasions of various kinds. Listening to prayers and sermons in mosques and churches, a universal phenomenon, was the most obvious activity of this sort. Educated people often made up a part of the audience of storytellers in public places even when a written copy of the same text lay on a shelf in their homes. Similarly, those who could both buy and read newspapers would still come to gathering places where the papers would be read out collectively. Numerous accounts can be found in the written and oral sources. "My father was a literate man," related Dr. Sulayman Jubran, who grew up in Buqay'ah (Peqi'in), in the upper Galilee. "Having learned how to read, he could make out written texts of any kind without difficulty. Nor was buying a daily newspaper beyond his reach. Still, he hardly ever bought a paper in order to read it at home. For that he would always go to the village café."[55] The habit was popular. When asked to explain, people who were interviewed for this study offered reasons of basically two kinds, one relating to the level of proficiency, the other to the unique quality of the oral experience itself.

The reason of the former type is of particular importance to our discussion, for it brings into sharp focus both the relativity of "literacy" in general and particularly in relation to Arabic, especially in its modern form. It will therefore be worth our while to consider it at some length. Between the ability to identify written passages from the Qur'an to the exclusion of all else and the capacity to read any kind of writing fluently lies a range of many intermediate situations. One's place in that range naturally depends on the scope and quality of one's training, a universal principle applicable in any language. Written Arabic, however, has certain features that make its reading and comprehension especially demanding. We shall recall Paul Saenger's theory, noted in the previous chapter, that the introduction of spaces between words had a watershed effect on reading fluency in medieval Europe. According to Saenger, spaces between words had always existed in written Arabic (and other Semitic languages) as an "intrinsic feature"; they compensated for the fact that the language was written without vowels. Had they not been separated by spaces, he has suggested, "identifying word boundaries would have been impracticable." Saenger even credited Arabic for influencing continental Europe in this matter, through the massive corpus of Arabic texts on Greek science and philosophy translated into Latin from the tenth century onward. The Latin West is thus "indebted to the Arab world for the transmission of the text format as well as the content of Aristotelian and other scientific works."[56]

This may or may not have been so.[57] But the absence of vowels (and, in some writing traditions of Arabic, also the more problematic absence of diacritical marks), for which the spaces presumably compensated, itself formed a considerable hurdle for the reader. It continues to do so to this day. This difficulty would often lead to instinctive vocalization for the sake of verification, as anyone who has tried to read such texts would readily confirm. Without vowels, written Arabic actually falls short of accurately corresponding to the language as it is heard. Unvowelled writing represents a kind of "raw" text that can invariably be read in more sensible ways than one. The reader is thus required to fill up the "missing parts," so to speak, out of his preexisting knowledge in order to obtain lexical access to the texts, namely, to make it comprehensible. This means, in fact, a two-tier reading process: visual—capturing the writing with the eye; and mental—"molding" it in accordance with grammatical rules known to the reader and turning the pliant words into meaningful sentences. This complex procedure inevitably slows down the act. Attaining the level of proficiency that allows smooth visual reading, therefore, involves much training. In particular, such training must include solid familiarization with Arabic grammar, an intricate field of study that traditionally lay beyond the most basic course of Islamic instruction. Graduates of a limited educational course, even when taught to identify letters and put them together to make words, may not be equipped with the grammatical tools needed for fluent reading.[58] Although in Arab society, just as in Europe, there was always a small class of people capable of silent visual reading, the bulk of those who received education were inadequately trained for such a task. This situation, common before the twentieth century, seems to have persisted after 1900 as well, even when more systematic educational efforts were made. The more gifted among those who attended schools in Palestine grappled successfully with the difficulties and attained a solid command of visual reading. Most others, however, acquired a less-than-complete reading capacity, either because the period of training was too short or because its quality was too low (see Chapter 1). Having gone through a course of learning, they would still have difficulties reading previously unseen texts. "Less-than-complete," again, represents a wide gamut of possible levels. Such people would often find it convenient to rely on someone more proficient who would clear the technical hurdles for them and lead them straight to the gist of the message.

A related problem in Arabic is one of vocabulary and, more broadly, expressive patterns. This problem initially stems from the historic gap between two layers of the language, *fushah* and *'amiyyah*—the written or literary language, with its infinitely rich lexicon and sophisticated structure, and the spoken idiom, with its rainbow of dialects. People capable of reading unvowelled Arabic are normally trained in making out the meaning of the written language as well. But for those without training or with incomplete one, the written text might be difficult and at times unintelligible, even if read to them by someone more proficient, unless it is interpreted. An old problem, it became infinitely more complex in modern Arabic. The exposure of Arabic-speaking societies to foreign ideas, the urge to discuss these ideas, and the subsequent endorsement of many of them engendered a process of linguistic adaptation in which numerous novel words were devised for notions that hitherto had no names in Arabic. In a development that had begun with the onset of the *nahdah,* writers and linguists experimented with all kinds of terminological solutions: they invented new words, changed the sense of old ones, revived obsolete terms and attached new meanings to them, and borrowed items from foreign lexicons when expedient. All these measures cast the language in flux. A colorful aspect of the cultural awakening, the process continued well into the twentieth century; in post-1900 Palestine it was at its peak. The old difficulties of the written language, produced without vowels and distinct from the spoken tongue, were thus immensely complicated by its semantic and lexical refurbishment. The result was a real crisis, during which the communicative quality of the language was seriously, if temporarily, compromised.[59]

How problematic this ongoing change could sometimes be, we may grasp from a typical story by a villager from Qaqun, who related his memoirs from the late 1930s:

> I went with my neighbor to hear the news-edition in the house of Abu Hantash [owner of the only radio receiver in the village]. We sat listening to the broadcasting, and when the announcer had finished the edition, I told my friend: "Let's go." He said: "Sit down man, so we can hear the news-edition." I said: "Would that God render your wife a widow! What [do you think] it was that you just heard?"[60]

In Kafr Yasif in the 1940s, people who had received education would come to listen to Abu Jiryis (Hanna Da'ud) read the news from the paper, related a local resident. Kafr Yasif had a proud tradition of education, and attending school was standard for the village children for many decades. Still, "to many, the language of the press was difficult and included many unfamiliar words. New words would pop up all the time. Abu Jiryis, a seasoned browser, would read and interpret for everybody."[61] Around the same time, the British brought a radio receiver to the village of 'Ar'arah and placed it in the home of one of the educated people there. "Men would come after work to his private *diwan* to listen. He would open it for the news, and when the broadcasting was over he would turn off the radio and 'translate' the news into a more comprehensible language."[62] Similarly, in Masmiyyat Hurani, as we have seen, it took a city-trained young man not just to read but also to interpret for the villagers "the obscure texts (*al-nusus al-ghamidah*) published in the newspaper."[63] And one more example, from a realistic novel whose setting is a Galilee village, depicting events during the 1936–1939 revolt:

> The newspaper, which Abu Ghassan used to bring from the town once a week, was a major source for news. A group of men would get together in front of Salim Farhud's shop and [Abu Ghassan] would read for them the news he deemed important in the paper. As soon as he would finish [reading] an issue Abu Nayif would say: "Go ahead, interpret for us." Abu Ghassan would then rephrase the piece in an understandable language, as if he were translating from a foreign tongue.[64]

Such difficulties were reported in many places. They underscored the relativity of being "literate" in twentieth-century Arab society. People who received training in reading came to possess practical skills that distinguished them from the illiterate in some important ways. That these skills had their limitations, however, is seen in the frequent preference of those with such training, imperfect as it was, to have modern texts read to them aloud. Those with different levels of proficiency would join the uneducated in listening to the reading of the most capable reader around. Hearing him vocalize the messages of a paper or a written proclamation, they would receive it properly pronounced, properly accentuated, and, when needed, also interpreted.

We now come to the second explanation for why educated people sometimes chose to listen to a text they could read for themselves. Touching upon the nub of the reading experience, it is more elusive than the previous kind of reasoning. In general, hearing is a more potent means of receiving messages than seeing. It has been observed that "sound unites groups of living beings as nothing else does"; in Walter Ong's words, once again, "through sound we can become present to a totality which is a fullness, a plenitude." On the other hand, the written word "is not sufficiently living and refreshing" for creating true contact between people. "A very small part of spoken speech can be put into writing that makes sense. . . . if words are written, they are on the whole far more likely to be misunderstood than spoken words are."[65] Writing is a useful device for informing an audience to which one has no direct access. But it is an imperfect device, for writing can communicate ideas, let alone emotions, only in a limited way. In written stories, journal articles, or handbills, writing may seek to move, excite, and alarm by using such technical devices as big headlines, exclamation marks, and graphic illustrations. But all of these fall short of the natural communicative quality of the human voice. This last quality is enhanced further when accompanied by the speaker's facial expression, body language, and gestures, and still more when the speaker performs in a communal forum, directly answering queries from the audience and responding to their expressed or implied expectations. A newspaper, then, has less potential than radio as a medium for transmitting news and commentary. Radio, in turn, is less effective than television, because of the latter's capacity to portray expressions and gestures. A person reading live to an audience has primacy over all of these media, due to the additional advantage of interactivity. In such a situation, the text turns into an "event" and takes on a life that it does not have in its written form. It takes a gifted and sensitive reader to mediate between the writer and his audience by translating the written text into the living experience that would have taken place had the writer himself faced the same audience. Obviously, the very same text can acquire different meanings and be turned into various kinds of experience when read by different people, or under different circumstances of time, place, and audience composition.

In relating their experience of participating as listeners in reading sessions, many Palestinian informants have acknowledged that the main attraction was the extra benefit of vocalization (and sometimes acting)—the "event" effect. "There were folk in our village who could read," Hajj Hasan Salim Abu 'Aql related, recalling the mandate years in 'Ar'arah. "Still, they would come to listen to our teacher reading the newspaper. He would spell it out loudly and make a drama of his reading. He would turn the reading of newspaper into a *hikayah* (tale, story)."[66] The sight was familiar. Serene Husseini Shahid, a high school student in Ramallah in the mid-1930s, related how copies of a newspaper edited by her father used to arrive in the school, where everybody was obviously literate. The students were "pouring over it and passing it from one group of ardent readers to another"[67]—not from one individual to another. Husni al-Salih, who grew up in the village of Tarshihah in the upper Galilee, described the same kind of practice under somewhat different circumstances. "We would spend the evenings in our homes, since there were no cafés at the time," he recalled, referring to the 1920s. "Those of us who had big houses would invite [the others] to spend the evenings at their homes":

> We would play some games in those evenings, then move on to reading (*qira'ah*). We would sit, and one of us would stand up and read, so everybody could hear him. We read from the book of the "Thousand and One

Nights," the book of "'Antarah," or the pamphlets of the "Islamic History series," which Jurji Zaydan used to publish then. Our evenings began to expand, involving youth as well as [adult] men. Any person of those present who excelled in reading would read in a loud voice (*bi-sawt murtafaʿ*) and the rest would listen.

Most participants in these gatherings were literate, Salih related. "When we realized that a few of them could not make out some of the read expressions, for insufficient education, the group moved to organize evening reading classes for them."[68]

Dr. Shukri 'Arraf, from Maʿiliya, has reported a similar custom in his village, a Greek-Orthodox community in the upper Galilee where education had been nearly universal for many decades. People would practice this custom as part of a "frozen tradition" in a peasant-society-turned-literate, he has suggested. It was performed with newspapers and political proclamations just as it was with traditional legends. 'Arraf offered the following charming explanation for the preference of educated people for listening to oral reporting: "Why do we click our wine glasses with those of our mates before drinking? Well, you see the wine, smell it, taste it and touch the glass. Four of the five senses are thus involved in the experience. The only one left out is hearing. To make the experience whole, we produce this sound with our glasses. By now we have become so accustomed to this sound that it is an indispensable part of the experience. It always evokes an association of drinking." Reading aloud in a group is the same, 'Arraf noted: conducted amidst a discussion and exchange of views, it becomes a rich and whole experience, nothing like the "flat" reading with the eyes. "No wonder even the educated readily prefer it."[69]

The advantages of vocal reading in company, if seldom accounted for, were regularly acknowledged. This came out in the instinctive responses by numerous informants, among them literate men, when asked about how they read the newspaper. The answer would almost invariably be "newspapers are read in the café!" as though this were a self-evident social axiom. "Read" in the café, that is, spelled out vocally, interpreted, listened to, and debated collectively, stirring passion and emotions—a truly whole experience. In the dynamics of the discussion, those better educated might have a weightier input; but eventually everybody would be rewarded. Where a skillful reader could offer his audience access to texts despite educational drawbacks and linguistic pitfalls, people with insufficient training would join his circle of listeners. When the reader was gifted enough to turn the act into a gratifying happening, literate, semi-literate, and illiterate people alike would be further attracted. The traditional lure of such sessions, successfully carried over into gatherings of the more practical kind, further ensured the smooth circulation of knowledge among all ranks of the community. At least in this last practical sphere, Palestinians, fully educated or not, by no means remained uninformed.

Conclusion

⊹≒⊨⊹

"Was there a reading revolution at the end of the eighteenth century?" the German historian Reinhard Wittmann has recently asked, his concern focusing on western Europe. Wittmann's probe into the matter has yielded findings that have led him to reply in the affirmative. During the half century before 1800, there was a dramatic rise in the scope of book production and in the number of their readers, amounting to a real "reading mania": education and literacy shot up; public and lending libraries, as well as the more elitist, private, reading societies, multiplied rapidly. Even the manufacturing of reading-related furniture, such as desks, suddenly became a prosperous trade. Within a few decades a "largely anonymous, unhomogeneous and fragmented—in short, modern" public of readers came into being. These changes, sweeping as they were, deserve to be entitled "revolutionary," Wittmann has concluded. The developments studied by Wittmann are in many ways akin to those studied here. Is the adjective he picked for describing them, then, equally applicable to pre-1948 Palestine?

Late to join the cultural transformation begun in the region during the nineteenth century, Palestine entered a phase of accelerated renovation after 1900. Signs of an approaching transition were already apparent before the First World War. But under a different government, with new norms and a new agenda, change was markedly stepped up after the war. It showed itself in all spheres of life, including those discussed in this study and far beyond. The growing importance of writing and the development of tools that enhanced its use redrew the cultural scene under new rules. By the end of the period, considerable strides had been made in preparing the grounds for this new scene, and more were to follow. The shift was clearly irreversible.

A major aspect of the cultural transition was that which took place in education—a background arena in the present study but one whose role in the changes explored here was crucial. Palestinian society recast its old standards, by which illiteracy was the convenient norm and enlightenment an elitist exception. Education now became a desired goal for a much larger segment of Palestinian society; its absence became a handicap. The make-over in the country's political circumstances provoked a widespread need for information, the access key to which was schooling. Beyond addressing the immediate need for news, education was vital in closing the recently dis-covered gaps between the local society and a range of others: the country's foreign rulers (and those seeking to propagate their faith in it); its dynamic neighbors in Egypt and Lebanon, where enviable progress had already been made; and, last but hardly least, the dangerously enterprising Zionists. The motivation induced by awareness of these facts was reflected in the readiness of lower-class urban families to draw on their meager resources so as to pay for their children's education, and in the efforts of humble vil-lagers to share the costs of school building. The demand for instruction was met with a vigorous, if still inadequate, response by the authorities and other, mostly foreign, organizations. These combined efforts laid solid foundations for a schooling system that was continuously expanding. There were enormous difficulties—material, administrative, and cultural—and by 1948 the achievements were only very partial. Still, of the country's younger Arab generation in that year, nearly half received systematic educa-tion that would allow them to take part in the cultural transformation in one way or another. The other developments in text production and con-sumption could not have occurred, or would have remained inconsiderable, without the profound advance in this field.

The government's role in molding the other sections of the scene was more limited, and progress resulted mostly from private initiative. Its sur-roundings transformed, Palestinian society exhibited a growing appetite for written and printed products, usable both as a compass and as a ladder for social mobility. This hunger was satiated, in large part, by the more vigorous print industries of neighboring countries, whose output was brought into Palestine in increasing quantities. It was also addressed by local produc-tion, practically nonexistent before 1900 and rapidly expanding thereafter. Written products of two kinds became particularly prominent. One was the periodical Palestinian press, a latecomer to the stage of Arab journalism, which followed a familiar pattern: it featured numerous ephemeral titles—a trend that mirrored at once exigencies and tenacity—but also some high-quality publications whose consumption became a public custom that would turn into addiction. The other was written messages of endless forms and purposes that came to pervade the open public domain, from street name signs to political banners. The latter was likewise a rarity-turned-standard, mostly in the cities. Once a peculiarity of little use to a largely illiterate society, public notices became organizing devices in the daily routine of urbanites, serving them in finding their way around, doing business, and engaging in dialogue. Books, imported and local, also circulated among educated consumers and accumulated in private collections in bigger quantities than before. But their cultural role remained markedly more limited than that of the former two types of texts. This was particularly so with the local book industry. On the periphery of developments in Arabic printing before 1900, Palestine remained a marginal producer of books until the end of the period and continued to rely on the output of Egypt and Lebanon.

The increasing presence of written texts both reactivated old conduits of dissemination and gave birth to new outlets. One colorful figure epitomizing these developments was the teenaged newspaper hawker, a new feature of the urban scene: vocally announcing his low-price merchandise in city streets and around the cafés, he was thereby placing relevant and affordable printed products at the center of public attention. Other effective, if still modest, channels were emerging, from bookstores through lending libraries to social club reading rooms. Those with the skills for exploiting books and journals independently and the means needed for buying them had at their disposal an increasing number of ways to access these materials. Other parts of the community, whose thirst for intelligence grew faster than their ability to read and buy, intuitively fell back on old circulation mechanisms. These proved to be as serviceable as ever. In traditional gatherings in cities and villages, printed texts were read, interpreted, and discussed in the familiar oral manner as a collective experience. The gap between appetite and ability, and the resort to old techniques for bridging it, were typical marks of the transition Palestine was undergoing, along with most other societies in its neighborhood.

In the historic shift to reliance on writing, progress was indeed remarkable. But as so often happens, it was not a balanced process engulfing the entire community symmetrically. While all parts of society were touched by these developments, directly or otherwise, certain sections were influenced less than others. Muslims, villagers, women, members of the lower classes, members of the older generation, were on the whole less affected than Christians, urbanites, men, upper- and middle-class members, and youth. Those from the former set of categories were less likely to order a printed work from an Alexandria publisher, borrow books for a fee from a lending bookstore in Jerusalem, make use of a Jaffa club library, or find themselves reading out to a circle of listeners. The change spread from the cities to the countryside piecemeal, reaching the smaller rural communities only marginally. It was equally slow to reach the female half of society. And there was a whole generation, or even two, of those who had been above schooling age when the system was set up, who for the most part remained without access to reading skills. By the end of the period the scene was far more diverse than at the outset, with many more dissimilarities within the community.

The cultural change was also uneven in another way, already alluded to. The entry of this society into the world of written texts, and the distribution channels that were devised to serve it, mainly revolved around writings of one type: products with a short life span usually made for fleeting reading, which could be read but also listened to, such as newspapers, political pamphlets, manifestoes, and street corner banners. Other printed items—books of a literary or scholarly nature, scientific studies, journals of intellectual discourse—were of secondary importance in the process. The demand for such serious publications, a domain of the small elite at first, spread more slowly to other sectors. In part this was due to the abysmal state of affairs at the start and the generally low level of education, which, even under the British, realistically aimed at fostering a basic practical competence of reading and writing rather than at developing a taste for literary discussion. This also resulted from the intensity of political life, which attracted much of the attention to publications addressing immediate needs at the expense of all else. And there was yet another, no less important factor, namely tradition. Accepting books of a nonreligious nature as standard sources of inspiration and mental gratification required a change of cultural norms, usually a slow process for a society. This type of change commenced during this period, but much of it still lay ahead in 1948. Palestinians thus moved from minimal use of any written texts to an extensive use of specific categories of them. In these specific categories, change was rapid. In the others it was slower. It was thus, perhaps inevitably, a lopsided process.

At this point we may return to the question that opened this concluding review: were the developments in text production and reading and, more broadly, the cultural transition in Palestine truly "revolutionary"? The question is by now little more than semantic. The term itself is, of course, relative: according to the *Oxford Advanced Dictionary*, "revolutionary" means "involving complete or drastic change," a definition as sound as any. The change in Palestine, representing a quantum leap forward within a short time, may well be depicted as drastic. But it was certainly less than complete by the time of the 1948 earthquake, which cut the process short before it could reach its full potential scope. Interrupted in the middle, if not to say in its outset, the "revolution" was not allowed to ripen. Quite likely, the shifts that had begun sometime before 1900 and had gathered momentum under the mandate would have evolved into a full-fledged cultural revolution if not for 1948. As it happened, they did not.

A quantitative assessment of the different modes of reading that would be at once reliable and meaningful is out of the question. What we may try instead is to look at different manners of reading and their respective pace of progress in a comparative way. Both individual and collective forms of using written texts expanded during the half century studied here. While there is no telling by what margin the former mode progressed, it clearly advanced in a more limited way than the latter. The number of independent readers grew steadily; if, beyond those who read books and journals, we also count those who now could decipher street signs independently, then the number must have increased several-fold. Yet, this increase was not nearly as intensive as the one occurring in the exposure to printed texts through collective and mostly vocal reading. Here the rise was indeed dramatic. Public communication of information had been customary in the past, but only rarely before 1900 had it been based on printed items of any kind, let alone ones with immediate relevance. Nor had it been conducted with the tremendous intensity it would assume later on. Thus, while the social mechanisms for this public communication of information were old, the twentieth-century version of the phenomenon was novel and its extent unprecedented.

The quality of the picture emerging from our findings is, on the whole, less than satisfactory. The inadequacy of extant evidence limits our ability to capture the scene in its multicolor variety. But the evidence does seem adequate for casting light on certain intricacies of the cultural reality in societies under comparable circumstances, in the Middle East and elsewhere. It shows, for example, how "literacy"—a pliant notion whose sense always depends on the function intended—becomes the more fluid in times of rapid change. Educational endeavor by multiple providers, leaning on a deficient infrastructure and available only to a part of the community, is bound to yield varying degrees of "literacy," however defined. Its graduates would take with them a wide range of abilities; moreover, these skills would not always be permanently retained. To what extent their training would prepare them to rely on reading for navigating in the modern world is a question that has to be examined individually for each section and sub-section of the educated community. Any attempt to chart literacy during this phase of transition—by census or otherwise—would be as fruitful as mapping shifting dunes.

A related aspect highlighted by these findings concerns the response of a society to a major cultural challenge for which it is initially ill-equipped. An instinctive reaction of this society would be turning to its own arsenal of proven traditional methods for answers. This might be paralleled by a long-term, gradual process of adopting or devising other tools for contending with the challenge. And when new needs are thus met with both old and novel methods simultaneously, gauging the effects of the change becomes a thorny business. As the present case has shown, data on the number of those who obtained proficiency in reading through education teach us little about the size of the public exposed to the texts in circulation, let alone affected by them. Nor do circulation figures of newspapers, evidence of printed proclamations, and the like necessarily indicate the size of the public actually exposed to these materials. Where one copy enlightens all the men in a neighborhood café or village guesthouse and through them the rest of the community, neither the level of literacy nor the number of copies is of much import. The size of an "audience"—readers and listeners—thus remains as elusive a quality as that of society's degree of "literacy."

One common way of ending a concluding chapter is by addressing the broader implications of the issues discussed in the study. Another is by look-ing briefly at later developments in the same arena, thus terminating with a historical epilogue. Adopting the former option would mean delving into a vast range of issues, for it is clear that the developments discussed here had a profound impact on every plain of Palestinian life—social, politi-cal, intellectual, religious, probably even economic. Examining this impact must be left for another book that should depart from the point at which the present work ends. Among other issues, such a book should explore the effect of reading, a potent new skill, on accepted conventions of social status. Most likely, this new factor would be found to have challenged, if not overshadowed, traditional criteria of public eminence such as noble descent, wealth, and old age. It also must have influenced intergenerational relations, since the new skill was to a large extent a youth domain. A re-lated and equally intriguing question should be the effect of these shifts on the prestige of the society's spiritual leaders, who lost the near-exclusive control they once shared with the rulers over the messages circulating in society. Yet another essential issue is the role of texts and reading in shaping Palestinian concepts of collective identity and communal orientation. Beyond such social and ideological spheres, there were political ramifications that merit separate exploration. Most prominent among these are the ways in which the government used printing and publication and their effect; the repercussions of popular access to printed knowledge for political relations—specifically, for the government's relationship with the governed; and the varied impact of the developments considered here on the Palestinian encounter with external enemies.

A future study of this kind, however, would entail a special handicap, unique to the case of Palestine. Nineteen-forty-eight was a disaster so staggering as to forcefully disrupt historic trends and diminish the relevance of earlier developments with regard to subsequent ones in that society's history. This brings us to the second option just mentioned, of concluding this discussion with a historical epilogue. As already noted, in the case of Palestine changes in the use of written texts and the spread of literacy were not granted much chance to produce the long-term effects they would have had given a more stable course of events. Moreover, the 1948 calamity eradicated much of the evidence for the earlier occurrences, as we have seen. Nevertheless, Palestinians, scattered as they have come to be, seem to have taken with them certain gains from this period. Whether under Arab or Israeli rule, post-1948 Palestinians would not revert to the cultural phase that preceded the changes considered here. High regard for education, respect for the value of the printed word, realistic appreciation of the tremendous power of writing, and keen awareness of its multiple uses are lessons born from Palestine's experience between 1900 and 1948 that seem to have been absorbed. These lessons are, yet again, a matter for another exploration.

Notes

Introduction

1. "Lebanon" was a loose term prior to the First World War, and only after the foundation of a state by that name did it become more specific. In studies on that country, "Lebanon" is often used to denote the place corresponding to the modern state of Lebanon, even when earlier periods are considered. In the present study I have followed that practice throughout, rather than use slightly more accurate but far more cumbersome names.

2. For developments in printing, see Sabat, pp. 103–105, 287, 299, and Chapter 2 below. For the post-1908 beginnings of journalism in these provinces, see Ayalon, *The Press,* pp. 62–69.

3. Palestine's demographic figures until the end of the Ottoman era are notoriously confused and controversial. For some evaluations that seem sounder than others, see Gilbar, *Megamot,* pp. 4ff.; Schölch, chap. 2; see also Assaf, *ha-Yahasim,* pp. 121–143.

4. Here, too, there is much variation in data presented by different sources. See Rafeq, who quotes many assessments on Jerusalem's population in the nineteenth century. Also Assaf, *ha-Yahasim,* pp. 126–131; Ben Arieh, "Population," pp. 50–53; Schölch, p. 38.

5. The 1922 population census showed that no town in Palestine had a population of 10,000 except for the three large cities, Haifa, Nablus, and Hebron. Mills, vol. 2, p. 16.

6. See the colorful description of public services in turn-of-the-century Jerusalem, in Yehoshuʿa, *Yerushalayim,* pp. 65–68.

7. Gilbar, "Growing Economic Involvement."

8. Details in Muhafazah, pp. 19–26.

9. Gilbar, "Growing Economic Involvement."

10. Gilbar, *Megamot,* pp. 10–12. Slightly different figures appear in Government of Palestine, Department of Statistics, *Statistical Abstract* (1944–45), pp. 21–22.

11. Gilbar, *Megamot,* pp. 3–10. According to the first population census, conducted by the British in 1922, Palestine then had a population of c. 750,000, of which c. 590,000 (78%) were Muslims and c. 71,000 (9.5%) Christians; see Government of Palestine, Department of Statistics, *Statistical Abstract* (1944–45), pp. 16–17. The more comprehensive and accurate census of 1931 showed a total population of c. 1,035,000, including c. 760,000 (73%) Muslims and c. 91,000 (9%) Christians; see Mills, vol. 2, pp. 18–19. According to a census conducted in 1945, the country's population had reached 1,810,000, among them c. 1,100,000 (c. 60%) Muslims and c. 139,000 (c. 8%) Christians; Government of Palestine, Department of Statistics, *Statistical Abstract* (1944–45), pp. 16–17. For the decline in the death rates under the mandate, see pp. 26–28.

12. Metzer and Kaplan, pp. 155–157. The average per capita growth of the Arab economic sector during these years was 3.6% annually. During the same period, the economy of Palestine's Jewish sector grew by a striking 13.2% annually on average; the

average per capita growth was 4.9% annually. There were, however, considerable fluctuations in growth rates during the period, in both sectors; see Metzer and Kaplan, pp. 167–170.

13. Metzer and Kaplan, pp. 159–160. The figures represent the share of employment in agriculture as part of the overall labor force during these years. In terms of production, agriculture in the Arab sector accounted for c. 42% of the total in 1922, declining to c. 39% in 1945.

14. Metzer and Kaplan, passim.

15. In 1925 there were 600 kilometers of paved roads in Palestine, increasing to 2,660 by 1945; Assaf, *ha-Yahasim,* p. 307, quoting a British source.

16. Najjar, pp. 58ff., quoting British documents; *Filastin,* 23 July 1921, p. 1; 1 October 1921, p. 1; *al-Nafa'is al-'Asriyyah,* year 9, issue 4, August 1922, cover page.

17. An ad for oil lamps, said to be "more gentle and prettier" than either gas or electric lamps, appeared in *Filastin,* 14 April 1925, p. 5. Ads for "electric implements" for lighting houses and businesses (residential generators) appeared, e.g., in *Filastin,* 13 February 1923, p. 4; 1 January 1924, p. 4. Shops also sold record players (*gramufunat*) operated manually or by batteries; *al-Nafa'is al-'Asriyyah,* year 9, issue 4, August 1922, p. III; *Filastin,* 20 April 1929, p. 7. See also Roaf, p. 399.

18. *Al-Nafa'is al-'Asriyyah,* year 9, issue 4, August 1922, p. III; *Filastin,* 4 January 1929, p. 3.

19. *Al-Difa',* 31 May 1934, pp. 6, 8; 1 June 1934, p. 4; 25 June 1934, p. 1.

20. See numerous ads in *Filastin* and *al-Difa',* beginning in early October 1935.

21. McCracken, p. 105.

22. The literature here is considerable and constantly increasing. Two volumes reflecting the state of the field in recent years are Cavallo and Chartier, *History,* and Chartier, *Histoires.* See also the opening remarks in Grafton's illuminating article.

23. Allen, passim. Many of the data appear in tables on pp. 38, 50, 59, and in appendices 2–14.

24. Allen, pp. 68–69.

25. Allen, pp. 143–176.

26. Allen, pp. 70–82.

Chapter 1

1. "Mawt al-adab fi filastin," *al-Munadi,* 21 May 1912, quoted in Yehoshu'a, *Ta'rikh al-sihafah . . . fi'l-'ahd al-'uthmani,* pp. 171–172; *Filastin,* 15 July 1911, p. 1; 22 July 1911, p. 1. Similarly, *Filastin,* 2 August 1911, p. 1; *al-Nafa'is al-'Asriyyah,* year 3, September 1911, pp. 377–380; and, sometime later, *Lisan al-'Arab,* 5 November 1921, p. 1; *al-Zahrah,* year 2, issue 9/10, 1922–1923, pp. 211–217.

2. A similar assessment would later be offered by a keen Israeli observer of Arab Palestinian society, Michael Assaf, putting the rate of those able to read in nineteenth-century Palestine at 1–3%; Assaf, *ha-'Aravim tahat ha-tzalbanim,* pp. 250–251.

3. Calculated according to Mills, vol. 1, p. 206; vol. 2, p. 110. The country's sedentary population then was c. 970,000, among them 71% Muslims and 9.5% Christians. The Jewish community in the country, c. 18% of the population at the time, had an overall literacy rate of 86% (men c. 93%, women c. 79%). If we add the all-Muslim nomad popu-

lation to the sedentary Muslim community, the ratio of literate Muslims will decrease to c. 13%; Mills, vol. 1, p. 334; vol. 2, p. 8.

4. Vaschitz, pp. 388–389.

5. Mills, vol. 1, p. 203.

6. Mills, vol. 1, Ibid. p. 205.

7. For a discussion of some of the problematic aspects of "literacy" as a concept, see Street, esp. chaps. 4 and 5; Schofield, pp. 313–314; Jonathan Boyarin, pp. 1ff.; and, more recently, Griffiths, esp. chap. 2; and Henkin, pp. 19–21.

8. Bowman, p. 268.

9. 'Asali, "al-Ta'lim," pp. 19–20. Similarly: Asad, *Ruhi al-khalidi,* pp. 11–12; Qasimiyyah, pp. 11–13; Hammad Husayn, pp. 178–179.

10. This section is based on the following works, among others: Tibawi, *Education;* Miller; Ichilov and Mazawi; Qatshan; Katul; Badran, *al-Ta'lim;* Asad, *Ittijahat;* Mustafa Dabbagh, *Madrasat al-qaryah;* Amin Hafiz al-Dajani; 'Asali, "al-Ta'lim"; Abu Hanna, *Dar al-mu'allimin;* Tuqan; Department of Education files in the ISA; and numerous personal interviews.

11. Tibawi, *Education,* p. 20.

12. For the role of the *madrasah* in the history of Islamic education, see George Makdisi, pp. 27–34 and passim; Berkey, *Transmission,* pp. 6–9 and passim. For its role in Palestine, see Hasan bin 'Abd al-Latif Husayni, pp. 14–63; 'Asali, *Ma'ahid al-'ilm;* 'Asali, *al-Ta'lim,* pp. 12–24; Ghanayim, pp. 267–269.

13. For details on this school, see Strohmeier.

14. Tibawi, *Education,* pp. 20, 270; Asad, *Ittijahat,* pp. 24–25; Ghanayim, pp. 296–297. Slightly different figures are quoted in 'Asali, *al-Ta'lim,* pp. 24–27. See also Husri, pp. 6–8, where he reproduces tables with a breakdown of data by district. The school-age population was assessed at c. 72,000.

15. Husri, pp. 8–9.

16. Data collected by the Palestinian educator Ahmad Samih al-Khalidi for the year 1911 suggest a similar scale—a total of some 17,000 students; quoted by Abcarius, p. 101. Husri (p. 8), relying on official Ottoman sources, gives the total figure of 18,108, not including a few thousand pupils who attended missionary schools. See also Abu Ghazaleh, "Arab Cultural Nationalism," pp. 38–39.

17. A partial list of the most famous of these appears in Qasimiyyah, pp. 32–34.

18. Bowman, p. 268.

19. Tibawi, *Education,* p. 218, quoting British documents. See also Miller, p. 90.

20. Tibawi, *Education,* p. 271; Government of Palestine, Department of Education, *Statistical Tables* (1944–45), tables on pp. 10, 20–23 (including a breakdown by religious denominations), 34.

21. Mills, vol. 1, pp. 203–220; Government of Palestine, Department of Education, *Statistical Tables* (1944–45), tables on pp. 10, 20, 21; Government of Palestine, Department of Statistics, *Statistical Abstract* (1944–45), pp. 185–188; Tibawi, *Education,* pp. 42–46, 227, and tables on pp. 270, 271; Abcarius, pp. 102–103; Vaschitz, pp. 236–244. The data in the various sources differ somewhat, but they all point to basically the same scale.

22. A letter from the village of Madamah to *al-Ittihad,* 23 July 1944, p. 3. See also CO/733/171/2, "Report on Palestine and Trans-Jordan, 1928," p. 47: "Marked enthusiasm for education is shown by many villagers and considerable amounts were collected by voluntary subscriptions to put up new or repair existing school buildings."

23. Report by the acting director of education, dated 1 September 1945–ISA/E/29/45.

24. Abcarius, p. 101.

25. A statistical survey for 1944–1945 still notes the existence of "a considerable number of *kuttabs*." Government of Palestine, Department of Statistics, *Statistical Abstract* (1944–45), p. 192. The report also indicates that "the standard in these remains low."

26. *Zawiyyah*—usually a Sufi gathering place, used for prayer and often also for instruction. This might suggest a Sufi context in this case.

27. Darwazah, pp. 145–146.

28. For some examples, see Niqula Khuri, p. 64 (reference to *kuttab* in Bir Zayt, the 1890s); Jirjis al-Khuri al-Maqdisi, pp. 747–748 (late nineteenth century, Syria/Palestine—location not mentioned); 'Abd al-Qadir al-Salih, p. 20 (Talfit, late Ottoman years); Aburish, pp. 131–132 (Bituniyya, late Ottoman years); Harb, p. 17 (Ramallah, around 1900); Shuqayri, pp. 21–23 (Tulkarm, around 1910); Husni al-Salih, pp. 5–6 (Tarshihah, mid-1910s); 'Abd al-Ra'uf Rimawi, pp. 150–53 (Dayr Ghasanah, 1918); Haykal, pp. 13–22 (Jaffa, 1910s); Sukayik, pp. 12–20 (Gaza, around 1920); Faysal Hurani, pp. 12–13 (Masmiyyat Hurani, early mandate years); 'Abd al-Rahim, pp. 22–24 (Nahaf, early 1930s); Muhammad Rimawi, pp. 191–228 (Kafr Rima, 1930s); Qadi, pp. 13–14 (Bayt Surif, 1930s); interview with Hanna Abu Hanna (Isdud, 1930s); Gorkin and Othman, pp. 109–110 (Qabu, early 1940s).

29. Cf. descriptions of similar systems in Yemen, in Messick, chap. 4; and in Morocco, in Eickelman, pp. 50–51, 65–66, 98–101.

30. Goldziher, pp. 201–202, quoting many such sayings, some of which (including the ones cited here) he ascribes to the ninth-century scholar Jahiz. I owe this reference to Prof. Michael Winter. For an instance of this in Palestine, see Kayyali, pp. 42–43. Kayyali, a graduate of the Teachers' College in Jerusalem around 1920, complained that upon returning to his hometown Majdal, he was jeered by local residents for the "disgraceful" career he had chosen. They greeted him with these proverbs.

31. Tamimi and Bahjat, p. 237.

32. Jirjis al-Khuri al-Maqdisi, pp. 747–748.

33. Niqula Khuri, p. 64.

34. Sukayik, pp. 12–14.

35. Sukayik, pp. 14–20; interview with Hanna Abu Hanna.

36. Seyyed Hossein Nasr, p. 65. "Scripture is meant to be recited, memorized and repeated; it is meant to be listened to, mediated upon, and internalized. It is written word that is spoken"; Graham, p. 27 and passim. Similarly, see Daniel Boyarin; Baker, pp. 102–104. We shall return to this important issue in Chapter 5 below.

37. See descriptions in Darwazah, pp. 145, 150; Sukayik, pp. 18–19; Salah, pp. 10–11; Kanafani, pp. 46–47; Abu Hanna, *Zill al-ghaymah*, pp. 40–41.

38. Sukayik, p. 19.

39. See Edward Lane's account from Egypt in the 1830s, of the shaykh who became a school headmaster even though he could neither read nor write. He would rely on the *'arif*, pretending that his eyes were too weak. Lane, pp. 62–63.

40. For a discussion of this point with regard to Qur'an learning in Indonesia, see Baker.

41. Jabra, p. 56. Cf. Street, pp. 132–158, where the author discusses this point in the context of education in the Iranian *maktab* (the equivalent of *kuttab*).

42. See also the persuasive study by Scribner and Cole, who have shown how, in a Liberian society whose spoken language is Vai but where some Arabic is also taught, people were able to read only certain Arabic texts presented to them in a familiar context, but nothing else. Paul Saenger, a leading historian of reading, has termed this type of skill "phonetic literacy," i.e., the capacity "to decode texts syllable by syllable and to pronounce them orally" but without comprehending their meaning; he distinguishes this from "comprehensive literacy," which he defines as permitting both decoding and understanding. Saenger, "Books of Hours," p. 142.

43. Nor is there necessary interdependence between reading and writing abilities. One can command the one without knowing the other. See, e.g., Sukayik, p. 17, where the author depicts training in writing, emulating the shaykh's example in producing lines that were "beyond our minds' grasp and understanding." This point, however, is beyond our concern here.

44. Tibawi, *Education,* p. 74.

45. Zu'bi, p. 7. Similarly, interview with Yunus al-'Azzi.

46. Sukayik, pp. 17–18.

47. Niqula al-Khuri, *Mudhakkirat,* pp. 63–64.

48. Abu Hanna, *Zill al-ghaymah,* p. 47, and interview with Hanna Abu Hanna.

49. Darwazah, pp. 147–149. Darwazah was a student in that school from 1895 to 1898.

50. Madrasat rawdat al-ma'arif, *Barnamaj* (1912), p. 2. The Lebanese-Egyptian writer Jurji Zaydan visited Palestine in 1914 and painted a rather bleak picture of the state of education there; *al-Hilal,* 1 May 1914, pp. 603–604.

51. See Tibawi, *Education,* pp. 218–219.

52. Diagram in Tibawi, *Education,* p. 44.

53. Hukumat Filastin, idarat al-ma'arif al-'umumiyyah, *Manhaj al-dirasah,* pp. 3–10.

54. Tibawi, *Education,* pp. 77–99. Books and libraries will be discussed further in the next two chapters.

55. E.g., Newton, pp. 29–30; Darwazah, pp. 149–150; Tamimi and Bahjat, pp. 237, 384–385; Ziyadah, vol. 1, pp. 41ff., 101; *Mir'at al-Sharq,* 3 December 1921, p. 1; *Filastin,* 3 November 1922, p. 2; 1 November 1924, p. 3; Jabra, pp. 28–32, 51, 52, 54.

56. E.g., Kanafani, pp. 45–46 (Haifa, the early 1930s); Muhammad Rimawi, pp. 191–228 (Kafr Rima, the 1930s and 1940s). Tibawi's *Education* abounds with examples (and criticism) of the deficiencies of education under the mandate.

57. Mustafa Dabbagh, pp. 4–5, 50. Dabbagh was an educator and inspector in the villages, and his book lays out comprehensive guidelines for conducting village schools. See also Tannous.

58. Details in Qatshan, pp. 83ff.

59. Miller, pp. 90ff.; 'Abd al-Ra'uf Rimawi; *al-Kulliyyah al-'Arabiyyah,* 15 December 1932, pp. 67–68; *al-Ittihad,* 23 July 1944, p. 3.

60. For a lively account of the experience of village boys commuting on foot to the nearby town school, see Abu Hanna, *Zill al-ghaymah,* pp. 176–177. Similarly, *al-Ittihad,* 23 July 1944, p. 3. In the late years of the mandate, guesthouses were opened in some towns to accommodate village students who came to study in them; Qadi, pp. 13–14; interviews with Hanna Abu Hanna (for Nazareth), Prof. Butrus Abu Manneh (for Lydda), Yunus al-'Azzi (for Masmiyyah), and 'Abd al-Hamid Abu Laban (for Falujah and Gaza).

61. Mustafa Dabbagh, pp. 4–5.

62. See, e.g., Hukumat Filastin, idarat al-maʿarif, *Manhaj al-taʿlim al-ibtidaʾi fi madaris al-qura*, pp. 2–3 and passim.

63. *Al-Zamr*, 16 July 1925, p. 3.

64. For a comparable situation in England throughout much of the nineteenth century, see Horn, esp. pp. 115–150. For England and France, see Lyons, pp. 324–327. For Russia, see Brooks, pp. 3–4, 43–45 and passim.

65. Mudawwar, p. 85.

66. CO/733/171/2, "Report on Palestine and Trans-Jordan, 1928," p. 47.

67. Faysal al-Hurani, p. 191, describing the situation in Masmiyyat Hurani in the 1940s.

68. In a report of the Department of Education for 1932–1933, for example, the number of pupils in all village schools was 4,392 in first-grade classes, but only 2,331 in fourth-grade classes; Mustafa Dabbagh, p. 70.

69. Qadi, p. 13.

70. For a discussion of this point, an account of tests that were conducted in this regard, and criticism leveled at the British administration for its alleged failure to assure permanent literacy in the villages, see Tibawi, *Education*, pp. 218–224; Qatshan, pp. 77–83. See also Katul, p. 8; Mustafa Dabbagh, p. 70.

71. Government of Palestine, Department of Education, *Statistical Tables* (1944–45), tables on pp. 34, 35; Abu Ghazaleh, "Arab Cultural Nationalism," p. 39.

72. Newton, p. 30.

73. According to Tibawi, *Education*, table on p. 270, a total of 1,400 girls attended girls' state schools in 1914. Ichilov and Mazawi (p. 10) report more than 5,600 girls in French schools in Palestine for the year 1912.

74. "Umm Mahmud," interviewed in Gorkin and Othman, pp. 18–19.

75. "Umm Khalid," interviewed in Gorkin and Othman, p. 163. For a different and exceptional attitude—an ʿalim from Nablus who in the 1930s sent his daughter to acquire education—see Salah, pp. 7–11.

76. Mudawwar, pp. 84–85.

77. Tibawi, *Education*, table on p. 270.

78. Government of Palestine, Department of Education, *Statistical Tables* (1944–45), tables on pp. 20, 21, 34, 35.

79. Madrasat al-banat al-islamiyyah, *Barnamaj*, introduction. See also Miller, pp. 102–108.

80. Tuqan, pp. 51–53, 74–75.

81. For example, in 1944–1945, as against an average of 38 pupils per teacher in state schools, the average in private Christian schools was 18; and as against a little less than 4 teachers per state school on average, the average in the private Christian schools was a little more than 8. Government of Palestine, Department of Education, *Statistical Tables* (1944–45), tables on pp. 20, 21, 34, 35.

82. Ichilov and Mazawi. For the curriculum see chap. 5. For the social composition see tables on pp. 87 and 90.

83. For similar descriptions, see, e.g., Toubbeh, pp. 65–80 (Catholic schools in Jerusalem); Haykal, pp. 11–12 (Catholic school in Jaffa); Vatikiotis, pp. 23, 26–27 (Greek-Orthodox school in Haifa).

84. Mustafa Dabbagh, p. 50. With comparable optimism, Dabbagh also exhorted village teachers to seek integration of the villagers in the educational activity, to play an active

role in adult education, and to disseminate books from the school library so as to "accustom [the villagers] to useful reading"; pp. 112–113.

85. Miller, pp. 97–98.

Chapter 2

1. The literature on Islamic libraries is extensive. One systematic study of the subject is by Eche. See also Sibai; Ibn Dohaish; Pinto; Chamberlain, pp. 133ff.; Kohlberg, pp. 71–74; Heffening and Pearson; Pedersen and Makdisi (esp. section 3).

2. Kohlberg, passim. For a few other examples of such collections see Crecelius; Haarmann; ʿAtallah, *al-Maktabah al-jawhariyyah;* ʿAtallah, *Maktabat aal al-qamhawi;* ʿAtallah, *Makhtutat aal tuffahah;* Salamah, *Maktabat al-masjid al-aqsa;* Salamah, *al-Maktabah al-budayriyyah.*

3. Shaykh Muhammad al-Khalili, owner of an important collection in eighteenth-century Jerusalem, quoted in ʿAsali, *Maʿahid al-ʿilm,* p. 374. Similarly ʿAsali, "Maktabat," p. 292; Sibai, chap. 6; Kurd ʿAli, pp. 196–200; Salamah, *al-Maktaba al-budayriyya,* vol. 1, pp. 3–4; Volney, pp. 261–263; Raghib al-Khalidi in two articles in *Filastin,* 19 July 1911, p. 1, and 22 July 1911, p. 1.

4. Russell, pp. 94–95. Russell was a British resident physician in Aleppo at the time. I am indebted to Yaron Ayalon for drawing my attention to this work.

5. Details in Kurd ʿAli, pp. 200–202; Husayni, *Tarajim ahl al-quds,* pp. 71–77; Salamah, *al-Maktabah al-budayriyyah,* vol. 1, pp. 6–13; ʿAsali, *Maʿahid al-ʿilm,* pp. 388–392; Qasimiyyah, pp. 37–42; introduction section in the following catalogues by ʿAtallah: *Maktabat aal al-qamhawi, Maktabat masjid al-hajj nimr,* and *Maktabat al-haram al-ibrahimi.*

6. ʿArif, *al-Mufassal,* pp. 449–450; Tarrazi, *Khazaʾin,* vol. 1, pp. 293–296.

7. ʿAtallah, *Maktabat al-haram al-ibrahimi,* p. 5. Arab authors normally employ the same term, *maktabah,* for both private stocks of books and public libraries, thereby introducing much ambiguity into their discussion of the subject.

8. Interview with Muhammad ʿAql.

9. Almost all sources mention 1900 as the opening year, and the library's printed catalogue indicates on its front cover that it was "established in Holy Jerusalem in the Hijri year 1318," corresponding to 1900. In a recent study, however, Lawrence Conrad presents clues which seem to suggest that the library may have been opened to the public several years earlier. Conrad, p. 198.

10. The most comprehensive study of the Khalidiyyah is Conrad's, on which the present discussion is primarily based. The library's printed catalogue of 1900 is *Barnamaj al-maktabah al-khalidiyyah.* On p. 78 it is indicated that many items in the collection had been left out of the catalogue for a variety of reasons. See also Mukhlis; Kurd ʿAli, pp. 200–201; Tarrazi, *Khazaʾin,* vol. 1, pp. 142–143; Conrad and Kellner-Heinkele; Ajami; Rashid Khalidi, pp. 43–46, 54–55.

11. Conrad and Kellner-Heinkele, pp. 292–293, and personal correspondence with L. Conrad.

12. *Barnamaj al-maktabah al-khalidiyya,* pp. 55–57.

13. Conrad and Kellner-Heinkele, pp. 292–293; Rashid Khalidi, pp. 44–45, 54. On the journals in the collection see further below.

14. Calculation based on Tarrazi, *Ta'rikh al-sihafah,* vol. 4, pp. 4–10, 106–110.

15. Nusayr, pp. 53–98.

16. Calculation based on Tarrazi, *Ta'rikh al-sihafah,* vol. 4, pp. 162–190, 212–224. Tarrazi's lists are not entirely devoid of errors, but are amply adequate for a sense of scale. The circulation figure is from *al-Hilal,* October 1897, p. 131, and is likewise approximate rather than precise.

17. Rashid Khalidi, p. 54, and note 62 on p. 227.

18. For details see Rashid Khalidi, pp. 54–55 and p. 227, note 63. See also Conrad and Salameh, pp. 574–575.

19. The data in this paragraph are based on findings elaborated in Ayalon, "Modern Texts."

20. "It is a great shame," one Palestinian intellectual charged in 1912, "that the number of readers of the scientific *al-Muqtataf,* the historic *al-Hilal* or the scholarly *al-Muqtabas* [a literary monthly from Damascus] does not exceed ten in each of the Palestinian towns"—a pessimistic estimate, if not quite far-fetched. Yehoshu'a, *Ta'rikh al-sihafah . . . fi'l-'ahd al-'uthmani,* pp. 171–172, quoting the editor of *al-Munadi,* 21 May 1912.

21. Asad, *Khalil baydas,* p. 11; Yehoshu'a, *Ta'rikh al-sihafah . . . fi'l-'ahd al-'uthmani,* pp. 85, 100, 168–169, 170; Yehoshu'a, "Nitzanei 'itonut," pp. 144–145; Nimr, p. 19; Darwazah, pp. 177, 179; Shumali, *Ittijahat,* p. 26; Rashid Khalidi, p. 54. See also note 23 below.

22. Ayalon, "Modern Texts," pp. 22–24.

23. In Yarka, a passage in the "incomes and expenses" record of the village *khilwah* (praying house) attests, somewhat more vaguely, to a spending in 1882 of 86 qurush for "the *kazitah*" (gazette). I am grateful to Mr. 'Ali Zghayyir from Yarka for providing me with copies of these documents. The 'Ar'arah document is from the private archive of Dr. Muhammad 'Aql of that village, to whom I am likewise grateful.

24. Details in Asad, *Ittijahat,* p. 42; *al-Kitab al-'arabi al-filastini,* passim; Khatib, appendix.

25. Centre d'études de politique étrangère, pp. 400, 415–416.

26. Mustafa, pp. 98–105.

27. *Al-Nafa'is,* 9 August 1922, p. 111; *Filastin,* 19 April 1929, p. 2; *al-Ittihad,* 17 December 1944, p. 4.

28. Snubar, p. 13; Ziyadah, vol. 1, pp. 90, 183 (Ziyadah first became acquainted with *al-Muqtataf* when he took his entry exam for the Teachers Seminar, in 1921); Yusuf, *Shay',* p. 26; 'Abbas, pp. 92–93; similarly, Haykal, pp. 124, 196–197.

29. HA/96/13, p. 5.

30. Details in Sulayman, *al-Sihafah al-filastiniyyah wa-qawanin al-intidab,* pp. 93–105.

31. Sawafiri, p. 70. See also: Asad, *Ittijahat,* pp. 53–54; Shumali, *Ittijahat,* pp. 94ff.; Yusuf, *Khamsun 'am^{an},* p. 14; Tuqan, pp. 80–81, 88–91; Buri and Shibl, pp. 105–106.

32. Examples and discussion in Shumali, *Ittijahat,* pp. 94ff.

33. Asad, *Ittijahat,* pp. 53–54.

34. *Al-Hilal* 1928, March, p. 633; May, p. 887; June, p. 1016; July, p. 1143; August, p. 1247; December, p. 248.

35. E.g., *al-Hilal,* December 1921, p. 280; January 1922, p. 379; June 1922, p. 877; August 1927, p. 1273; December 1927, p. 247; December 1936, pp. 236, 238; January 1937, p. 358.

36. Sawafiri, p. 70. Sawafiri mentions the following writers: Is'af al-Nashashibi, Ahmad Samih al-Khalidi, Qadri Hafiz Tuqan, 'Adil Zu'aytar, Khayri Hammad, 'Ali Sirtawi, Najati Sidqi, Hamdi al-Husayni, Hilmi al-Idrisi, and Muhammad al-Bustami. The poets he mentions are 'Abd al-Karim Karmi, Muhammad 'Adnani, 'Abd al-Rahim Mahmud, and Fadwa Tuqan. See also Tuqan, pp. 88–89, 110–112. *Al-Risalah* was launched in Cairo in 1933 by Ahmad Hasan al-Zayyat. Sawafiri himself also wrote for the Lebanese *al-Adib,* begun in 1942, as did Ishaq Musa al-Husayni, Ahmad Samih al-Khalidi, and Mahmud Sayf al-Din al-Irani.

37. See the section entitled *athar adabiyyah* in the journal. E.g.: year 3, 1911—issue 1, pp. 46, 47; issue 2, p. 96; issue 8, p. 376; issue 10, p. 472; issue 12, p. 567.

38. E.g., year 9, 1922, issue 4, pp. 49–50, 111, 135, 137, 138.

39. Such references appeared in almost every issue of the 1921–1922 volume.

40. Yusuf, *Khamsun 'am^{an},* pp. 18–21. Yusuf's business is discussed further in the next chapter.

41. *Filastin,* 5 February 1929, literary section on p. 7. Similarly *Bayt Lahm,* June 1920, pp. 78, 80; November 1920, p. 239; *al-Jazirah,* 26 February 1925, p. 4; 9 March 1925, p. 4; 2 April 1925, p. 4; *al-Ittihad al-'Arabi,* 18 July 1925, p. 4.

42. E.g., *al-Zahrah* 2, no. 6, 1922–1923, p. 160.

43. E.g., *Filastin,* 25 January 1924, p. 4; *al-Difa',* 25 June 1934, p. 1.

44. Sawafiri, pp. 70–71; Abu Ghazaleh, *Arab Cultural Nationalism,* pp. 91–92; Yusuf, *Khamsun 'am^{an},* p. 30; Dajani, *Jabhat al-tarbiyyah,* p. 99.

45. Sawafiri, pp. 71–72; Ziyadah, vol. 1, p. 183; Haykal, pp. 123–124, 137–138. See also Asad, *Ittijahat,* pp. 53–54.

46. Tuqan, p. 80.

47. The stock was stored in a container on the premises of the Jaffa Orthodox community. It included many hundreds of books and bound journal volumes that had been collected by the Israeli authorities in 1948, mostly from communal libraries in that city. Torrential rains in winter 2002 badly damaged the entire collection. I am grateful to Sami Abu Shihadah, who arranged for me and a group of students to inspect the books before they were ruined.

48. For a partial list of such visits, see Sawafiri, pp. 71–72; see also Asad, *Ittijahat,* pp. 53–54; Haykal, pp. 161–164.

49. Palestine [Mandatory Government], *Blue Book 1929,* pp. 225, 230, 235, 300; *Blue Book 1936,* p. 301.

50. HA/96/13, p. 1. The figures were quoted by Moshe Shertok (later Sharet). David Siton, a Jewish journalist in Jerusalem in the 1930s and 1940s, noted that Egyptian dailies were sold in the country in "thousands of copies," as were Egyptian periodicals—a sweeping and quite likely inflated appraisal; Siton, p. 161.

51. Shim'oni, pp. 396–398. Vaschitz, p. 279, noted that books from that series were read in Palestine of the 1940s "in hundred of copies." For the relatively low price of items from this series, see next chapter.

52. Non-Muslim minorities—Jews, Greeks, Armenians—were allowed to use printing in their own languages, but not in the languages of Islam, Arabic, and Turkish. The literature on the beginning of printing in the Middle East is extensive and growing. For recent studies on the subject, see issue no. 16 of *Culture and History* (Oslo, 1997), based on papers from a conference on the subject, and the volume edited by Hanebutt-Benz, Glass, and Roper.

53. Jbarah's bibliography of Arabic publications in Palestine includes as many as 65 works which the Franciscans printed prior to 1900 and another 51 between 1900 and 1948. The Jbarah bibliography is discussed later on in this chapter.

54. An official Ottoman document from 1898 mentions the existence of private Arabic printing shops in the narrow alleys of Jerusalem, Jaffa, and Haifa. Having searched for evidence on them for many years, Muhammad Sulayman, a Palestinian scholar, has recently noted that "extensive toiling and all forms of exploring and inquiring" has yielded no clue on such places, save for some fragmentary references to a few small presses in Jerusalem. Sulayman, "al-Matabi'," pp. 77–78. See also note 58 below.

55. Al-Quds, 5–18 September 1908, quoted in Sulayman, "al-Matabi'," p. 82.

56. Al-Quds, 18 September 1908, quoted by Yehoshu'a, Ta'rikh al-sihafah . . . fi'l-'ahd al-'uthmani, pp. 41–43.

57. Jbarah's bibliography—the fullest we have at our disposal (though certainly incomplete)—lists only 5 works printed in Hananiyya's press, none of them prior to 1900; Jbarah, passim.

58. For the evolution of Arabic printing in Palestine, see Sabat, pp. 299–304; Yehoshu'a, Ta'rikh al-sihafah . . . fi'l-'ahd al-'uthmani, pp. 7–13, 41–43; Sulayman, "al-Matabi'," pp. 76–84. Sulayman also mentions (on p. 82) three other private presses which operated briefly in Jerusalem between 1892 and 1894, of which little is known beyond their names. By his count (p. 84), no fewer than 11 printing presses were opened in Jerusalem during the last quarter of the nineteenth century. On Hananiyya see further in Mana', p. 89.

59. Sulayman, Ta'rikh al-sihafah, pp. 83–84.

60. Al-Akhbar, 19 September 1919; 24 December 1919, p. 4.

61. Al-Karmil, 19 November 1920, p. 4.

62. Al-Yarmuk, 30 April 1925, p. 3.

63. Mir'at al-Sharq, 23 June 1920, p. 4; 28 July 1921, p. 1.

64. E.g., al-Akhbar, 13 September 1919, p. 3; Mir'at al-Sharq, 25 March 1921, p. 4; al-Yarmuk, 21 September 1924, p. 4; 18 January 1925, p. 4; 30 April 1925, p. 4; al-Jazirah, 2 February 1925, p. 4; al-Zamr, 9 July 1925, p. 2; 1 April 1926, p. 4; 28 October 1926, p. 4.

65. Filastin, 2 April 1929, p. 1. Similarly, al-Jazirah, 29 April 1926, p. 4.

66. The history of the Palestinian press is laid out in detail in Yehoshu'a's three volumes. See also Yusuf Khuri; Sulayman, Ta'rikh; 'Aqqad; Najjar; and Kabhah. A more concise survey appears in Ayalon, The Press, pp. 65–69, 95–101.

67. For a more detailed discussion of the economic angle, see Ayalon, The Press, pp. 195–202, 216–230.

68. For the timidity of the press under 'Abd al-Hamid, see Ayalon, The Press, pp. 113–115.

69. Yehoshu'a, Ta'rikh al-sihafah . . . fi'l-'ahd al-'uthmani, p. 104. Al-Quds printed close to 1,500 copies and al-Nafa'is al-'Asriyyah ca. 1,800, but both also circulated out of Palestine (as well as beyond the Middle East)—Yehoshu'a, Ta'rikh al-sihafah . . . fi'l-'ahd al-'uthmani, pp. 44, 96; al-Nafa'is al-'Asriyyah, year 3, issue 1, January 1911, p. 1. The Jaffa-based Filastin, which may have been the country's most popular newspaper before the First World War, claimed having 1,121 subscribers in 1912 (Filastin, 18 December 1912, p. 3), a figure to be taken with caution.

70. Malul, p. 449.

71. The Arab population of Palestine grew during this period from c. 600,000 to c. 850,000. For the British appraisal of press circulation in 1929, see Palestine [Mandatory

Government], *Blue Book 1929*, p. 159. The figure quoted refers to leading newspapers only; the total circulation of all newspapers in the country was bigger. For comparison, in Syria, with its equally stormy public life, per capita newspaper consumption reached roughly the same rate as in Palestine: c. 33,000 copies with a population of c. 2.2 million in 1930. In Iraq the figure was far smaller until mid-century and beyond—perhaps half the rate of Palestine and Syria—for various political and cultural reasons. See Ayalon, *The Press*, pp. 84ff., 92–95, 151, 153.

72. *Mir'at al-Sharq*, 1 October 1924, p. 3. Such notices became very common after the First World War. For a few more examples, see 30 September 1921, p. 6; 15 October 1921, p. 5; 28 August 1922, p. 4; 20 September 1924, p. 3; 1 October 1924, pp. 3, 4; *Lisan al-ʿArab*, 10 March 1922, p. 3; 11 July 1925, p. 5; *al-Zamr*, 29 January 1925, p. 4; 18 February 1926, p. 3; *al-Yarmuk*, 16 March 1927, p. 3; 1 April 1928, p. 3; *al-Jamiʿah al-ʿArabiyyah*, 16 January 1928, p. 3; 23 January 1928, p. 4; 19 April 1928, p. 3.

73. Aba Hushi, in a meeting of the political committee of Mapai (the Jewish Labor Party), July 1936; HA/96/13, p. 8.

74. For an extensive discussions of this role, see Najjar and Kabha.

75. Assessments for the 1930s in Arnon-Ohana, *Herev mi-bayit*, pp. 200–201; Assaf, *ha-Yahasim*, p. 284; CZA/25/22760. For the 1940s, see Shimʿoni, pp. 403–414; Abu Ghazaleh, "Arab Cultural Nationalism," p. 56.

76. In the case of Christian societies printing their own tracts, however, the operation was somewhat more akin to a publishing enterprise.

77. During the period from 1900 to 1948, according to Jbarah's Palestinian bibliography (see below), 123 books and other items were printed in *matbaʿat bayt al-maqdis*, at least 99 in *matbaʿat dar al-aytam*, 51 in the Franciscan press, 33 in *al-matbaʿah al-tijariyyah*, 18 in *al-matbaʿah al-ʿasriyyah*, and at least 16 in *matbaʿat al-ʿarab*, in Jerusalem; 10 in *matbaʿat filastin al-jadidah* in Jaffa; at least 29 in *matbaʿat al-zahrah* in Haifa, and 18 in *al-matbaʿah al-wataniyyah* in Acre. Jbarah, passim. See also note 86 below.

78. *Al-Kitab al-ʿarabi*, and Jbarah, *al-Biblyughrafiya* (both discussed below). For a short but solid survey, see Shimʿoni, pp. 396–403.

79. Mills, vol. 1, pp. 214, 219.

80. Ishaq Musa al-Husayni, pp. 37–40. Husayni also provides a detailed table by topic for the years 1938 and 1939: in 1938, 15 items were published, including 8 schoolbooks; in 1939, 12 items, including 5 schoolbooks.

81. For example, for the year 1926 Husayni indicates a total of 7 books, as against 17 recorded in the government's annual report for that year; and for 1936 he indicates 12, while the official publication puts it at 39; quoted in Tibawi, *Education*, p. 98. The data in the official publications, however, included not only textbooks but apparently also pamphlets. For the year 1928, Husayni indicates only 4 books, while a report in *Filastin* (6 June 1929, p. 5) mentions a total of 18 Arabic books published in that year.

82. Vaschitz, p. 277; Assaf, *ha-Yahasim*, pp. 276–277; Shimʿoni, p. 398.

83. Khatib, appendix. See also lists in Sawafiri, pp. 96, 283, 290, 301, 312, 317, 334, 364, 376.

84. *Al-Kitab al-ʿarabi*, pp. 3–4. The introduction was written by Ishaq Musa al-Husayni, committee secretary. On the committee, see Ziyadah, vol. 2, p. 62.

85. Other places were Damascus, Amman, Baghdad, Sidon, Mecca, Istanbul, Tripoli, Qazan, and locations in Europe and the United States.

86. The list also features some 30–40 items authored by Jewish individuals or insti-

tutions and printed in Jewish presses. These are not included in the statistics presented below.

87. Interview with Jbarah. The bibliography is a part of Jbarah's personal and ambitious project to build a collection comprising everything ever printed in Palestine. I am grateful to him for allowing me to study this impressive collection and his draft bibliography. Of the 962 items, 673 (70%) were printed in Jerusalem, 112 in Haifa, 103 in Jaffa, 33 in Acre, 5 in Nazareth, 4 in Nablus, and 9 in Bethlehem, Safad, Hebron Gaza, Ramallah, and Lydda (1 or 2 in each). For another 23, no place of publication is given.

88. Assaf, *ha-Yahasim*, pp. 276–277.

89. Ishaq Musa al-Husayni, p. 37. Husayni ascribes this sad situation in the book market to widespread illiteracy: "The rate of the educated in our country is no higher than a fifth or a quarter [of the population] at most. The rate of those educated enough to fathom their rights and duties is still less. We are, then, only a quarter of a nation, or even a fifth or sixth of it . . . How many writers can [such a small segment] produce? How many books can it yield annually? And how many copies of such books can be sold in a stagnant market?" (pp. 36–37).

90. For a recent intriguing study of the subject, see Henkin, especially chaps. 3 and 4.

91. Photographers of the period were often interested in capturing the view of holy sites, of which they sometimes had a prior image. They, and perhaps others who sought to highlight the country's "exotic" face, may have been careful to avoid such mundane items as written signs so as not to "contaminate" the authentic timeless scene.

92. Schiller and Levin, p. 98 (a photograph by Bonfils from 1875. Bonfils was the most famous photographer of Palestine and of adjacent countries in the late nineteenth and early twentieth centuries); Schiller, *Tsilumey yerushalayim*, p. 29 (showing the gate in 1870, without the "Cook" sign); Schiller, *Yerushalayim, halifot u-tmurot*, p. 16; *In Arab Lands*, picture 15; Landau, p. 41; Gidal, p. 102, picture 62 (picture 63, of a somewhat later time, also shows a nearby shop with a board in Greek); Osman, p. 53; CZA/PHG/2259.

93. Gilbert, p. 163, a picture from the 1880s; Zacharia, p. 96, produces a similar view with a somewhat different text, taken in 1905.

94. Matson, vol. 1, pp. 4, 74; Landau, p. 41; Schiller and Levin, p. 114; Schiller, *Tsilumey yerushalayim*, pp. 33, 34, 35; Schiller, *Yerushalayim, halifot u-tmurot*, p. 14; Gilbert, p. 147; Faber et al., p. 13; Hummel, pp. 260–262, 267, 272; Osman, pp. 41, 42, 54; CZA/PHG/22850, CZA/PHG/12779. For pictures from the same neighborhood taken after the turn of the century, see Farkash, p. 30; Zacharia, pp. 42, 99.

95. E.g., Landau, p. 54; Schiller and Levin, p. 145; Gidal, p. 105, picture 68; Zacharia, pp. 102, 104; CZA/PHG/17438/1, CZA/PHG/19433/1, CZA/PHG/19433/2, CZA/PHG/12905; HA, pictures 3102, 8708.

96. Faber et al., pp. 75–76; Farkash, p. 73; Landauer, p. 94; photographs from the CZA showing streets in Jaffa around 1912, nos. PHG/2512, PHG/3198/1, PHG/3198/2, PHG/3211/1, PHG/3211/2, PHG/3211/3, PHG/3216/2, PHG/3635; similarly HA, pictures 3896, 8714. The photographic collection of the Central Zionist Archive contains hundreds of items showing streets scenes from Palestinian towns (Jerusalem, Jaffa, Haifa, Nablus, Habron, Nazareth, Bethlehem, Acre) in the late nineteenth and early twentieth centuries. Written signs are visible only in a handful of them.

97. E.g., Schiller, *Tsilumey yerushalayim*, pp. 158, 159; Schiller and Levin, p. 209; Gilbert, p. 107; Landau, pp. 54–55; Zacharia, picture on the book's front cover; CZA/PHG/2891.

98. Ayalon, *The Press,* pp. 166–173.

99. Gidal, p. 88, picture 48. See also Conrad, p. 203.

100. E.g., CZA/PHG/15173, CZA/PHG/3478, CZA/PHG/20662, all showing the sign "Palestine Flour Mills" in Haifa, in 1912 and later, with signs in English, French, and Arabic; CZA/PHG/26734, showing signs on stores in a Jaffa street in 1912, some of them in Arabic.

101. E.g., Walid Khalidi, p. 100, picture 90; p. 109, picture 109; p. 151, picture 188; Diyab and Sharabi, pp. 81, 156, 192, 194–195; Yusuf, *Khamsun ʿamᵃⁿ,* p. 19; HA, picture 3869.

102. Diyab and Sharabi, p. 194, and similarly p. 81; HA, picture 1582.

103. Walid Khalidi, p. 95, picture 82. Similarly p. 103, picture 97; p. 104, picture 98; p. 322, picture 389. Banners with inscriptions identifying groups and organizations appeared in the 1918 Nabi Musa festival in Jerusalem—HA, pictures 1299, 1301. See also HA/80/145/13 (report from 9 March 1920); CZA/J1/300 (a report from 2 November 1929 indicating the use of flags and collar badges); CZA photographs nos. PHG/11405, PHG/11406, PHG/11407/1, and PHG/11407/2 (written banners from the 1935 Nabi Musa parade); Diyab and Sharabi, p. 102 (banners on a Jaffa store in 1936 reading "Long live free Arab Palestine").

104. *Al–Jamiʿah al-ʿArabiyyah,* 9 April 1928, p. 4.

105. See, e.g., Jouhaud, pp. 235–238, discussing the impact of placards in sixteenth-century France.

106. Jabarti, *Taʾrikh muddat al-faransi,* pp. 53, 64, 66 of the Arabic text. See also Sawi, pp. 36–37, 73. The French may well have been the first to introduce this practice into the region. It remains to be explored whether local rulers adopted it subsequently.

107. Antonius, pp. 79–84; Tauber, pp. 16–20, 315 (who also mentions the appearance of such manifestoes in Baghdad, in the summer of 1881); see also Jouhaud, pp. 235–238. Butrus Dalleh, a fairly knowledgeable source from Kafr Yasif, has claimed in an interview that similar activities took place in northern Palestinian towns such as Haifa, Acre, and Tiberias. I could not find evidence to corroborate this.

108. Darwazah, pp. 216–217.

109. Ghuri, p. 18.

110. Musa, p. 81; Tibawi, *Anglo-Arab Relations,* p. 166.

111. WO/157/728/144888.

112. Interview with Butrus Dalleh, and similarly with Musa Basal, Hanna Abu Hanna, and Iliyas Hamati. See also Sakakini, p. 138; CZA/S25/227954 (letter from 13 June 1936); CZA/S25/22741 (report from 24 June 1936); Arnon-Ohana, *Falahim,* pp. 64–65; *Thawrat filastin ʿam* 1936, p. 174; Abu Hanna, *Zill al-ghaymah,* pp. 141–142.

113. CZA/S25/3437 and CZA/J1/300. A great number and variety of such printed announcements are kept in the Central Zionist Archive in Jerusalem, often with a description of the manner in which they were distributed. In addition to the two files quoted above, see CZA files J1/204, J1/311, S25/9358, S25/22191, and S25/22207. Similarly, HA/80/145/11 (report from 3 July 1920) and HA/80/145/12 (reports from 4, 12, and 14 July 1920); HA/80/145/13 (reports from 7 March and May 1920); HA/80/145/15 (report from 3 June 1920). See also Porat, p. 63; ʿAql, p. 28; ʿAbbas, p. 96; Arnon-Ohana, *Herev mi-bayit,* pp. 286–287, 300–302; Arnon-Ohana, *Falahim,* p. 176; and interview with Hanna Abu Hanna.

114. FO/371/45422, report by the Public Information Office (PIO) in Jerusalem, 1945.

Chapter 3

1. Tarrazi, *Khaza'in*, vol. 3, pp. 909–917.

2. For the use of this method and the difficulties it involved during the early decades of the Arab press, see Ayalon, *The Press*, pp. 206–211.

3. *Hadiqat al-Akhbar*, 10 May 1858, p. 1; *al-Ahram*, 5 August 1876, p. 4.

4. Ayalon, "Modern Texts," pp. 22–24.

5. Fyfe, p. 114; *Lisan al-ʿArab* (Damascus), 21 October 1918, p. 4.

6. Yehoshuʿa, *Ta'rikh al-sihafah . . . fi'l-ʿahd al-ʿuthmani*, p. 18, 30: "in those days, newspapers were not sold on the street, but were placed in some shops for that purpose."

7. *Filastin*, 21 March 1967, p. 3. In its issue of 29 September 1929, p. 5, the paper presented a list of spots in different town where the paper was sold, as well as hawkers or "roving sellers." Also McCracken, p. 83 (depicting a similar practice in Jerusalem immediately after the First World War). See also the charming photo of a child hawker selling copies of *Filastin* around 1925, in Diyab and Sharabi, p. 160.

8. See discussion of newspaper hawkers and their role in nineteenth-century Manhattan in Henkin, pp. 110–113. The role of the traditional city crier will be discussed in Chapter 5, below.

9. Ziyadah, vol. 1, p. 54. Similarly, interview with ʿAbd al-Hamid Abu Laban, who related his memories from Kafr Zakariyyah (near Hebron).

10. *Al-Jawa'ib*, 21 April 1868, p. 1. The ad does not mention the book's title, only a description. For the broad circulation of *al-Jawa'ib*, see Ayalon, *The Press*, pp. 30–31.

11. Warren, pp. 491–492. There were also 7 bookbinders—6 Jews and a Muslim.

12. Darwazah, p. 160.

13. See Hummel, p. 261 (presenting a photograph from c. 1881); Walid Khalidi, p. 62, no. 40, where the sign appears in a section covering the period prior to 1918; Faber et al., p. 13, showing the same sign and dating it to "the late nineteenth century."

14. Their postwar ads in the local press indicated that the shop had been in operation since 1910; e.g., *Filastin*, 9 September 1921; *al-Nafa'is al-ʿAsriyyah*, year 9, issue 4 (August 1922), p. 111; *al-Jazirah*, 2 April 1925, p. 4. Bulus and Wadiʿ Saʿid were, respectively, the uncle and father of a subsequently famous intellectual, Edward Said.

15. *Al-Zahrah*, year 2, issue 7/8, 1922–23, pp. 185–186.

16. Rashid Khalidi (*Palestinian Identity*, p. 45) has suggested that new bookstores in prewar Palestine were "catering to the demand for foreign books, periodicals and other works in Arabic and foreign languages." This seems to overstate the case for that period, however, and suggests the need for more evidence.

17. Much can be learned about these shops from their own advertisements. For some examples see *Filastin*, 13 July 1923, p. 4, and 15 December 1935, p. 6 (ads for *maktabat filastin al-ʿilmiyyah* in Jerusalem and Jaffa, the latter one indicating that the shop had expanded its activities to selling games and gifts for children as well as Christmas trees); 8 February 1924, p. 3 (*maktabat bayt al-maqdis* in Jerusalem); 19 April 1927 (for *al-maktabah al-jadidah* in Jerusalem); 4 January 1929, p. 5, and 1 February 1929, p. 5 (*maktabat filastin al-jadidah* in Jaffa); 1 January 1933, p. 7 (*maktabat haddad* in Haifa, which offered, in addition to the usual supplies, gifts for the holidays and housewares); 3 October 1935, p. 6; and 11 December 1935, p. 2 (*al-maktabah al-ʿasriyyah* in Jaffa); *al-Difaʿ*, 24 May 1934, p. 7 (*al-maktabah al-ʿarabiyyah al-wataniyyah* in Haifa).

18. *Al-Nafa'is*, year 9, issue 4, August 1922, p. 111; *Filastin*, 9 November 1921, p. 4; 30 April 1929, p. 7.

19. *Zahrat al-Jamil,* year 1, issue 7/8, 1–15 August 1921, p. 4; *al-Zahrah,* year 2, 1922–23—issue 7/8, pp. 185–186; issue 23/24, p. 511.

20. *Filastin,* 1 February 1929, p. 5.

21. Advertisement in Maktab al-sihafah wa'l-nashr, *Man huwa,* p. 190.

22. E.g., *al-Jazirah,* 2 April 1925, p. 4; *al-Iqdam,* 1 November 1929, p. 4.

23. Yusuf, *Khamsun ʿamᵃⁿ,* pp. 16–22, 27, 30; Yusuf, *Shayʾ,* pp. 47–49.

24. Figures of production gathered from Jbarah's bibliography, passim. See also Shimʿoni, pp. 397–398, and ads of *al-maktabah al-ʿasriyyah* in *Filastin,* 10 May 1946, p. 2, and of *maktabat filastin al-ʿilmiyyah* in *al-Kitab al-ʿarabi,* last page. Simʿoni, a knowledgeable source, mentions the Saʿid brothers' bookstore among the upcoming businesses of book production in the 1940s. Jbarah, however, lists only 7 books published by them.

25. *Al-Difaʿ,* 6 September 1943; Shimʿoni, p. 398; Vaschitz, pp. 279–280; interview with Hanna Abu Hanna.

26. ISA/P326/630. The union's name as appearing on its letterhead was "The Union Arab Libraries Association in Palestine." A letter by the union's president to Khalil al-Sakakini, dated 11 March 1945, included a name list of 51 booksellers. By Sakakini's own count, the number was 53 (adding one name in Jerusalem and one in Acre).

27. The value of the Ottoman pound during the empire's last decades was roughly 90% of the English pound. The Egyptian pound, or *gineh*—also divided into 100 qurush—was roughly equivalent to the English pound. The buying power of these units is discussed below.

28. For instances of book prices during the later decades of the nineteenth century, see, e.g., the price list of books sold by the owners of *al-Muqtataf* in Cairo—*al-Muqattam,* 12 March 1889, p. 4. The Egyptian biweekly/monthly *al-Hilal* featured a regular literary section from its inception in 1892, in which it often quoted book prices. Similar ads appeared frequently in many journals of the period.

29. *Al-Nafaʾis al-ʿAsriyyah,* year 5, issue 1 (January 1913), inner back cover. Prices were marked in French francs. The pound was divided to 100 qurush, and the franc was roughly equivalent to 4 qurush.

30. E.g., *al-Jazirah,* 2 April 1925, p. 4; *Lisan al-ʿArab,* 1 October 1921, p. 3.

31. *Al-Nafaʾis,* year 9, issue 4, August 1922, pp. 49–50; similarly *Bayt Lahm,* June 1920, p. 78; *Mirʾat al-Sharq,* 21 June 1921, p. 4; *Filastin,* 13 July 1923, p. 4; 8 February 1924, p. 3; 4 June 1929, p. 3; *al-Jazirah,* 2 April 1925, p. 4. See also the price list of books offered for sale by *al-Hilal* in Cairo, on the back cover of the March 1924 issue of the journal, and of books sold by *al-Muqtataf* on the back cover of its May 1932 issue.

32. E.g., *al-Difaʿ,* 5 September 1943, p. 3; *Filastin,* 1 March 1944, p. 3; 5 May 1945, p. 3; 10 May 1946, p. 2; 28 May 1946, p. 4. A 20-volume encyclopedia entitled *Muʿjam al-udabaʾ* was offered for 175 qurush.

33. *Al-Nafaʾis al-ʿAsriyyah* (later *al-Nafaʾis*) regularly listed people who donated such subscriptions to others, beginning in 1909 and continuing after the First World War. The lists appeared under the title "*ihdaʾ al-Nafaʾis,*" and those mentioned in them came from all over Palestine, as well as from other countries. See also Chapter 4, note 19.

34. ISA/P350/01671. The document does not mention the paper's name, but in all likelihood it refers to subscribers of the Islamic Jerusalem daily *al-Liwaʾ.*

35. Issawi, pp. 34, 90–91, 428. Issawi's tables are often lacking with regard to Palestine, but reasonable inferences may be made from his data on other places in the Fertile Crescent.

36. Issawi, pp. 90–91; see also p. 37; Assaf, *ha-Yahasim,* pp. 158, 161–162.

37. Metzer and Kaplan, pp. 155–164.

38. Government of Palestine, Department of Statistics, *Statistical Abstract* (1936), p. 58; Government of Palestine, Department of Statistics, *Statistical Abstract* (1939), p. 97; Government of Palestine, Department of Statistics, *Statistical Abstract* (1944–45), pp. 155–156; Assaf, *ha-Yahasim,* pp. 225–228.

39. Government of Palestine, Department of Statistics, *Statistical Abstract* (1939), p. 107; Government of Palestine, Department of Statistics, *Statistical Abstract* (1944–45), pp. 113–119; Nadan, p. 156, figure 5.8.

40. Calculated according to tables in Gurevich, p. 175, and Government of Palestine, Department of Statistics, *Statistical Abstract* (1939), p. 107.

41. Jabra, pp. 29, 43, 136–137.

42. Jabra, p. 176; Government of Palestine, Department of Statistics, *Statistical Abstract* (1936), p. 58. We will return to this story in the next chapter.

43. Lyons, pp. 331–336; Allen, pp. 44–46; Richter, *La lecture,* pp. 101–108; Richter, *Introduction,* pp. 32–38, 40–42.

44. Rashid Khalidi, p. 54, and details in note 63. See also above, Chapter 2, "Impact of the Neighborhood." Khalidi has found scores of volumes of imported periodicals from the late nineteenth and early twentieth centuries in that library—*al-Muqtataf, al-Manar, al-Hilal,* and *al-Muqtabas.*

45. Al-Majlis al-shar'i al-islami al-a'la, p. 32; Dagher, p. 68.

46. And perhaps, as Conrad has recently suggested, it was a political statement as well; Conrad, pp. 202–203.

47. *Barnamaj al-maktabah al-khalidiyyah,* introduction. See also the rules devised by the library's caretaker for some five decades, Amin al-Ansari, quoted in Conrad, pp. 201–202.

48. Conrad calculates that the collection included 2,168 volumes in 1900. He also estimates that the reading room, which also served as storage room, could take c. 6,000–7,000 "as an absolute maximum." Conrad, pp. 200, 205–206. For 1917, see Mukhlis, p. 366; for 1936, Tarrazi, *Khaza'in,* vol. 1, p. 143. Later assessments—e.g., 12,000 in 1945, as noted by 'Arif, *Mufassal,* p. 449, or 11,000 in 1951, as noted by Dagher, p. 68—appear to have been exaggerated.

49. Al-Maktabah al-khalidiyyah, *Barnamaj al-maktabah al-khalidiyyah,* introduction.

50. Niqula Ziyadah, who as a student in 1992 visited the Coptic monastery in Jerusalem, was permitted to borrow books such as Mustafa Lutfi al-Manfaluti's short stories and Shibli Shumayyil's study on Darwin and evolution—an impressive mark of openness for an institution of religious learning; Ziyadah, vol. 1, pp. 88–89. See also Tarrazi, *Khaza'in,* vol. 2, pp. 475–482; Dagher, pp. 71–76.

51. In his study of libraries in the West Bank (including Jerusalem) and the Gaza Strip, Abu Diyah mentions a total of 10 school and college libraries dating to the pre-1948 years: 3 in Tulkarm, 2 in Hebron, and one each in Jerusalem, Bir Zayt, Jenin, Ramallah, and Sebastia. Six of these were set up in the 1940s. Abu Diyah, pp. 34, 40, 46, 56, 58, 61, 62, 63, 73, and 74.

52. Madrasat al-najah al-wataniyyah, *Barnamaj* (1929–1930), p. 18. See also the description of the library in the Jerusalem Teachers' Seminar, in Ziyadah, vol. 1, pp. 70–71, 101–102.

53. *Al-Jazirah,* 23 February 1925, p. 3, announcing the opening of a library in the Jaffa Orthodox School, to which "nice quantities of books" had been donated.

54. Wittmann, pp. 303, 305, 308–311; Barbéris and Duchet, pp. 440–445; Richter, *La lecture,* pp. 24–27, 83–85, 114, 213–215; Whitmore, pp. 119–129.

55. Zaydan, vol. 4, p. 78.

56. Eli Smith, an American missionary and one of the founders, in a 1848 letter to the German Oriental Society; "Gesellschaft der Künste," p. 378. See also *al-Jam'iyyah al-suriyyah,* introduction, pp. 7–22. The Syrian Society is reported to have been preceded by an association calling itself "The Edification Society" (*majma' 'al-tahdhib*), founded several months earlier in Beirut by local Christians; *al-Jam'iyyah al-suriyyah,* pp. 5–6. In 1857 the Syrian Society was reorganized under the name "The Syrian Scientific Society" (*al-jam'iyyah al-'ilmiyyah al-suriyyah*).

57. Zaydan, vol. 4, pp. 78–105, offering a survey of these societies that, though incomplete and somewhat confused, is nonetheless illuminating. A report on the library for the year 1847 appeared in "Gesellschaft der Künste," pp. 382–384. See also Sarkis, *al-Jam'iyyah al-suriyyah,* pp. 21–22.

58. *Al-Ahram,* 19 August 1876; *al-Jinan,* 29 February 1876; Zaydan, vol. 4, pp. 126–127 (also reporting the opening of such reading rooms in Lebanese villages). For similar reports on the opening of reading rooms, see *Hadiqat al-Akhbar,* 2 August 1858, p. 4; 6 August 1859, p. 4; *al-Jawa'ib,* 21 April 1861, pp. 1, 4; *al-Jinan,* 1 April 1876, back cover (facing p. 252); *al-Muqtataf,* April 1900, pp. 313–314; Commins, p. 132.

59. Finn, chap. 21. The society, regarded as forerunner of the Palestine Exploration Fund, was active apparently until the mid-1850s. It had its own library as well as coin and antique collections, and its members used to meet periodically to discuss their readings and studies. See also Muhafazah, p. 55.

60. Tibawi, "Jam'iyyat al-aadab." According to Tibawi, the society was also known as *jam'iyyat al-aadab al-'arabiyyah* and *jam'iyyat al-aadab al-'ilmiyyah al-'arabiyyah.* See also Muhafazah, pp. 55–56; Yaghi, pp. 94–95; Shumali, *Ittijahat,* pp. 34–35; Asad, *Ittijahat,* pp. 41–42; Kahati, pp. 33–35; Sakakini, p. 9 (introduction by the Hebrew translator) and pp. 21–57 (entries for the years 1907–14. Sakakini's diaries, which provide ample accounts on his own routine from 1907 onward, frequently mention meetings with his society colleagues in private homes and in cafés, but none in a special club); Yehoshu'a, *Ta'rikh al-sihafah . . . fi'l-'ahd al-'uthmani,* p. 168; Yehoshu'a, "Nitzanei 'itonut," pp. 142–143. Yehoshu'a, a Jewish writer, was a child in Jerusalem before the First World War who later befriended some of these cultural figures.

61. WO/157/728/144888, reports from May and June 1918.

62. *Al-Zahrah,* year 2, issue 7/8, 1922–23, p. 188.

63. Abu Ghazaleh, *Arab Cultural Nationalism,* pp. 96–98.

64. White, p. 1; interview with YMCA director Rizek Abusharr (Rizq Abu Sharr). Dagher, p. 76, indicates 25,000 as the figure for 1951. The YMCA had been active in Jerusalem since the 1870s. Its library will be discussed further in the next chapter.

65. Interview with Fakhri Jdai.

66. *Mir'at al-Sharq,* 14 January 1919, p. 2.

67. *Al-Jazirah,* 26 February 1925, p. 3; *al-Karmil,* 10 March 1925, p. 2; *al-Ittihad al-'Arabi,* 16 May 1925, p. 4.

68. E.g., *al-Jazirah,* 2 April 1925, p. 3; 28 December 1925, p. 3 (reporting similar activities of the Islamic Youth Club).

69. Buri and Shibl, pp. 94–95, and similarly p. 98. For some more examples see *Mira't al-Sharq,* 7 January 1919, p. 2; *al-Zahrah,* year 2, 1922–23, issue 7/8, pp. 186–189; *al-Yarmuk,* 1 February 1925, p. 2; *Filastin,* 18 January 1929, p. 4; 29 January 1929, p. 4. See also Shumali, *Ittijahat,* pp. 66–71, 93–94, 215–216; Yaghi, pp. 95–100; Sawafiri, pp. 71–72; ISA/347/1513; ISA/349/1577; ISA/349/1591.

70. Wittmann, pp. 306–308; Allen, pp. 44–45.

71. Darwazah, p. 160.

72. *Al-Zahrah,* year 2, 1922–23—issue 7/8, p. 186, and issue 23/24, p. 511.

73. See sources quoted in note 25 above.

74. Bowman, p. 272; al-Durr, p. 206. See also Tibawi, *Education,* pp. 97–98; interview with Yunus al-ʿAzzi.

75. For some historic descriptions, see Hattox, pp. 101–103; Lane, pp. 334–335, 386–420; Tietze, p. 37; Georgeon, "Les cafés à Istanbul"; Deguilhem; Marino; Ukers, pp. 657–670.

76. Fyfe, p. 113.

77. Fyfe, p. 113. For a discussion of the café in the Egyptian context, see Ayalon, "Political Journalism," pp. 113–116.

78. Georgeon, "Lire et écrire," p. 178; see also pp. 67–70; Hanioğlu, p. 109. The term has remained in use in Turkey to this day as a name for "café"; the 1992 edition of the *Oxford Turkish Dictionary* defines *kiraathane* as "public reading room; coffee house providing newspapers."

79. Darwazah, pp. 107, 114–115; Ben-Arieh, *Jerusalem,* pp. 45–46, and illustrations on pp. 50, 51. For an extensive discussion of café life in pre-1914 Jerusalem, see Yehoshuʿa, *Yerushalayim,* pp. 144–158. Also Snubar, p. 4; Ziyadah, vol. 1, p. 50.

80. HA/80/1660/11, report on a meeting in Café Ballur by Yitzhak Hoz, dated 12 February 1923 (original in English).

81. Interview with Hamati. At the age of 102 when interviewed (October 2002), Hamati was remarkably alert and vivacious, displaying a sharp memory of episodes and details from his pre–First World War youth.

82. Ayalon, *The Press,* pp. 69–72.

83. WO/157/728/144888, reports from May and June 1918.

84. Yehoshuʿa, *Ta'rikh al-sihafah . . . fi'l-ʿahd al-ʿuthmani,* pp. 177–178; Yehoshuʿa, *Yerushalayim,* pp. 150–151; Abu Khalil, pp. 11–12; Haddad, *Khalil al-Sakakini,* pp. 68–72; *al-Bilad* (Amman, daily), 30 October 1960, p. 2.

85. HA/80/145/20, a report dated 25–30 January 1920.

86. *Al-Karmil,* 11 November 1939, p. 1.

87. The memoirs of "Abu Bandali" in the last issue of *Filastin,* 21 March 1967, p. 3; Yehoshuʿa, *Yerushalayim,* pp. 150, 155; Interview with Lutfi Zurayyiq.

88. See description in the next chapter.

89. *Al-Karmil,* 4 October 1922, quoted in Nassar, pp. 15–16. Similarly, Duwayik; Tawfiq Zaybaq in *al-Zahrah,* year 2, issue 9/10, 1922–23, p. 214; Yehoshuʿa, *Yerushalayim,* p. 152.

90. Thomsen, p. 211.

91. Jabra, p. 113. For a similar practice as late as the 1980s, see Shinar, p. 74.

92. For some descriptions, see Ahmad, pp. 74–77; Fattash, pp. 30–32; Muhammad Rimawi, pp. 23–29; Amin Hafiz al-Dajani, pp. 130–131; Abu Ghush, pp. 134–135; ʿAbd al-Rahim, pp. 16–17; ʿAbbas, pp. 17–18; Haddad, *al-Mujtamaʿ,* p. 63; see also *Mir'at al-*

Sharq, 1 November 1928, p. 1. A description from the second half of the twentieth century, which in principle is much the same as reports on the first half, appears in Shinar, pp. 84–86. Similar meetings by groups of men to discuss cardinal issues are sometimes described for town quarters as well; see, e.g., Snubar, p. 4 (Nablus); Shuqayri, p. 24 (Tul Karm); 'Abd al-Rahim Ahmad Husayn, p. 78 (Majdal).

93. E.g., in 'Imwas; Abu Ghush, pp. 134–135.

94. Interview with Hajj Hasan Salim Abu 'Aql.

95. Ziyadah, vol. 1, p. 118.

96. Faysal Hurani, p. 267.

97. Muhawi and Kanaana, pp. 4–6 and passim.

98. See above, Chapter 2, p. 50.

99. *Filastin,* 29 September 1913, quoted by Yehoshu'a, *Ta'rikh al-sihafah . . . fi'l-'ahd al-'uthmani,* pp. 18–19. Also interview with Iliyas Hamati.

100. In Salfit, where several *madafah*s had existed due to intramural rivalries, a coffee-house was opened in 1944. People abandoned their guesthouses and moved to the new place, a change that had a favorable effect on social relations in the village. See Fattash, pp. 31–32. The existence of cafés in several villages in the 1940s is also reported in the "village files" of the Haganah Archive (series 8), e.g., HA/8/203/20 (Bassah); HA/8/194/5 (Masmiyyah); HA/8/201/75 (Yahudiyyah). In Kafr Yasif a café was opened as early as 1924; Rafa'il Bulus, pp. 152–153 and interviews with Jamil Bulus and Butrus Dalleh. In Bituniyya, according to Aburish, one had been in operation at least since the early 1930s; Aburish, pp. 41, 63–64.

Chapter 4

1. Jabra, pp. 176–177.

2. Casson, chap. 2; Svenbro, pp. 50–52.

3. Saenger, *Space between Words,* pp. 1–13, 256–259, and passim; Saenger, "Silent reading"; Saenger, "Reading." See also Chartier, *Culture of Print,* pp. 2–3; Manguel, pp. 47–50.

4. Cavallo and Chartier, *History,* introduction, pp. 23–26; Wittmann. The "revolutionary" significance of the invention of printing is still a matter of hot controversy. See, e.g., the exchange between Elizabeth Eisenstein and Adrian Johns in *American Historical Review,* pp. 87–128.

5. Henkin; Petrucci, esp. pp. 362–367.

6. An inquiry into this aspect in Arab societies might quickly reveal that the ground to be explored there is just as tricky as in the European experience. Quite probably, it is trickier, due to certain peculiarities of the Arabic language and a particular crisis that language sustained in modern times, both of which had a direct bearing on reading modes (this last point will be considered later on). The state of the evidence, too, seems to be considerably more problematic in the Arab case.

7. This point is discussed in the next chapter, "The Old, Familiar Conduits."

8. Rosenthal, "Classical Muslim View," p. 47; Cook, esp. pp. 437–441, 519–523. Cook explains Islam's failure to adhere to the purely oral principle and its "capitulation to writing" in the lack of an "organization of learning" and the absence of a division of labor for

drilling in the oral retention of tradition. Rather, "it was everyone's business to memorize everything," a state of affairs that made it impossible to carry on with it for too long.

9. Muhammad Nasir al-Din al-Tusi, quoted by Berkey, *Transmission,* p. 25.

10. Rosenthal, *Technique,* esp. pp. 6–20; Rosenthal, "Classical Muslim View."

11. See next chapter, "The Old, Familiar Conduits."

12. Quoted in Pinto, p. 212, along with several other such statements.

13. Jahiz, *Hayawan,* pp. 41–42 (the chapter is entitled "In Praise of Books"). I am grateful to Prof. Andras Hamori for this reference.

14. Quoted in Pinto, pp. 215–216.

15. Rosenthal, *Technique,* pp. 8–10; Sibai, pp. 105–106.

16. The speaker is Muhammad bin 'Abdallah bin 'Abd al-Hakam, referring to the library of his father, a ninth-century Maliki scholar. Quoted in Brockopp, p. 29. I owe this reference to Professor Etan Kohlberg.

17. Eche, pp. 368–380; Rosenthal, *Technique,* pp. 6–12; Sibai, pp. 100–115; 'Asali, *Maktabat,* pp. 291–292.

18. Eche, pp. 378–379.

19. Khalil Baydas's journal, whose readership grew markedly thanks to this fashion, used to publicize the names of those involved in it on a regular basis. In 1911, for example, out of 73 readers of the journal who gave or received such gifts, 25 were from Palestine— from Jerusalem, Jaffa, Acre, Haifa, Nazareth, Ramallah, Bethlehem, and Bayt Jalah; *al-Nafa'is al-'Asriyyah* 4, 1911; see section entitled "Ihda' al-Nafa'is" in almost every issue. A similar phenomenon is reflected in the Haifa literary journal *Zahrat al-Jamil,* launched in 1921 (and becoming *al-Zahrah* in 1922), whose first volume carries many names of donors and recipients of such gifts—from Haifa, Acre, Jerusalem, Tulkarm, and Ma'iliyah. This fashion may have evolved at an earlier time and been applied to journals published and acquired from abroad.

20. E.g., *al-Nafa'is al-'Asriyyah,* January 1911, p. 47; August 1911, p. 376; August 1922, p. 138.

21. See Muensterberger, esp. chaps. 1 and 6.

22. Some such cases in twentieth-century Palestine were reported in Jaffa, Nazareth, Kafr Reynah, and villages in the Wadi 'Arah region; interviews with Dr. André Mazawi, Dr. Muhammad 'Aql, and Hanna Abu Hanna.

23. One private collection of manuscripts, that of the Qamhawi family in Nablus, was put at the public's disposal by Waqf, apparently sometime during the nineteenth century. The *waqfiyyah* prescribed that books should be lent to those interested, provided that a loan slip was used (a recommended method in classical sources). There is no telling whether and to what extent this procedure was implemented; if it was, it must have been quite limited. See 'Atallah, *Maktabat aal qamhawi,* introduction, fifth page.

24. E.g., Nashashibi, p. 16; Tuqan, p. 49.

25. Husseini-Shahid, p. 84 (also reporting the storing of books in the house attic and basement—pp. 41, 101). Serene Husseini-Shahid was the daughter of Palestinian political leader Jamal al-Husayni. See, similarly, Salah, pp. 9, 10; Tuqan, pp. 104–105.

26. *Al-Muqtataf,* June 1906, pp. 496–499.

27. *Al-Muqtataf,* October 1913, pp. 349–353.

28. *Filastin,* 30 September 1911, pp. 3–4; 4 October 1911, pp. 3–4.

29. See Duwayik.

30. E.g., Sakakini, p. 41 (1 January 1912).

31. Sakakini adhered to this routine even when away from home: "I get up in the morning," he reported from his exile in Damascus, "I drink coffee, smoke, then write or read the daily issues of *al-Sharq* and *al-Muqtabas*." Sakakini, p. 27 (12 September 1908); p. 35 (12 November 1908); p. 41 (1 January 1912); p. 49 (20 February 1914); p. 93 (11 January 1918). For a detailed study of Sakakini's life and thought, see Kahati, pp. 26–144.

32. Nuwayhid, pp. 23, 26. Nuwayhid translated Lothrop Stoddard's *The New World of Islam*.

33. Ziyadah, vol. 1, p. 102; see also pp. 70–71, 89–90, 183.

34. Zuʿbi, p. 7.

35. Jabra, pp. 84, 136–137.

36. *Al-Muqtataf*, 1 December 1924, pp. 577–578.

37. Abu Hanna, *Zill al-ghaymah*, p. 65; and interview with Abu Hanna.

38. Ziyadah, vol. 1, p. 183; interviews with Salim Makhuli, Butrus Dalleh, and Salim Jubran.

39. Interview with ʿAbd al-Hamid Abu Laban. Sometime later, still a teenager, Abu Laban became a correspondent for the Jaffa-based daily *al-Difaʿ*.

40. ʿAbbas, p. 75.

41. Personal communication with Rashid Khalidi and Lawrence Conrad. According to Conrad, two of the figures in the picture were not readers but rather Ottoman policemen, attracted to the place by the commotion of the photo opportunity.

42. Quoted in Conrad, pp. 201–202.

43. Interview with Rizek Abusharr. Similarly, interview with Fakhri Jdai with respect to the St. Anthony club library in Jaffa.

44. Rashid Khalidi, p. 54.

45. Rashid Khalidi, p. 227, note 65.

46. Conrad, p. 205.

47. Personal communication with Lawrence Conrad. See also Conrad, pp. 202, 206–208.

48. *Filastin*, 18 January 1924, p. 4.

49. Al-Majlis al-sharʿi al-islami al-aʿla, p. 32.

50. Interview with Rizek Abusharr. Cf. CO/733/230/4—letter from the American consul in Jerusalem depicting the club's activities. For the club in Jaffa, see BW/47/1, report from August 1943.

51. For a detailed and amply illustrated study of the library structure, see Walls. See also the famous picture of the reading room featuring some personalities of note, taken shortly after the library was first opened, reproduced above; and a picture from 1986, reproduced in Conrad, p. 204. ʿAbdallah Mukhlis, a prominent man-of-letters who visited the Khalidiyyah in 1917, noted that there was "nothing comely or splendid" either in its "simple bookcases [or] in its arrangement along public libraries lines"; Mukhlis, p. 366.

52. ʿAsali, *Maʿahid*, pp. 104–110; Burgoyne, pp. 368–372. For pictures of the al-Aqsa reading room in Qubbat al-Nahwiyyah and of the Jaffa Islamic library, see al-Majlis al-sharʿi al-islami al-aʿla, photographs following p. 32.

53. *Lisan al-ʿArab*, 22 March 1922, p. 1.

54. *Al-Ittihad al-ʿArabi*, 10 April 1926, p. 3—a gloomy account of the editor's visit to the club.

55. *Filastin*, 1 January 1929, pp. 7–8. A photograph of this club, an imposing building, is reproduced in Gharbiyyah, p. 105. See also Haykal, pp. 168–169.

Chapter 5

1. Ong, *Presence,* pp. 233–234.

2. Webb, pp. 32–34; Schofield, p. 312; Lyons, pp. 340–341, 343–344; Wittmann, pp. 290–291.

3. Manguel, pp. 110–114.

4. Brooks, pp. 29–34.

5. Dégh, pp. 149ff.

6. Ong, *Presence,* pp. 111–138; Ong, *Orality and Literacy,* pp. 31–33. The literature dealing with the Qur'an as an "oral text" is extensive. The present discussion is based primarily on Nelson; Nasr; Denny; Graham. See also Daniel Boyarin (discussing the parallel Hebrew biblical experience); and Griffiths, esp. pp. 40ff.

7. Nasr, p. 58. See also Makdisi, pp. 99–104.

8. Berkey, *Transmission,* p. 26.

9. Berkey, *Transmission,* pp. 26–30, 59–60; Chamberlain, pp. 141, 145.

10. Berkey, *Transmission,* p. 27.

11. Leder, pp. 288–292, describing such sessions in medieval Damascus. The sessions were known as *sama'at,* "auditions." On *ijazah*s, see Makdisi, pp. 140–146, and Witkam. I owe this last reference to Petra Sijpesteijn.

12. Berkey, *Popular Preaching.* For the early development of this phenomenon, see 'Athamina.

13. See, e.g., Jabarti, *'Aja'ib,* where appearances of the *munadi* are reported regularly and, during certain periods of critical developments (such as the French invasion of Egypt), nearly daily. An illustration showing a public crier in Istanbul in 1877 appeared in *The Graphic* (London), 15 September 1877, p. 245. For references to the practice in Ottoman Palestine, see Ziyadah, vol. 1, p. 48; Sakakini, pp. 59, 60, 61 (reports from 1914–15); Yusuf, *Shay',* p. 10.

14. Ziyadah, vol. 1, p. 48, offering a detailed description of the *munadi* practice.

15. Grant, pp. 149–150; Yusuf, *Shay',* p. 40; Rafa'il Bulus, p. 166; interviews with Dr. Muhammad 'Aql, Butrus Dalleh, Hanna Abu Hanna, and Butrus Abu Maneh.

16. For the tradition of mentioning the Prophet, or God, at the beginning (as well as the end) of various speech acts, see Caton, pp. 99–100.

17. Abu Hanna, *Zill al-ghaymah,* p. 111, and interview with Abu Hanna.

18. Dégh, pp. 165–186. Dégh's *Folktales and Society* is an enlightening study of the universal phenomenon of storytelling, with most examples taken from the Hungarian tradition. See also Manguel, pp. 119–121.

19. Most famous among them were *sirat 'antar, sirat bani hilal* (or *abu zayid al-hilali*), *sirat baybars, sirat al-amirah dhat al-himma,* and *sirat sayf bin dhi yazan.* Details in Connelly, pp. 4–8; see also Dégh, pp. 146ff.

20. Connelly, pp. 10–17; see also Berkey, *Popular Preaching,* pp. 55ff.

21. Deguilhem, pp. 133–135, describing *hakawati*s in Damascus in the 1990s.

22. E.g., Muhawi and Kanaana, pp. 2–3; Ahmad Zaki al-Dajani, p. 125.

23. See, e.g., Muhawi and Kanaana, pp. 4–5, 55, 68, 84, 93, 115, 255; 'Abdallah Ahmad al-Hurani, pp. 65ff., 73, 80.

24. See the study by Muhawi and Kanaana. On pp. 1–3 they explain the differences between stories for men and for women—the distinction was quite clear both in contents and in the fashion of telling. See also Tamimi and Bahjat, p. 100; Salah, p. 12.

25. Ahmad Zaki al-Dajani, pp. 125–126. For similar descriptions see Tamimi and

Bahjat, p. 100; Asad, *Khalil baydas,* pp. 6–9; Ahmad, pp. 76–77; Wilson, p. 278; Grant, pp. 164–165; Ziyadah, vol. 1, pp. 50–51; Yusuf, *Shayʾ*, pp. 36–37; Rafaʾil Bulus, p. 153; Abu Ghush, p. 135; Bsaysu, p. 27; Amin Hafiz al-Dajani, pp. 130–131; Faysal Hurani, p. 281; Haddad, *al-Mujtamaʿ*, p. 63; Weigert, pp. 37–39; Shimʿoni, pp. 392–393; Forte (describing a similar session in a Galilee village in the 1990s).

26. Ibrahim al-Dabbagh, p. 117.

27. Darwaza, vol. 1, p. 160; Niqula Khuri, p. 64; Zuʿbi, p. 7.

28. Manguel, p. 47. See also Chartier, *Culture of Print,* p. 8.

29. *Al-Ahlam,* September 1908, quoted in Yehoshuʿa, *Taʾrikh al-sihafah . . . fiʾl-ʿahd al-ʿuthmani,* pp. 79–84.

30. *Al-Asmaʿi,* August–September 1908, quoted in Yehoshuʿa, *Taʾrikh al-sihafah . . . fiʾl-ʿahd al-ʿuthmani,* p. 89.

31. *Al-Zahrah,* year 2, issue 9/10, 1922–23, p. 217.

32. *Filastin,* 10 September 1929, p. 1.

33. *Al-Ittihad,* 3 December 1944, p. 3.

34. *Filastin,* 15 October 1929, p. 1.

35. *Mirʾat al-Sharq,* 22 October 1919, p. 3. Similarly 8 October 1919, p. 3.

36. Antonius, pp. 79–81; Ayalon, *The Press,* pp. 156–158, and more examples quoted in Ayalon, "Political Journalism," pp. 115–116.

37. Avner (Yitzhak Ben-Zvi) in *ha-Ahdut* (Jerusalem), year 3, 1911, issue 5, p. 6.

38. See above, Chapter 3, "Accessing without Buying: Open Public Places."

39. Quoted in Sulayman, *Taʾrikh al-sihafah al-filastiniyyah,* p. 141.

40. WO157/728/144888, report from May–June 1918.

41. Jabra, p. 76.

42. Abu Hanna, *Zill al-ghaymah,* relating his own memoirs in the third person. See also ʿAbd al-Rahim, pp. 45–46; ʿAbbas, p. 60.

43. Kabhah, p. 24, quoting oral testimonies; interview with Hanna Abu Hanna.

44. Al-Mudawwar, p. 86.

45. Interview with Hajj Hasan Salim Abu ʿAql.

46. Interviews with Jamil Bulus, Dr. Salim Makhuli, and Butrus Dalleh (all from Kafr Yasif). See also Rafaʾil Bulus, pp. 152–153. See also Chapter 3, note 100, above.

47. Aburish, pp. 41–42, and similarly pp. 45–46. Ibrahim was the author's uncle.

48. Faysal Hurani, p. 267; for some similar descriptions, see pp. 122, 265–266, 281; Mudawwar, p. 86; CZA/S25/3539 (report by A. H. Cohen, dated 30 November 1937); *al-Ittihad,* 23 July 1944, p. 3. Similar stories came up in interviews with Dr. Salim Makhuli, Jamil Bulus, Dr. Muhammad ʿAql, Hajj Hasan Salim Abu ʿAql, Butrus Dalleh, Hanna Abu Hanna, Shukri ʿArraf, Yunus al-ʿAzzi, and Lutfi Zurayyiq.

49. Najjar, pp. 64, 90, quoting British documents; *Great Britain and Palestine,* p. 28.

50. CZA/S25/227954; Arnon-Ohana, *Fallahim,* pp. 64–65, 177. See also above, Chapter 2.

51. Sakakini, p. 153 (entry for 17 March 1932).

52. Jabra, p. 176. For similar testimonies see Kabhah, p. 24 (quoting oral evidence). While conducting research for a previous study, I had a chance to discuss the phenomenon of group reading of newspapers with the late Professor Charles Issawi. With rich recollections of life in both Cairo and Beirut during the interwar period, and a keen eye that was reputed throughout the profession, Issawi noted that reading aloud to illiterates in cafés and other public places, so common in Egypt, was far rarer in Beirut. The reason for that, he suggested, was that Lebanese, even if illiterate, would be "too vain" to show their il-

literacy in public. This was especially true of the social groups who normally frequented the cafés. A master of framing human conditions, Issawi may well have put his finger on a major disparity between the two societies. Possibly, the urban segment of Palestinian society was closer in that respect to its Lebanese counterpart than to the Egyptian one.

53. Faysal Hurani, p. 122. For the British policy of distributing radio receivers during the late years of the mandate, see FO/371/45422, a report by the Public Information Office (PIO) in Jerusalem, 1945.

54. Screened on Israeli TV sometime in November 2000. Its name is unknown but is immaterial for our purpose.

55. Interview with Dr. Sulayman Jubran; similarly, interview with Yunus al-'Azzi.

56. Saenger, *Space between Words,* pp. 123–130. "Word separation in Arabic was not an optional characteristic to be added in some epochs and omitted in others. It was an intrinsic feature, and as such a continuation of an ancient Semitic practice clearly evident in the earliest examples of Hebrew writings" (p. 124).

57. A cursory examination of early Arabic manuscripts seems to cast some doubt on the part of Saenger's thesis relating to Arabic. Spaces may not have been such an obvious and firm feature of the old Arabic script; see, e.g., Déroche, p. 616. I am grateful to Professor Patricia Crone and to Petra Sijpesteijn for referring me to some early Arabic texts on papyri containing evidence seemingly incompatible with Saenger's argument, and to the latter for drawing my attention to Déroche's article. A more systematic study is needed before this point is fully clear.

58. I am indebted to Professor Reinhard Schulze for discussing this point with me.

59. Ayalon, "Language as a Barrier."

60. Mudawwar, p. 86.

61. Interview with Butrus Dalleh.

62. Interview with Hajj Hasan Salim Abu 'Aql.

63. Faysal Hurani, p. 267.

64. Ibrahim, p. 71. I owe this reference to Sasson Somekh.

65. Ong, *Presence,* pp. 115–130. For further discussion of this point see Chartier, "Reading Matter," pp. 274–277; Caton, pp. 249–251; Street, p. 20.

66. Interview with Hajj Hasan Salim Abu 'Aql.

67. Husseini-Shahid, p. 78.

68. Husni al-Salih, p. 6.

69. Interview with Dr. Shukri 'Arraf.

Sources

Archival Material

BW—British Council Palestine files, London (Public Record Office). Series BW/47.
CO—Colonial Office, London (Public Record Office). Series CO/733.
CZA—Central Zionist Archive, Jerusalem. Sections: J/1; S/25; photograph collection.
FO—Foreign Office, London (Public Record Office). Series FO/371.
HA—Haganah Archive, Tel Aviv. Sections: 8; 80; 105; photograph collection.
ISA—Israel State Archive, Jerusalem. Sections: 2; 8; 65; 123/1.
WO—War Office, London (Public Record Office). Series WO/157.

Newspapers and Journals

al-Akhbar (Jaffa), 1919–1924
Barid al-Yawm (Jerusalem), 1920
Bayt Lahm (Bethlehem), 1920–1921
al-Difaʿ (Jaffa), 1934–1948
al-Dustur (Jerusalem), 1910–1911
Filastin (Jaffa), 1911–1914, 1920–1948
al-Hayat (Jerusalem), 1930–1931
al-Hilal (Cairo), 1892–1914
al-Iqdam (Haifa/Jaffa) 1929–1935
al-Ittihad (Haifa), 1944–1948
al-Ittihad al-ʿArabi (Tul Karm), 1925–1927
al-Jamiʿah al-ʿArabiyyah (Jerusalem), 1928–1930
al-Jamiʿah al-Islamiyyah (Jerusalem), 1932
al-Jawaʾib (Istanbul), 1868–1884
al-Jazirah (Jaffa), 1924–1927
al-Jinan (Beirut), 1870–1886
al-Karmil (Haifa), 1921–1938
al-Kuliyyah al-ʿArabiyyah (Jerusalem), 1932–1933
Lisan al-ʿArab (Jerusalem), 1921–1922
al-Liwaʾ (Jerusalem), 1935–1939
al-Majallah al-Tijariyyah (Haifa), 1925
Majallat Dar al-Muʿallimin (Jerusalem), 1921–1926
Majallat al-Nadi al-Siryani (Jerusalem), 1946
Majallat Rawdat al-Maʿarif (Jerusalem), 1922, 1932–1936
al-Minbar (Jerusalem), 1947–1948
Mirʾat al-Sharq (Jerusalem), 1919–1937

al-Muqtataf (Beirut/Cairo), 1876–1914
al-Nafa'is (Jerusalem), 1919–1922
al-Nafa'is al-'Asriyyah (Haifa/Jerusalem), 1908–1914
al-Quds al-Sharif (Jerusalem), 1920
Sawt al-Sha'b (Bethlehem), 1924–1927
al-Yarmuk (Haifa), 1924–1930
al-Zahrah (Haifa), 1922–1923
Zahrat al-Jamil (Haifa), 1921–1922
al-Zamr (Acre), 1925–1927

Interviews Quoted in the Text

Abu Hanna, Hanna—Haifa, 12 December 2000
Abu Laban, 'Abd al-Hamid—Ramlah, 17 October 2002
Abu Manneh, Prof. Butrus—Haifa, 12 December 2000
Abu 'Aql, Hajj Hasan Salim—'Ar'arah, 23 September 2000
Abusharr, Rizek—Jerusalem, 17 October 2001
'Aql, Dr. Muhammad—'Ar'arah, 23 September 2000
'Arraf, Dr. Shukri—Ma'iliyah, 5 August 2000
al-'Azzi, Yunus—Masmiyyah, 8 December 2002
Basal, Musa—Kafr Yasif, 2 December 2000
Bulus, Jamil—Kafr Yasif, 20 November 1999
al-Dalleh, Butrus—Kafr Yasif, 2 December 2000
Hamati, Iliyas—Jaffa, 11 October 2002
Jdai, Fakhri—Jaffa, 7 May 2002
Jbarah, Rasim Yusuf—Tayyibah, 1 October 2002
Jubran, Salim—Tel Aviv, 21 December 1999
Jubran, Sulayman—Tel Aviv, 22 October 1999
Makhuli, Dr. Salim—Kafr Yasif, 20 November 1999
Mazawi, Dr. André—Tel Aviv, 10 April 2000
Zghayyir, 'Ali—Haifa, 30 March 2002
Zurayyiq, Lutfi—Jaffa, 7 May 2002

Works in Arabic Quoted in the Text

'Abbas, Ihsan. *Ghurbat al-ra'i: sirah dhatiyyah.* Amman: dar al-shuruq, 1996.
'Abd al-Rahim, Matar. *Idfinuni hunak: sirat filastini yahlum bi'l-watan.* [Damascus: 'Abd al-Rahim], 1995.
Abu Diyah, Khalid Hafiz. *Dalil al-maktabat wa'l-maktabiyyin fi'l-daffah al-gharbiyyah wa-qita' ghazza.* Nablus: jami'at al-najah, 1986.
Abu Ghush, Ya'qub Haydar. *Qaryat 'imwas.* Bir Zayt: jami'at bir zayt, 1994.
Abu Hanna, Hanna. *Dar al-mu'allimin al-rusiyyah fi'l-nasirah "al-siminar" (1886–1914) wa-athruha 'ala al-nahdah al-adabiyyah fi filastin.* Nazareth: da'irat al-thaqafah al-'arabiyyah fi wizarat al-ma'arif wa'l-thaqafah, 1994.
———. *Zill al-ghaymah.* al-Nasira: dar al-nahdah li'l-tiba'ah wa'l-nashr, 1997.

Abu Khalil, Shawqi. *Bandali al-jawzi: ʿasruhu, hayatuhu, atharuhu.* Damascus: dar al-fikr, 1993.

Ahmad, Fathi. *Taʾrikh al-rif al-filastini fiʾl-ʿahd al-ʿuthmani, mintaqat bani zayd namu-dhaj[an].* Ramallah: al-matbaʿah al-ʿarabiyyah al-hadithah, 1992.

ʿAql, Muhammad. *al-Mufassal fi taʾrikh wadi ʿarah: ʿarah wa-ʾarʿarah min bidayat thawrat 1936 ila nihayat harb 1948.* Jerusalem: matbaʿat al-sharq al-ʿarabiyyah, 1999.

al-ʿAqqad, Ahmad Khalil. *al-Sihafah al-ʿarabiyyah fi filastin.* Damascus: dar al-ʿurubah, 1967.

al-ʿArif, ʿArif. *al-Mufassal fi taʾrikh al-quds.* Jerusalem: maktabat al-andalus, 1961.

———. *Taʾrikh ghazza.* Jerusalem: matbaʿat dar al-aytam al-islamiyyah, 1943.

al-Asad, Nasir al-Din. *al-Ittijahat al-adabiyyah al-hadithah fi filastin waʾl-urdunn.* Cairo: jamiʿat al-duwal al-ʿarabiyyah, maʿhad al-dirasat al-ʿarabiyyah al-ʿaliyyah, 1957.

———. *Muhadarat ʿan khalil baydas, raʾid al-qissah al-ʿarabiyyah al-hadithah fi filastin.* Cairo: jamiʿat al-duwal al-ʿarabiyyah, maʿhad al-dirasat al-ʿarabiyyah al-ʿaliyyah, 1963.

———. *Muhammad ruhi al-khalidi, raʾid al-bahth al-taʾrikhi fi filastin.* Cairo: maʿhad al-buhuth waʾl-dirasat al-ʿarabiyyah, 1970.

al-ʿAsali, Kamil Jamil. *Maʿahid al-ʿilm fi bayt al-maqdis.* Amman [author's publication], 1981.

———. "al-Maktabat al-filastiniyyah mundh al-fath al-ʿarabi al-islami hatta 1985." In *al-Mawsuʿah al-Filastiniyyah.* 2nd series (*al-dirasat al-khassah*). Vol. 3. Beirut: Encyclopaedia Palaestina Corporation, 1990, pp. 286–290.

———. "al-Taʿlim fi filastin min al-fath al-islami hatta bidayat al-ʿasr al-hadith." In *al-Mawsuʿah al-Filastiniyyah.* 2nd series (*al-dirasat al-khassah*). Vol. 3. Beirut: Encyclopaedia Palaestina Corporation, 1990, pp. 3–34.

———. *Wathaʾiq maqdisiyyah taʾrikhiyyah.* Vol. 1. Amman: matbaʿat al-tawfiq, 1983.

ʿAtallah, Mahmud ʿAli. *Fihris makhtutat aal tuffahah bi-nablus.* Nablus: jamiʿat al-najah, 1993.

———. *Fihris makhtutat al-maktabah al-jawhariyyah.* Nablus: jamiʿat al-najah, 1990.

———. *Fihris makhtutat maktabat aal al-qamhawi bi-nablus.* Amman: al-jamiʿah al-ur-dunniyyah; Nablus: jamiʿat al-najah, 1992.

———. *Fihris makhtutat maktabat al-haram al-ibrahimi al-khalil.* Nablus: jamiʿat al-najah, 1983.

———. *Fihris al-makhtutat, maktabat masjid al-hajj nimr al-nabulsi fi nablus.* Amman: majmaʿ al-lughah al-ʿarabiyyah al-urdunni, 1983.

Badran, Nabil. "al-Rif al-filastini qabl al-harb al-ʿalamiyyah al-ula." *Shuʾun Filastiniyyah,* no. 7 (March 1972), pp. 116–129.

———. *al-Taʿlim waʾl-tahdith fiʾl-mujtamaʿ al-ʿarabi al-filastini.* Vol. 1: *ʿahd al-intidab.* Beirut: markaz al-abhath al-filastiniyyah, 1969.

al-Barghuthi, ʿUmar al-Salih, and Khalil Tawtah. *Taʾrikh filastin.* Jerusalem: matbaʿat bayt al-maqdis, 1923.

Bsaysu, Muʿin. *Dafatir filastiniyyah.* Beirut: dar al-farabi, 1978.

Bulus, Rafaʾil Bulus. *Kafr yasif bayna asalat al-madi wa-rawʿat al-hadir.* Acre: matbaʿat abu rahmun, 1985.

Buri, Samʿan Matta, and Yusuf Ahmad Shibl. *ʿAkka: turath wa-dhikrayat.* Beirut: dar al-hamraʾ liʾl-tibaʿah waʾl-nashr, 1992.

al-Dabbagh, Ibrahim. *Hadith al-sawmaʿah: rasaʾil fiʾl-adab waʾl-fukahah waʾl-naqd waʾl-falsafah.* Jaffa: maktabat al-tahir ikhwan, n.d.

al-Dabbagh, Mustafa. *Madrasat al-qaryah.* Jerusalem: matba'at al-'arab, 1935.

al-Dajani, Ahmad Zaki. *Madinatuna yafa wa-thawrat 1936.* [Cairo: author's publication, 1989].

al-Dajani, Amin Hafiz. *Jabhat al-tarbiyyah wa'l-ta'lim wa-nidaluhah didd al-isti'mar: al-baramij wa'l-manahij wa'l-mu'allimun wa'l-tullab 'abra arba'at 'uhud.* Vol. 1: *al-intidab al-baritani 1918–1948.* [Ramallah, 1996].

Darwazah, Muhammad 'Izzat. *Mudhakkirat 1305–1404/1887–1984.* Vol. 1. Beirut: dar al-gharb al-islami, 1993.

Daya, Jan. "al-Nafa'is al-'asriyyah." *Shu'un Filastiniyyah,* no. 87–88 (February–March 1979), pp. 168–180.

Diyab, Imtiyaz, and Hisham Sharabi. *Yafa: 'itr madinah.* Beirut: dar al-fatiy al-'arabi, 1991.

al-Durr, Ibrahim Farid. *Shafa 'amr: fustat al-sultan salah al-din al-ayyubi.* Beirut: mu'assasat al-abhath al-'arabiyyah, 1988.

Duwayik, Mahmud. "al-Maktabah." *Majallat Dar al-Mu'allimin* 3, nos. 9–10 (July 1923), pp. 209–213.

al-Fattash, Ibrahim. *Ta'rikh qada' salfit (al-jama'iniyyat).* n.p., 1992.

Ghanayim, Zuhayr Ghanayim 'Abd al-Latif. *Liwa' 'akka fi 'ahd al-tanzimat al-'uthmaniyyah 1281–1337h/1864–1918m.* Beirut: mu'assasat al-dirasat al-filstiniyyah, 1999.

Gharbiyyah, 'Izz al-Din. *Qissat madinah—yafa.* Beirut: al-munazzamah al-'arabiyyah li'l-tarbiyyah wa'l-thaqafah wa'l-'ulum, 198–?

al-Ghuri, Emile. *Filastin 'abr sittin 'am^{an}.* Beirut: dar al-nahar li'l-nashr, 1972.

Haddad, Yusuf Ayyub. *Khalil al-sakakini: hayatuhu, mawaqifuhu wa-atharuhu.* [Nicosia]: al-ittihad al-'amm lil-kuttab wa'l-sihafiyyin al-filastiniyyin, 1981.

———. *al-Mujtama' wa'l-turath fi filastin: qaryat al-bassa.* Nicosia: markaz al-abhath al-filastiniyyah, 1985.

Hanna, 'Abdallah. "Nafa'is al-khizanah al-khalidiyyah fi'l-quds al-sharif." *al-Katib al-Filastini,* no. 19 (April–May–June 1990), pp. 102–110.

Harb, Tal'at. *Tidhkarat tal'at harb.* Bir Zayt: jami'at bir zayt, markaz dirasat wa-tawthiq al-mujtama' al-filastini, 1994.

Haykal, Yusuf. *Ayyam al-siba, suwar min al-hayat wa-safahat min al-ta'rikh.* Amman: dar al-jalil l'il-nashr wa'l-dirasat wa'l-abhath al-filastiniyyah, 1988.

Hukumat Filastin. Idarat al-ma'arif al-'umumiyyah. *Manhaj al-dirasah li'l-madaris al-hukumiyyah al-ibtida'iyyah li'l-banin fi'l-mudun wa'l-qura.* Jerusalem, 1921.

———. *Manhaj al-ta'lim al-ibtida'i.* Jerusalem, 1927

———. *Manhaj al-ta'lim al-ibtida'i fi madaris al-qura.* Jerusalem, 1929.

al-Hurani, 'Abdallah Ahmad. *Masmiyyat al-hurani: min qura filastin al-mubadah.* Amman: al-sharikah al-dawliyyah li'l-tiba'ah wa'l-nashr, 1988.

al-Hurani, Faysal. *al-Watan fi'l-dhakirah: durub al-manfa.* Damascus: dar kana'an li'l-dirasat wa'l-nashr, 1994.

Husayn, 'Abd al-Rahim Ahmad. *Qissat madinah: al-majdal wa-'asqalan.* Beirut: al-munazzamah al-'arabiyyah li'l-tarbiyyah wa'l-thaqafah wa'l-'ulum, 1987.

Husayn, Hammad. "Qadaya al-tarbiyyah wa'l-ta'lim fi'l-sihafah al-filastiniyyah khilal fitrat al-intidab al-baritani." In *al-Ta'lim al-filastini: ta'rikh^{an} waqi'^{an} wa-dururat al-mustaqbal; al-mu'tamar al-dawli al-thani li'l-dirasat al-filastiniyyah, 1996.* Beirut: jami'at bayrut, 1997, pp. 177–211.

al-Husayni, Hasan bin ʿAbd al-Latif. *Tarajim ahl al-quds fiʾl-qarn al-thani ʿashar al-hijri.* Amman: al-jamiʿah al-urdunniyyah, 1985.

al-Husayni, Ishaq Musa. *ʿAwdat al-safinah.* Jerusalem: maktabat filastin al-ʿilmiyyah, 1945.

al-Husayni, Muhammad Yunis. *al-Tatawwur al-ijtimaʿi waʾl-iqtisadi fi filastin al-ʿarabiyyah.* Jaffa: maktabat al-tahir ikhwan, 1946.

al-Husri, Satiʿ. *Hawliyyat al-thaqafah al-ʿarabiyyah.* Cairo: dar al-riyad liʾl-tabʿ waʾl-nashr, 1952.

Ibrahim, Hanna. *Musa al-filastini.* Shafa ʿAmr: dar al-mashriq liʾl-tarjamah waʾl-tibaʿah waʾl-nashr, 1998.

al-Jabarti, ʿAbd al-Rahman. *ʿAjaʾib al-athar fiʾl-tarajim waʾl-akhbar.* 3 Vols. Beirut: dar al-jabal, n.d.

———. *Taʾrikh muddat al-faransis bi-misr.* Trans. Shmuel Moreh. Leiden: Brill, 1975.

Jabra, Jabra Ibrahim. *al-Biʾr al-ula.* London: riyyad al-rayyis liʾl-kutub waʾl-nashr, 1987.

al-Jahiz, ʿAmr ibn Bahr. *Kitab al-hayawan.* Ed. Fawzi ʿAtawi. Beirut: maktabat al-talib wa-sharikat al-kitab al-lubnani, 1968.

al-Jamʿiyyah al-suriyyah liʾl-ʿulum waʾl-funun, 1847–1852. Beirut: dar al-hamraʾ, 1990.

Jbarah, Rasim Yusuf. *al-Biblyughrafiya al-ʿarabiyyah fi filastin 1847–1947.* al-Tayyibah: dar al-kutub al-ʿarabiyyah, 1996.

Kanafani, ʿAbd al-Latif. *15 Shariʿ al-burj—haifa: dhikrayat wa-ʿibar.* Beirut: baysan liʾl-nashr waʾl-tawziʿ, 1996.

al-Katul, Jibraʾil. *Nizam al-taʿlim fi filastin (silsilat maqalat nushirat fi majallat "al-muntada").* Jerusalem: maktab al-akhbar li-hukumat filastin, 194–?

Kayyali, Fawzi. "al-Muʿallim fi biladina." *Majallat Dar al-Muʿallimin* 3, no. 2 (November 1922), pp. 42–45.

Khalifah, Shaʿban ʿAbd al-ʿAziz. *Harakat nashr al-kutub fi misr.* Cairo: dar al-thaqafah, 1974.

Khatib, Husam. *Harakat al-tarjamah al-filastiniyyah: min al-nahdah hatta awakhir al-qarn al-ʿishrin.* Beirut: al-muʾassasah al-ʿarabiyyah liʾl-dirasat waʾl-nashr, 1995.

Khuri, Niqula. "Mudhakkirat kahin al-quds al-khuri niqula al-khuri, biʾr zayt 1885–bayrut 1954." *Dirasat ʿArabiyyah* 30 nos. 5–6 (March–April 1994), pp. 62–76.

Khuri, Yusuf. *al-Sihafah al-ʿarabiyyah fi filastin, 1876–1948.* Beirut: muʾassasat al-dirasat al-filastiniyyah, 1976.

al-Kitab al-ʿarabi al-filastini: maʿrad al-kitab al-ʿarabi al-filastini al-awwal fi nadi al-ittihad al-urthuduksi fiʾl-quds, min 11–20 tishrin al-awwal 1946. Jerusalem: lajnat al-thaqafah al-ʿarabiyyah fi filastin, 1946.

al-Kulliyyah al-islamiyyah. *Nizam al-kulliyyah al-islamiyyah biʾl-quds al-sharif.* Jerusalem: dar al-aytam al-islamiyyah, n.d.

Kulliyyat rawdat al-maʿarif al-wataniyyah. *Barnamaj li-sanat 1932–1933.* Jerusalem: matbaʿat bayt al-maqdis, 1350 [1931–1932].

Kurd ʿAli, Muhammad. *Khitat al-sham.* Vol. 6. Damascus: matbaʿat al-mufid, 1928.

Madrasat al-banat al-islamiyyah (Jerusalem). *Barnamaj sanat 1348–1349/1929–1930.* Jerusalem: matbaʿat dar al-aytam [1930].

Madrasat mar jiryis (Jerusalem). *Barnamaj durus, 1906.* Jerusalem: matbaʿat dar al-aytam, 1906.

Madrasat al-najah al-wataniyyah (Nablus). *Barnamaj ʿamihah al-thani ʿashar, 1348/1929–1930.* Jerusalem: matbaʿat dar al-aytam [1930].

———. *Barnamaj ʿamihah al-rabiʿ ʿashar, 1350/1931–1932.* Jerusalem: matbaʿat dar al-aytam, 1933.

————. *Barnamaj 'amihah al-ithnayn wa' l-'ishrin, 1358/1939–1940.* Jerusalem: matba'at dar al-aytam, 1940.

Madrasat rawdat al-ma'arif. *Barnamaj.* Jerusalem: matba'at al-munadi, 1331 [1911–1912].

————. *Barnamaj li-sanat 1924–1925.* Jerusalem: matba'at dar al-aytam, 1342 [1923–1924].

Madrasat san jurj fi'l-quds. Jerusalem: matba'at bayt al-maqdis, 1928.

Mahamid, 'Umar. *Safahat min ta'rikh madaris al-jam'iyyah al-rusiyyah-al-filastiniyyah fi filastin bayn a'wam 1882–1914.* al-Tayyibah: markaz ihya' al-turath al-'arabi, 1988.

al-Majlis al-shar'i al-islami al-a'la fi filastin. *Bayan li-sanat 1341–1342/1923–1924.* Jerusalem: matba'at madrasat al-aytam al-islamiyyah, 1924.

al-Maktabah al-Khalidiyyah. *Barnamaj al-maktabah al-khalidiyyah al-'umumiyyah.* Jerusalem: matba'at jurji habib hananiyya, 1900.

Maktab al-sihafah wa'l-nashr. *Man huwa li-rijal filastin sanat 1945–1946.* Jaffa: matba'at al-'arab, 1946.

Mana', 'Adil. *A'lam filastin fi awakhir al-'ahd al-'uthmani 1800–1918.* Jerusalem: jam'iyyat al-dirasat al-'arabiyyah, 1986.

al-Maqdisi, Jirjis al-Khuri. "al-Ta'lim qadim^{an} wa-hadith^{an} fi suriyah." *al-Muqtataf* 31 (1906), pp. 745–751.

al-Mudawwar, 'Abd al-Rahim Badr. *Qaryat qaqun.* Bir Zayt: jami'at bir zayt, 1994.

Muhafazah, 'Ali. *al-Harakat al-fikriyyah fi 'asr al-nahdah fi filastin wa'l-urdunn.* Beirut: al-ahliyyah li'l-nashr, 1987.

al-Mukhlis, 'Abdallah. "Khaza'in al-kutub al-'arabiyyah: nafa'is al-khizanah al-khalidiyyah fi'l-quds al-sharif." *Majallat al-Majma' al-'Ilmi al-'Arabi* 4, no. 8 (August 1924), pp. 366–379; 4, no. 9 (September 1924), pp. 409–413.

Musa, Sulayman, ed. *al-Thawrah al-'arabiyyah al-kubra, watha'iq wa-asanid.* Amman: da'irat al-thaqafah wa'l-funun, 1961.

Mustafa, Kamal. *'Ali mahir basha: al-mathal al-a'la li'l-ummah wa'l-watan wa'l-sihafah wa'l-adab.* Cairo: maktab nashr al-mu'allafat al-'ilmiyyah wa'l-i'lanat al-tijariyyah, 1938.

Namlah, 'Ali al-Din Ibrahim. *al-Wiraqah wa-ashhar a'lam al-warraqin: dirasah fi'l-nashr al-qadim wa-naql al-ma'lumat.* al-Riyadh: matbu'at maktabat al-malik fahd al-wataniyyah, 1995.

Nassar, Najib. *Rasa'il sahib al-karmil: al-masirah al-maydaniyyah fi arja' filastin wa-sharq al-urdunn.* Ed Walid Khulayf. Nazareth: matba'at al-hakim, 1992.

Nawfal, Yusuf. *al-Maktabah al-'arabiyyah: ta'rikhuha, turathuha, hadiruha.* Cairo: dar al-ghad al-'arabi, 1989.

al-Nimr, Ihsan. *Ta'rikh jabal nablus wa'l-balqa'.* Vol. 4. Nablus: matba'at jam'iyyat 'ummal al-tabi' al-ta'awwuniyyah, 1975.

Nusayr, 'Aydah Ibrahim. *Harakat nashr al-kutub fi misr fi'l-qarn al-tasi' 'ashr.* Cairo: al-hay'ah al-misriyyah al-'ammah li'l-kitab, 1994.

Nuwayhid, 'Ajjaj. *Hadir al-'alam al-islami.* Translation of Lothrop Stoddard, *The New World of Islam,* 2nd printing. Beirut: dar al-fikr, 1971.

————. *Sittun 'am^{an} ma'a al-kafilah al-'arabiyyah.* Ed. Bayan Nuwayhid al-Hut. Beirut: dar al-istiqlal li'l-dirasat wa'l-nashr, 1993.

al-Qadi, Mahmud. *Shay' min al-dhakirah.* Damascus: dar kana'an li'l-dirasat wa'l-nashr, 1995.

Qasimiyyah, Khayriyyah. *al-Hayat al-fikriyyah fi filastin awakhir al-'ahd al-'uthmani.* Beirut: al-ruwad, 1994.

Qatshan, ʿAbdallah. *al-Taʿlim al-ʿarabi al-hukumi iban al-hukm al-turki waʾl-intidab al-baritani 1516–1948*. Amman: dar al-karmil-samid, 1987.

Rimawi, ʿAbd al-Raʾuf. "Madrasat dayr ghasana." *Majallat Dar al-Muʿallimin* 5, no. 5 (January 1925), pp. 150–153.

al-Rimawi, Muhammad. *Waqaʾiʿ tufulah filastiniyyah*. Damascus: al-sharikah al-muttahidah liʾl-tawziʿ, 1984.

Sabat, Khalil. *Taʾrikh al-tibaʿah fiʾl-sharq al-ʿarabi*. Cairo: dar al-maʿarif, 1958.

Salah, Yusrah. *Tadhakkurat*. Bir Zayt: jamiʿat bir zayt, markaz dirasat wa-tawthiq al-mujtamaʿ al-filastini, 1992.

Salamah, Khadir Ibrahim. *Fihrist makhtutat al-maktabah al-budayriyyah (maktabat al-shaykh muhammad bin hubayish)*. 2 Vols. Jerusalem: idarat al-awqaf al-ʿammah, maktabat al-masjid al-aqsa, 1987.

———. *Fihrist makhtutat maktabat al-masjid al-aqsa*. 2nd ed. Vol. 1. Jerusalem: matbaʿat dar al-aytam al-islamiyyah, 1983.

al-Salih, ʿAbd al-Qadir. *Dhikrayat*. Amman: matbaʿat rafidi, 1985.

al-Salih, Husni. *Filastin, dhikrayat muʾlimah: sirah dhatiyyah*. Beirut: dar al-hadatha, 1997.

Sarkis, Yusuf Iliyan. "al-Jamʿiyyah al-mashriqiyyah fi bayrut." *al-Mashriq* 12 (1909), pp. 32–38.

Sawafiri, Kamil Salih Mahmud. *al-Adab al-ʿarabi al-muʿasir fi filastin min sanat 1860–1960*. Cairo: dar al-maʿarif 1979.

al-Sawi, Ahmad Husayn. *Fajr al-sihafah fi misr: dirasah fi aʿlam al-hamlah al-faransiyyah*. Cairo: al-hayʾa al-misriyyah al-ʿammah liʾl-kitab, 1975.

Sharubim, Mikhaʾil. *al-Kafi fi taʾrikh misr al-qadim waʾl-hadith*. Bulaq: al-matbaʿah al-amiriyyah, 1900.

Shaykhu, Luis. *al-Aadab al-ʿarabiyyah fiʾl-qarn al-tasiʿ ʿashar*. Beirut: al-matbaʿah al-kathulikiyyah liʾl-aabaʾ al-yasuʿiyyin, 1924.

Shumali, Qustandi. *al-Ittijahat al-adabiyyah waʾl-naqdiyyah fi filastin: dirasat li-hayat al-naqd al-adabi al-hadith fi filastin min khilal jaridat filastin*. Jerusalem: dar al-ʿawdah, 1990.

———. *Jaridat filastin 1911–1967: dirasah naqdiyyah wa-fihris taʾrikhi*. Jerusalem: markaz abhath al-quds, 1992.

al-Shuqayri, Ahmad. *Arbaʿun ʿaman fiʾl-hayat al-ʿarabiyyah waʾl-dawliyyah*. Beirut: dar al-ʿawdah, 1973.

Snubar, Ibrahim. *Tadhakkurat*. Bir Zayt: jamiʿat bir zayt, markaz dirasat wa-tawthiq al-mujtamaʿ al-filastini, 1992.

Sukayik, Bahjat ʿAta. *Dhikrayat al-sinin al-haniyyah fi rubuʿ ghazza al-hashimiyyah*. [Gaza, 1995?]

Sulayman, Muhammad. "al-Matabiʿ al-filastiniyyah wa-atharuhah al-thaqafi fiʾl-ʿahd al-turki." *Ruʾyah* (Gaza) 13 (October 2001), pp. 72–98.

———. *al-Sihafah al-filastiniyyah wa-qawanin al-intidab al-baritani*. Nicosia: al-ittihad al-ʿamm liʾl-kuttab waʾl-sihafiyyin al-filastiniyyin, 1988.

———. *Taʾrikh al-sihafah al-filastiniyyah, 1876–1976*. Vol. 1: *1876–1918*. Nicosia: al-ittihad al-ʿamm liʾl-kuttab waʾl-sihafiyyin al-filastiniyyin, 1987.

Talas, Asʿad. "Dur kutub filastin wa-nafaʾis makhtutatiha." *Majallat al-Majmaʿ al-ʿIlmi al-ʿArabi, dimashq* 20, nos. 5–6 (May–June 1945), pp. 234–241.

Tamari, Salim. "al-Hadathah fi'l-quds al-ʿuthmaniyyah: al-mudhakkirat al-jawhariyyah 1904–1917." *Majallat al-Dirasat al-Filastiniyyah*, no. 44 (Winter 2000), pp. 69–96.

al-Tamimi, Muhammad Rafiq, and Muhammad Bahjat. *Wilayat bayrut.* Vol. 1: *al-qism al-janubi.* Beirut: matbaʿat al-iqbal [1917].

di-Tarrazi, Filib. *Khazaʾin al-kutub al-ʿarabiyyah fiʾl-khafiqayn.* 3 Vols. Beirut: manshurat wizarat al-tarbiyyah al-wataniyyah waʾl-funun al-jamilah, dar al-kutub, 1948.

———. *Taʾrikh al-sihafah al-ʿarabiyyah.* 4 Vols. Beirut: al-matbaʿah al-adabiyyah, 1913, 1914, 1933.

Thawrat filastin ʿam 1936. Jaffa: jaridat al-jamiʿah al-islamiyyah, 1937.

Tibawi, ʿAbd al-Latif. "Jamʿiyyat al-aadab al-ʿarabiyyah fi'l-quds." *Majallat Majmaʿ al-Lughah al-ʿArabiyyah bi-Dimashq* 49, no. 4 (September 1974), pp. 871–881.

Tuqan, Fadwa. *Rihlah jabaliyyah rihlah saʿbah, sirah dhatiyyah.* 4th printing. Amman: dar al-shuruq, 1999.

Yaghi, ʿAbd al-Rahman. *Hayat al-adab al-filastini al-hadith, min awwal al-nahdah hatta al-nakbah.* Beirut: al-maktab al-tijari liʾl-tibaʿah waʾl-nashr waʾl-tawziʿ, 1968.

Yehoshuʿa, Yaʿacov. *Taʾrikh al-sihafah al-ʿarabiyyah fi filastin fiʾl-ʿahd al-ʿuthmani (1908–1918).* Jerusalem: matbaʿat al-maʿarif, 1974.

———. *Taʾrikh al-sihafah al-ʿarabiyyah al-filastiniyyah fi bidayat ʿahd al-intidab al-baritani ʿala filastin (1919–1929).* Haifa: al-markaz al-yahudi al-ʿarabi, 1981.

———. *Taʾrikh al-sihafah al-ʿarabiyyah al-filastiniyyah fi nihayat ʿahd al-intidab al-baritani ʿala filastin, 1930–1948.* Jerusalem: maʿhad harry truman liʾl-abhath, 1983.

Yusuf, Fawzi. *Khamsun ʿamᵃⁿ fi khidam al-harakah al-thaqafiyyah: maktabat al-andalus 1935–1985.* Jerusalem: matbaʿat al-maʿarif, 1985.

———. *Shayʾ min hayati.* Jerusalem: maktabat al-andalus, 1980.

Zaydan, Jurji. *Taʾrikh aadab al-lughah al-ʿarabiyyah.* 4 Vols. Cairo: al-hayʾah al-misriyyah al-ʿammah liʾl-kitab, 1957.

Ziyadah, Niqula. *Ayyami, sirah dhatiyyah.* 2 Vols. Paris: Hazar, 1992.

al-Zuʿbi, Sayf al-Din. *Shahid ʿiyan: mudhakkirat.* Shafa ʿAmr: dar al-mashriq liʾl-tarjamah waʾl-tibaʿah waʾl-nashr, 1987.

Works in Other Languages Quoted in the Text

Abcarius, M. F. *Palestine through the Fog of Propaganda.* London: Hutchinson, 1946.

Abu Ghazaleh, Adnan. *Arab Cultural Nationalism in Palestine.* Beirut: Institute for Palestine Studies, 1973.

———. "Arab Cultural Nationalism in Palestine during the British Mandate." *Journal of Palestine Studies* 1, no. 3 (Spring 1972), pp. 37–63.

Aburish, Said K. *Children of Bethany: The Story of a Palestinian Family.* London: I. B. Tauris, 1988.

Ajami, Jocelyn M. "The Khalidi Library: A Hidden Treasure." *Aramco World* 4, no. 6 (November–December 1993), pp. 2–9.

Allen, James Smith. *In the Public Eye: A History of Reading in Modern France, 1800–1940.* Princeton: Princeton University Press, 1991.

Antonius, George. *The Arab Awakening.* New York: Capricorn, 1965.

Arnon-Ohana, Yuval. *Falahim ba-mered ha-ʿaravi be-eretz Israel 1936–1939.* Tel Aviv: Shiloah Center for Middle Eastern and African Studies, 1978.

————. *Herev mi-bayit: ha-maʾavaq ha-pnimi ba-tnuʿah ha-leumit ha-falastinit.* Tel-Aviv: yariv hadar, 1981.

Ashbee, C. R. *Jerusalem 1920–1922.* London: Murray, 1924.

Assaf, Michael. *ha-ʿAravim tahat ha-tsalbanim, ha-mamlukim veha-turkim.* Tel Aviv: davar and mossad bialik, 1941.

————. *ha-Yahasim bein aravim vi-yhudim be-eretz israel, 1860–1948.* Tel Aviv: tarbut ve-hinukh, 1970.

ʿAthamina, Khalil. "Al-qasas: Its Emergence, Religious Origin and Its Socio-Political Impact on Early Muslim Society." *Studia Islamica* 76 (1992), pp. 53–74.

Auld, Sylvia, and Robert Hillenbrand, eds. *Ottoman Palestine.* 2 Vols. London: Altajir World of Islam Trust, 2000.

Ayalon, Ami. "Language as a Barrier to Political Reform in the Middle East." *International Journal of the Sociology of Language* 137 (June 1999), pp. 67–80.

————. "Modern Texts and Their Readers in Late Ottoman Palestine." *Middle Eastern Studies* (October 2002), pp. 17–40.

————. "Political Journalism and Its Audience in Egypt, 1875–1914." *Culture and History* 16 (1997), pp. 100–121.

————. *The Press in the Arab Middle East: A History.* New York: Oxford University Press, 1995.

Baker, James N. "The Presence of the Name: Reading Scripture in an Indonesian Village." In Jonathan Boyarin, ed., *The Ethnography of Reading.* Berkeley: University of California Press, 1992, pp. 98–138.

Barbéris, Pierre, and Claude Duchet, eds. *Manuel d'histoire littéraire de la France.* Vol. 4: *1789–1848.* Paris: Editions Sociales, 1972.

Baudrillard, Jean. "The System of Collecting." In John Elsner and Roger Cardinal, eds., *The Culture of Collecting.* Cambridge, MA: Harvard University Press, 1994, pp. 7–24.

Ben-Arieh, Yehoshuʿa. *Jerusalem in the Nineteenth Century: The Old City.* Jerusalem: Yad Izhak Ben Zvi, 1984.

————. "The Population of the Large Towns in Palestine during the First Eighty Years of the Nineteenth Century, according to Western Sources." In Moshe Maʿoz, ed., *Studies on Palestine during the Ottoman Period.* Jerusalem: Magnes, 1975, pp. 49–69.

Berkey, Jonathan. *Popular Preaching and Religious Authority in the Medieval Islamic Near East.* Seattle: University of Washington Press, 2001.

————. *The Transmission of Knowledge in Medieval Cairo: A Social History of Islamic Education.* Princeton: Princeton University Press, 1992.

Bierman, Irene. *Writing Signs: The Fatimid Public Text.* Berkeley: University of California Press, 1998.

Bowman, Humphrey. *Middle East Window.* London: Longman and Green, 1942.

Boyarin, Daniel. "Placing Reading: Ancient Israel and Medieval Europe." In Jonathan Boyarin, ed., *The Ethnography of Reading.* Berkeley: University of California Press, 1992, pp. 10–37.

Boyarin, Jonathan, ed. *The Ethnography of Reading.* Berkeley: University of California Press, 1992.

Brockopp, Jonathan E. *Early Maliki Law.* Leiden: Brill, 2000.

Brooks, Jeffrey. *When Russia Learned to Read: Literacy and Popular Literature, 1861–1917.* Princeton: Princeton University Press, 1985.

Burgoyne, Michael Hamilton. *Mamluk Jerusalem, an Architectural Study.* London: World of Islam Festival Trust, 1987.

Casson, Lionel. *Libraries in the Ancient World.* New Haven: Yale University Press, 2001.

Caton, Steven C. *"Peaks of Yemen I Summon": Poetry and Cultural Practice in a North Yemeni Tribe.* Berkeley: University of California Press, 1990.

Cavallo, Guglielmo, and Roger Chartier, eds. *A History of Reading in the West.* Amherst: University of Massachusetts Press, 1999.

Centre d'études de politique étrangère, Groupe d'études de l'Islam. *L'Égypte indépendente.* Paris, 1938.

de Certau, Michel. *The Practice of Everyday Life.* Berkeley: University of California Press, 1984.

Chamberlain, Michael. *Knowledge and Social Practice in Medieval Damascus, 1190–1350.* Cambridge: Cambridge University Press, 1994.

Chartier, Roger. *Histoires de la lecture: Un bilans de recherches; actes du colloque des 29 et 30 janvier 1993, Paris.* Paris: Institut mémoires de l'édition contemporaine, 1995.

———. "Reading Matter and 'Popular' Reading: From the Renaissance to the Seventeenth Century." In Guglielmo Cavallo and Roger Chartier, eds., *A History of Reading in the West.* Amherst: University of Massachusetts Press, 1999, pp. 269–283.

———, ed. *The Culture of Print: Power and the Use of Print in Early Modern Europe.* Cambridge: Polity Press, 1989.

Commins, David Dean. *Islamic Reform: Politics and Social Change in Late Ottoman Syria.* New York: Oxford University Press, 1990.

Connelly, Bridget. *Arab Folk Epic and Identity.* Berkeley: University of California Press, 1986.

Conrad, Lawrence I. "The Khalidi Library." In Sylvia Auld and Robert Hillenbrand, eds., *Ottoman Palestine.* Vol. 1. London: Altajir World of Islam Trust, 2000, pp. 191–209.

Conrad, Lawrence I., and Barbara Kellner-Heinkele. "Ottoman Resources in the Khalidi Library in Jerusalem." In Amy Singer and Amnon Cohen, eds., *Aspects of Ottoman History: Papers from CIEPO IX, Jerusalem.* Jerusalem: Magnes, 1994, pp. 280–293.

Conrad, Lawrence I., and Khader Salameh. "Palestine." In Geoffrey Roper, ed., *World Survey of Islamic Manuscripts.* Vol. 3. London: Al-Furqan Islamic Heritage Foundation, 1993, pp. 563–600.

Cook, Michael. "The Opponents of the Writing Tradition in Early Islam." *Arabica* 46, no. 4 (October 1977), pp. 437–523.

Crecelius, Daniel. "The Waqf of Muhammad Bey Abu al-Dhahab in Historical Perspective." *International Journal of Middle East Studies* 23 (1991), pp. 57–81.

Dagher, Joseph A[sad]. *Répertoire des bibliothèques du proche et du moyen orient.* Paris: UNESCO, 1951.

Darnton, Robert. "First Steps toward a History of Reading." In *The Kiss of Lamourette.* New York: Norton, 1990, pp. 154–187.

Davis, Natalie Zemon. "Printing and the People." In *Society and Culture in Early Modern France.* Stanford: Stanford University Press, 1965, pp. 187–226.

Dégh, Linda. *Folktales and Society: Story-Telling in a Hungarian Peasant Community.* Bloomington and Indianapolis: Indiana University Press, 1989.

Deguilhem, Randi. "Les cafés à Damas (XIXe–XXe siècles)." In Hélène Desmet-Grégoire and François Georgeon, eds., *Cafés d'Orient revisitée.* Paris: CNRS, 1997, pp. 128–139.

Denny, Frederick Mathewson. "Qur'an Recitation: A Tradition of Oral Performance and Transmission." *Oral Tradition* 4, nos. 1–2 (1989), pp. 5–26.

Déroche, François. "New Evidence about Umayyad Book Hands." In *Essays in Honor of Salah al-Din al-Munajjid.* London: al-Furqan Islamic Heritage Foundation, 2002, pp. 611–641.

Diggs, Diana, and Joanne Rappaport. "Literacy, Orality and Ritual Practice in Highland Colombia." In Jonathan Boyarin, ed., *The Ethnography of Reading.* Berkeley: University of California Press, 1992, pp. 139–155.

Doumani, Beshara. *Rediscovering Palestine: Merchants and Peasants in Jabal Nablus, 1700–1900.* Berkeley: University of California Press, 1995.

Eche, Youssef. *Les bibliothèques arabes publiques et semi-publiques en Mésopotamie, en Syrie et en Égypte au Moyen Age.* Damascus: Institut Français de Damas, 1967.

Eickelman, Dale F. *Knowledge and Power in Morocco: The Evolution of a Twentieth-Century Notable.* Princeton: Princeton University Press, 1985.

Eisenstein, Elizabeth L. "An Unacknowledged Revolution Revisited." *American Historical Review* 107, no. 1 (February 2002), pp. 87–105, 126–128.

Faber, Paul, et al. *Beelden vour Volkenkunde (Rotherdam, Netherlands).* Amsterdam: Fragment, 1986.

Farkash, Rinat, and Aharon. *Me-az ve-ʿad ʿolam: tsilumim rishonim shel eretz yisrael ʿad ha-shilton ha-briti.* Jaffa: galeria farkash, 1998.

Finn, James. *Stirring Times, or Records from Jerusalem Consular Chronicles of 1853 to 1856.* London: Kegan Paul, 1878.

Forte, Tanya. "Elef laylah va-laylah 'ha-amitiyyim' shel abu hanna: shiluv sipur ha-ani be-tokh historia be-mifneh ha-meʾah ba-galil." *Jamaʿah* 6 (2000), pp. 33–57.

Fyfe, Hamilton H. *The New Spirit in Egypt.* Edinburgh and London: Blackwood, 1911.

Georgeon, François. "Les cafés à Istanbul à la fin de l'Empire ottoman." In Hélène Desmet-Grégoire and François Georgeon, eds., *Cafés d'Orient revisitée.* Paris: CNRS, 1997, pp. 39–78.

———. "Lire et écrire à la fin de l'Empire ottoman: Quelques remarques introductives." *Revue du monde musulman et de la Méditerranée* 75–76 (1995), pp. 169–179.

"Gesellschaft der Künste und Wissenschaften in Beirut." *Zeitscrift der Deutschen Morgenländischen Gesellschaft* 2 (1848), pp. 378–388.

Gidal, Nachum Tim. *Jerusalem in 3000 Years.* Edison, NJ: Knickerbocker Press, 1996.

Gilbar, Gad. "The Growing Economic Involvement of Palestine with the West, 1865–1914." In David Kushner, ed., *Palestine in the Late Ottoman Period: Political, Social and Economic Transformation.* Jerusalem: Yad Izhak Ben Zvi, 1986, pp. 188–210.

———. *Megamot ba-hitpathut ha-demografit shel ha-falastinim, 1870–1987.* Tel Aviv: Moshe Dayan Center, 1989.

Gilbert, Martin. *Jerusalem: Rebirth of a City.* London: Chatto and Windus, 1985.

Goldziher, I[gnatz]. "Education (Muslim)." In James Hastings, ed., *Encyclopaedia of Religion and Ethics.* Vol. 5. New York: Charles Scribner, 1951, pp. 198–207.

Goody, Jack, ed. *Literacy in Traditional Societies.* Cambridge: Cambridge University Press, 1968.

Gorkin, Michael, and Rafiqa Othman. *Three Mothers, Three Daughters: Palestinian Women's Voices.* Berkeley: University of California Press, 1996.

Government of Palestine. Department of Education. *Statistical Tables and Diagrams for the Scholastic Year 1944–45.* Jerusalem: Government Printing Office, 1947.

Government of Palestine. Department of Statistics. *Statistical Abstract of Palestine 1936.* Jerusalem: Government Printing Press, 1937.

————. *Statistical Abstract of Palestine 1939*. Jerusalem: Government Printing Press, 1939.

————. *Statistical Abstract of Palestine 1944–45*. Jerusalem: Government Printer, 1946.

Grabar, Oleg. "Graffiti or Proclamations: Why Write on Buildings?" In Doris Behrens-Abouseif, ed., *The Cairo Heritage: Essays in Honor of Laila Ali Ibrahim*. Cairo: American University in Cairo Press, 2000, pp. 69–76.

Grafton, Anthony. "Is the History of Reading a Marginal Enterprise? Guilloume Budé and His Books." *The Papers of the Bibliographical Society of America* 91, no. 2 (June 1997), pp. 139–157.

Graham, William A. "Qur'an as a Spoken Word: An Islamic Contribution to the Understanding of Scripture." In Richard C. Martin, ed., *Approaches to Islam in Religious Studies*. Tucson: University of Arizona Press, 1985, pp. 23–40.

Grant, Elihu. *The People of Palestine*. Philadelphia and London: J. B. Lippincott, 1921.

Great Britain and Palestine 1915–1936. London: Royal Institute of International Affairs, 1937.

Griffiths, Paul J. *Religious Reading: The Place of Reading in the Practice of Religion*. New York: Oxford University Press, 1999.

Gröber, Karl. *Palästina, Arabien und Syrien: Baukunst, Landschaft, Volksleben*. Berlin: Ernst Wasmuth, 1925.

Gurevich, David. *Statistical Abstract of Palestine*, 1929. Jerusalem: Keren ha-Yesod, 1930.

Haarmann, Ulrich. "The Library of a Fourteenth-Century Jerusalem Scholar." *Der Islam* 61 (1984), pp. 327–333.

Hanebutt-Benz, Eva, Dagmar Glass, and Geoffrey Roper, eds. *Middle Eastern Languages and the Print Revolution: A Cross-Cultural Encounter*. Mainz: Gutenberg Museum and Internationale Gutenberg-Gesellschaft, 2002.

Hanioğlu, M. Şükrü. *The Young Turks in Opposition*. New York: Oxford University Press, 1995.

Hattox, Ralph. *Coffee and Coffeehouses: The Origins of a Social Beverage in the Medieval Near East*. Seattle: University of Washington Press, 1985.

Heffening, W., and J. D. Pearson. "Maktaba." In *Encyclopaedia of Islam*. 2nd ed. Leiden: Brill.

Henkin, David M. *City Reading: Written Words and Public Space in Antebellum New York*. New York: Columbia University Press, 1998.

Horn, Pamela. *Education in Rural England 1800–1914*. Dublin: Gill and Macmillan, 1978.

Hourani, Albert. "Bustani's Encyclopaedia." *Journal of Islamic Studies* 1 (1990), pp. 111–119.

Hummel, Ruth Victor. "Reality, Imagination and Belief: Jerusalem in Nineteenth- and Early Twentieth-Century Photographs (1839–1917)." In Sylvia Auld and Robert Hillenbrand, eds., *Ottoman Palestine*. Vol. 1. London: Altajir World of Islam Trust, 2000, pp. 235–275.

Husseini-Shahid, Serene. *Jerusalem Memoirs*. Beirut: Naufal, 1999.

Ibn Dohaish, Abdul Latif Abdullah. "Growth and Development of Islamic Libraries." *Der Islam* 66 (1989), pp. 289–302.

Ichilov, Orit, and André Elias Mazawi. *Between State and Church: Life-History of a French-Catholic School in Jaffa*. Frankfurt: Peter Lang, 1996.

In Arab Lands: The Bonfils Collection of the University of Pennsylvania Museum. Cairo: Zeitouna, 1999.

Issawi, Charles. *The Fertile Crescent 1800–1914*. New York: Oxford University Press, 1988.

Jagodzinski, Cecile M. *Privacy and Print: Reading and Writing in Seventeenth-Century England.* Charlottesville: University Press of Virginia, 1999.

Johns, Adrian, "How to Acknowledge a Revolution." *American Historical Review* 107, no. 1 (February 2002), pp. 106–125.

Jouhaud, Christian. "Readability and Persuasion: Political Handbills." In Roger Chartier, ed., *The Culture of Print: Power and the Use of Print in Early Modern Europe.* Cambridge: Polity Press, 1989, pp. 235–260.

Kabhah, Mustafa. *Tafqidam shel ha-ʿitonut ve-hasiyah ha-ʿitonaʾi ba-maʾavaq ha-leʾumi ha-ʿaravi ha-falastini, 1929–1939.* Unpublished Ph.D. dissertation. Tel Aviv University, 1996.

Kahati, Yoram. *The Role of Some Leading Arab Educators in the Development of the Ideology of Arab Nationalism.* Unpublished Ph.D. dissertation. University of London, London School of Economics and Political Science, 1991.

Khalidi, Rashid. *Palestinian Identity: The Construction of Modern National Consciousness.* New York: Columbia University Press, 1997.

Khalidi, Tarif. "Palestinian Historiography: 1900–1948." *Journal of Palestine Studies* 10, no. 3 (1981), pp. 59–76.

Khalidi, Walid. *Before Their Diaspora: A Photographic History of the Palestinians, 1876–1948.* 2nd ed. Washington, DC: Institute for Palestine Studies, 1991.

Kohlberg, Etan. *A Medieval Muslim Scholar at Work: Ibn Tawus and His Library.* Leiden: Brill, 1992.

Landau, Jacob M. *Abdul-Hamid's Palestine.* London: André Deutsch, 1979.

Landauer, Georg. *Palästina.* Munich: Meyer and Jessen, 1925.

Lane, Edward William. *An Arabic–English Lexicon.* 8 Vols. London: Williams and Norgate, 1863–1893.

———. *Manners and Customs of the Modern Egyptians.* First published 1836. London: East-West Publications, 1978.

Leder, Stefan. "Charismatic Scripturalism, the Hanbali Maqdisis of Damascus." *Der Islam* 74 (1997), pp. 279–304.

Luke, Harry Charles, and Edward Keith-Roach. *The Handbook of Palestine and Trans-Jordan.* 2nd ed. London: Macmillan, 1930.

Lyons, Martin. "New Readers in the Nineteenth Century: Women, Children, Workers." In Guglielmo Cavallo and Roger Chartier, eds., *A History of Reading in the West.* Amherst: University of Massachusetts Press, 1999, pp. 313–344.

Makdisi, George. *The Rise of Colleges: Institutions of Learning in Islam and the West.* Edinburgh: Edinburgh University Press, 1981.

Malul, Nissim. "Ha-ʿitonut ha-ʿaravit." *ha-Shiloah* 31 (1914), pp. 364–374, 439–450.

Manguel, Alberto. *A History of Reading.* New York: Penguin, 1997.

Marino, Brigitte. "Cafés et cafeteries de Damas aux xviiiᵉ et xixᵉ siècles." *Revue du Monde Musulman et de la Méditerranée* 75–76 (1995), pp. 275–292.

Matson, Eric G. *The Middle East in Pictures.* 4 Vols. New York: Arno Press, 1980.

McCracken, W. D. *The New Palestine.* London: Jonathan Cape, 1922.

Messick, Brinkley. *The Calligraphic State: Textual Domination and History in a Muslim Society.* Berkeley: University of California Press, 1993.

Metzer, Jacob, and Oded Kaplan. *Mesheq yehudi u-mesheq ʿaravi be-eretz yisrael; totzar, taʿasuqah u-tzmihah bi-tqufat ha-mandat.* Jerusalem: The Maurice Falk Institute for Economic Research in Israel, 1990.

Miller, Ylana M. *Government and Society in Rural Palestine, 1920–1948.* Austin: University of Texas Press, 1985.

Mills, E. *Census of Palestine 1931.* 2 Vols. Alexandria: Printed for the Government of Palestine by Whitehead Morris, 1933.

Muensterberger, Werner. *Collecting: An Unruly Passion.* Princeton: Princeton University Press, 1994.

Muhawi, Ibrahim, and Sharif Kanaana. *Speak, Bird, Speak Again: Palestinian Arab Folktales.* Berkeley: University of California Press, 1989.

Nadan, Amos. *The Arab Rural Economy in Mandate Palestine, 1921–1947: Peasants under Colonial Rule.* Unpublished Ph.D. dissertation. University of London, London School of Economics and Political Science, 2001.

Najjar, Aida Ali. *The Arab Press and Nationalism in Palestine 1920–1948.* Unpublished Ph.D. dissertation, Syracuse University, 1975.

Nashashibi, Nasser Eddin. *Jerusalem's Other Voice: Ragheb Nashashibi and Moderation in Palestinian Politics, 1920–1948.* Exeter: Ithaca Press, 1990.

Nasr, Seyyed Hossein. "Oral Transmission and the Book in Islamic Education: The Spoken and the Written Word." In George N. Atiyeh, ed., *The Book in the Islamic World.* Albany: SUNY Press, 1995, pp. 57–70.

Nassar, Issam. *Photographing Jerusalem: The Image of the City in Nineteenth-Century Photography.* New York: Columbia University Press, 1997.

Nelson, Kristina. *The Art of Reciting the Qur'an.* Austin: University of Texas Press, 1985.

Newton, Frances E. *Fifty Years in Palestine.* Wortham, England: Coldharbour Press, 1948.

Ong, Walter. *Orality and Literacy: The Technologizing of the Word.* London: Methuen, 1982.

———. *The Presence of the Word: Some Prolegomena for Cultural and Religious History.* Minneapolis: University of Minnesota Press, 1981.

Onne, Eyal. *Photographic Heritage of the Holy Land 1839–1914.* Manchester: Institute for Advanced Studies, Manchester Polytechnic, 1980.

Osman, Colin. *Jerusalem Caught in Time.* London: Garnet Publishing, 1999.

Palestine [Mandatory Government]. *Blue Book 1929.* Alexandria, 1930.

———. *Blue Book 1936.* Jerusalem: Government Printer [1937?].

Patai, Raphael. *Journeyman in Jerusalem: Memoirs and Letters 1933–1947.* Salt Lake City: University of Utah Press, 1992.

Pedersen, J., and G. Makdisi. "Madrasa, Part I." In *Encyclopaedia of Islam.* 2nd ed. Leiden: Brill.

Petrucci, Armando. "Reading to Read: A Future for Reading." In Guglielmo Cavallo and Roger Chartier, eds., *A History of Reading in the West.* Amherst: University of Massachusetts Press, 1999, pp. 345–367.

Pinto, Olga. "The Libraries of the Arabs during the Time of the Abbasides." *Islamic Culture* 3 (1929), pp. 210–243.

Porat, Yehoshu'a. *Tzmihat ha-tnu'ah ha-'aravit ha-leumit ha-palestinait 1918–1929.* Tel-Aviv: 'Am 'Oved, 1976.

Rafeq, Abdul-Karim. "The Political History of Ottoman Jerusalem." In Sylvia Auld and Robert Hillenbrand, eds., *Ottoman Palestine.* Vol. I. London: Altajir World of Islam Trust, 2000, pp. 25–36.

Richter, Noë. *Introduction à l'histoire de la lecture publique.* Bernay: La Queue du Chat, 1995.

———. *La lecture et ses institutions.* Vol. I: *La lecture populaire 1700–1918.* Paris: Université du Maine, 1987.

Roaf, Susan. "Life in Nineteenth-Century Jerusalem." In Sylvia Auld and Robert Hillenbrand, eds., *Ottoman Palestine.* Vol. I. London: Altajir World of Islam Trust, 2000, pp. 389–413.

Rosenthal, Franz. "'Of Making Many Books There Is No End:' The Classical Muslim View." In George N. Atiyeh, ed., *The Book in the Islamic World*. Albany: SUNY Press, 1995, pp. 33–55.

———. *The Technique and Approach of Muslim Scholarship*. Analecta Orientalia, no. 24. Rome: Pontificium Institutum Biblicum, 1947.

Russell, Alex. *The Natural History of Aleppo*. Vol. 2. London: Robinson, 1974.

Saenger, Paul Henry. "Books of Hours and the Reading Habits of the Later Middle Ages." In Roger Chartier, ed., *The Culture of Print: Power and the Use of Print in Early Modern Europe*. Cambridge: Polity Press, 1989, pp. 141–173.

———. "Reading in the Late Middle Ages." In Guglielmo Cavallo and Roger Chartier, eds., *A History of Reading in the West*. Amherst: University of Massachusetts Press, 1999, pp. 120–148.

———. "Silent Reading: Its Impact on Late Medieval Script." *Viator* 13 (1982), pp. 366–414.

———. *Space between Words: The Origins of Silent Reading*. Stanford: Stanford University Press, 1997.

Sakakini, Khalil. "*Kazeh ani rabotai*": *mi-yomano shel khalil al-sakakini* [Hebrew translation of Sakakini's *Kadha ana ya dunya*]. Jerusalem: keter, 1990.

Schiller, Ely. *Tsilumey yerushalayim ve-eretz yisrael ha-rishonim*. Jerusalem: Ariel, 1980.

———. *Yerushalayim, halifot u-tmurot ba-dorot ha-aharonim*. Jerusalem: Ariel, 1977.

Schiller, Ely, and Menahem Levin. *Tsilumei eretz yisrael ha-rishonim*. Tel Aviv: Misrad ha-Bitahon, 1991.

Schofield, R. S. "The Measurement of Literacy in Pre-Industrial England." In Jack Goody, ed., *Literacy in Traditional Societies*. Cambridge: Cambridge University Press, 1968, pp. 311–325.

Schölch, Alexander. *Palestine in Transformation 1856–1882: Studies in Social, Economic and Political Development*. Washington, DC: Institute for Palestinian Studies, 1993.

Scribner, Sylvia, and Michael Cole. *The Psychology of Literacy*. Cambridge, MA: Harvard University Press, 1981.

Shahla, George D. "Private Schools and the Government Systems for the Arab Population in Palestine." *Open Court* 44, no. 935 (October 1935), pp. 241–244.

Shimʿoni, Yaʿacov. *ʿAravey eretz yisrael*. Tel Aviv: ʿAm ʿOved, 1947.

Shinar, Dov. *Palestinian Voices: Communication and Nation Building in the West Bank*. Boulder, CO: Lynne Rienner, 1987.

Sibai, Mohamed Maki. *Mosque Libraries: An Historical Study*. London and New York: Mansell, 1987.

Siton, David. "ha-ʿItonut ha-ʿaravit be-eretz yisrael bi-shnot ha-mandat." In Yitzhaq Tischler, ed., *ʿAl ʿitonim ve-ʿitonaut*. Jerusalem: Yuval Tal, 1976, pp. 155–163.

Street, Brian V. *Literacy in Theory and Practice*. Cambridge: Cambridge University Press, 1984.

Strohmeier, Martin. "Al-Kulliyya al-Salahiyya, a Late Ottoman University in Jerusalem." In Sylvia Auld and Robert Hillenbrand, eds., *Ottoman Palestine*. Vol. 1. London: Altajir World of Islam Trust, 2000, pp. 57–62.

Svenbro, Jesper. "Archaic and Classical Greece: The Invention of Silent Reading." In Guglielmo Cavallo and Roger Chartier, eds., *A History of Reading in the West*. Amherst: University of Massachusetts Press, 1999, pp. 37–63.

Tamari, Salim. "Factionalism and Class Formation in Recent Palestinian History." In Roger Owen, ed., *Studies in the Economic and Social History of Palestine in the Nineteenth and Twentieth Centuries.* Carbondale and Edwardsville: Southern Illinois University Press, 1982, pp. 177–202.

Tannous, Afif I. "The Village Teacher and Rural Reconstruction in Palestine." *Open Court* 44, no. 935 (October 1935), pp. 236–240.

Tauber, Eliezer. *The Emergence of the Arab Movements.* London: Frank Cass, 1993.

Thomsen, P[eter]. "Verzeichnis der Arabischen Zeitungen und Zeitschriften Palästinas." *Zeitschrift des Deutsches Palästina-Vereins* (1914), pp. 211–215.

Tibawi, A[bdul] L[atif]. *Anglo-Arab Relations and the Question of Palestine 1914–1921.* London: Luzac, 1978.

———. *Arab Education in Mandatory Palestine: A Study of Three Decades of British Administration.* London: Luzac, 1956.

Tietze, Andreas. *Mustafa ʿAliʾs Description of Cairo of 1599: Text, Translation, Notes.* Vienna: Verlag der Österreichischen Akademie Wissenschaften, 1975.

Toubbeh, Jamil I. *Days of the Long Night: A Palestinian Refugee Remembers the Nakba.* Jefferson, NC: McFarland, 1998.

Ukers, William H. *All about Coffee.* New York: The Tea and Coffee Trade Journal, 1922.

Vaschitz, Yossef. *ha-ʿAravim be-eretz yisrael: kalkalah ve-hevrah, tarbut u-mediniyut.* Merhaviya: Sifriyat Poʿalim, 1947.

Vatikiotis, P. J. *Among Arabs and Jews: A Personal Experience 1936–1990.* London: Weidenfeld and Nicolson, 1991.

Volney, M. C-F. *Masa be-mitsrayim uve-suriya.* Translated from the French by Aharon Amir. Jerusalem: Yad Izhak Ben Zvi and Mossad Bialik, 1997.

Walls, A. G. "The Turbat Barakat Khan or Khalidi Library." *Levant* 6 (1974), pp. 25–50.

Warren, Charles. *Underground Jerusalem.* London: Richard Bentley, 1876.

Webb, R. K. *The British Working-Class Reader, 1790–1848: Literacy and Social Tension.* London: Allen and Unwin, 1955.

Weigert, Gideon. *My Life with the Palestinians.* Jerusalem: The Jerusalem Times, 1997.

White, Ruth M. *Report on the Jerusalem International YMCA Library.* Unpublished typescript at the Jerusalem YMCA, 1988.

Whitmore, Harry E. "Readers, Writers, and Literary Taste in the Early 1830s: The *Cabinet de lecture* as Focal Point." *Journal of Literary History* 13, no. 2 (Spring 1978), pp. 19–30.

Wilson, Charles Thomas. *Peasant Life in the Holy Land.* London: J. Murray, 1906.

Witkam, Jan Just. "The Human Element between Text and Reader: The *Ijaza* in Arabic Manuscript." In Yasin Dutton, ed., *The Codicology of Islamic Manuscripts. Proceedings of the Second Conference of al-Furqan Islamic Heritage Foundation, 4–5 December 1993.* London: Islamic Heritage Foundation, 1995, pp. 123–136.

Wittmann, Reinhard. "Was There a Reading Revolution at the End of the Eighteenth Century?" In Guglielmo Cavallo and Roger Chartier, eds., *A History of Reading in the West.* Amherst: University of Massachusetts Press, 1999, pp. 284–312.

Yehoshuʿa, Yaʿacov. "Nitzanei ʿitonut ve-sifrut ʿaravit ba-aretz be-reshit ha-meʾah." *Qeshet* 68 (Summer 1975), pp. 142–150.

———. *Yerushalayim tmol shilshom: pirqey havay.* Jerusalem: Reuven Mass, 1977.

Zacharia, Shabtai. *Soharim u-vaʿaley melacha yehudim bi-yerushalaim ha-ʿatiqa be-ʿavar.* Jerusalem: Tzur-Ot, 2002.

Index